B: Iacobus.

B: Ioseph.

Vita Activa

Vita Contemplativa

DIVA VIRGO CANDIDA
CANDIDI ORDINIS
PRÆMONSTRATENSIS
MATER TVTELARIS
ET DOMINA.

B: Giselbertus

B: Wilhelmus

Cœlo et terrâ glorioso
S.S.P. NORBERTO, PRÆMONSTRATI ORDINIS PATRIARCHÆ,
MAGNO ANTVERPIÆ APOSTOLO,
Quingentesimo Anno æternâ Gloriâ iam fruenti,
V. hoc Iubilæum Parenti Opt. Max.
Chrysostomus Abbas et Canonici S. Michaelis
Antuerpiensis gratulantur.
FIDE ET PATIENTIA

HISTORY OF SAINT NORBERT

APOSTLE OF THE EUCHARIST
AND
FOUNDER OF THE
NORBERTINE (PREMONSTRATENSIAN) ORDER
ARCHBISHOP OF MAGDEBURG

BY THE
REV. CORNELIUS J. KIRKFLEET, ORD. PRAEM.

En Norbertinae sunt haec compendia Vitae
Hic quod mireris, quodque sequaris, habes.

This is the story of the Life of St. Norbert—
Here one finds things to admire and to imitate.

MMXVII

ISBN: 978-1-953746-55-9

APPROBATIO ORDINIS. B. H. Pennings, O. Praem.
Prior Provinciae Americanæ

NIHIL OBSTAT
Sti. Ludovici, die 23. August 1916
F. G. Holweck
Censor Librorum

IMPRIMATUR
Sti. Ludovici, die 23. August 1916
✠ Joannes J. Glennon, Archiepiscopus Sti. Ludovici

Mediatrix Press
http://www.mediatrixpress.com/
607 E. 6th Ave
Ste 230
Post Falls, ID 83854

Cover: *The Citizens of Antwerp bring the Monstrance and other Sacramentals they had hidden from Tankelin*, 1630
Cornelis de Vos

Table of Contents

PREFACE. ix

FIRST PERIOD: FROM HIS BIRTH UNTIL HIS COMING TO PRÉMONTRÉ; 1080-1119

CHAPTER I
His Birth and Education. 1

CHAPTER II
Norbert's Conversion. 11

CHAPTER III
The Penitent. 21

CHAPTER IV
The Missionary. 33

CHAPTER V
The Peacemaker. 43

CHAPTER VI
Prémontré. 57

SECOND PERIOD: FROM THE TIME THE ORDER IS FOUNDED UNTIL NORBERT BECOMES ARCHBISHOP OF MAGDEBURG; 1120-1126

CHAPTER I
The Founder. 69

CHAPTER II
Trials. 81

CHAPTER III
Solemn Profession. 93

CHAPTER IV
The Monastery. 105

CHAPTER V
The Church at Prémontré. 115

CHAPTER VI
Godfrey of Cappenberg. 127

CHAPTER VII
The Third Order of St. Norbert. 137

CHAPTER VIII
The Apostle of Antwerp. 147

CHAPTER IX
The Approbation of the Order. 157

CHAPTER X
St. Bernard and St. Norbert. 169

CHAPTER XI
The Wonder-worker. 179

CHAPTER XII
His Second Journey to Rome. 189

CHAPTER XIII
Farewell to Prémontré. 201

THIRD PERIOD: FROM THE TIME NORBERT BECOMES ARCHBISHOP UNTIL HIS DEATH; 1126-1134

CHAPTER I
THE ARCHBISHOP. 215

CHAPTER II
A SUCCESSOR AT PRÉMONTRÉ. 227

CHAPTER III
PERSECUTION. 239

CHAPTER IV
DRIVEN FROM HIS SEE. 251

CHAPTER V
THE DEFENDER OF THE PAPACY. 261

CHAPTER VI
THE ITALIAN EXPEDITION. 273

CHAPTER VII
THE DEATH OF ST. NORBERT. 285

CHAPTER VIII
TRANSLATION OF RELICS. 297

PREFACE

HE life of Norbert, a Saint of the twelfth century, has been written repeatedly in almost every language. In the "Acta SS." (T. XX. et 1 Junii app. p. 38) one of the Bollandists, Father Conrad Jannick, says: "I hardly know of an illustrious man—king, emperor, or saint—whose life has been written more often than Norbert's." Of Norbert it has been said in very truth, that his deeds have been glorified by numerous historians in their annals, by poets in their verses, by artists on their canvas.

As to its historical value, the life-story of Norbert, as Founder of a Religious Order, is a reflection of the ecclesiastical conditions in his days—while as almoner at the court of Henry V, and later as Archbishop of one of the most important sees of Germany, his life gives an insight into the political conditions of a great historical period.

When we consider that at one time there were no less than 67 abbeys of Norbertine or White Canons in England, Scotland and Ireland, it seems very strange that Norbert is but little known among English-speaking nations. However, in the first place, we should remember that since the Protestant Reformation, when all these houses were lost, more than three hundred years passed before the sons of Norbert returned to England; secondly, only a very short account of Norbert's life was thus far ever written in the English language. Today, therefore, as the Premonstratensian Fathers are once more engaged in missionary activity among English-speaking people on both sides of the Atlantic, a more detailed life of St. Norbert, will, we trust, be welcomed.

We shall here give a list of biographies of St. Norbert; first, for the benefit of students of this historical period, and secondly, because we shall often have occasion to refer to these in the course of our history.

Until the middle of the last century, the principal source of information for the biographer of St. Norbert was a MS. attributed to Bl. Hugh, the Saint's first disciple and successor. At different times copies were made of this MS. Thus, one may be seen to-day in the British Museum in London. (No. 15621.) The Public Library of Soissons (Aisne) has two copies, one of the twelfth and one of the thirteenth century. The Library of Bourgogne at Brussels has one copy of the twelfth and one of the fifteenth century. All are entitled: "Vita Norberti, auctore Canonico, praeadjuvante Hugone abbate, Fossense."

This Life was generally used by all compilers until the year 1856, when Mr. Roger Wilmans discovered in the Royal Library at Berlin, a manuscript Life of Norbert of the thirteenth century. This valuable document he published in vol. XII of Pertz "Monumenta Germaniae Historica." When compared with the MS. generally in use, it was found to agree in everything; but in the latter is related in a more detailed manner the Life of the Archbishop of Magdeburg, his dealings with the Emperor, and the expedition of Lothaire and Norbert to Italy (1132-1133). Although no one has been able to find out who was the author of this MS., it is now generally believed, that he was a German; this is clear from the contents and the expressions he uses; also that the MS. is a copy of the MS. by Bl. Hugh, but with additions, especially that on Norbert's influence in Germany. This MS. is referred to as "Vita A" while the one by Hugh is called "Vita B." These observations are based on a series of articles published in the "*Katholiek*," a Holland publication, in the year 1885. The author, Father G. VandenElsen, O. Praem., has made a thorough study of these two oldest biographies of St. Norbert.

The first printed Life of St. Norbert came out in the year 1572 and was published by Surius in his: "*De Probatis Sanctorum Historiis.*" (T. III., p. 517-547.) This is an abridgement of the old MS. now known as the "Vita B."

Since that date Norbert's Life has been printed and reprinted in various languages. Thus appeared in:

1599: "Divi Norberti vita metrica"—Leodii—publ. by Malcorp.

1623: "Vita S. Norberti iconibus expressa." Theod. Galleus excudit. Antverpiae.

1623: "Het leven van den H. Norbertus"—Van der Sterre—Antwerp.

1627: "Vie de Saint Norbert" by Maurice du Pre— Paris.

1632: "Compendia della vita, miracoli ed istituto del glorioso Patriarca San Norberto" by Cornelius Hanegravius. Rome.

1633: "Vita S. Norberti" T. I. "Bibliotheca Ordinis Praemonstratensis" by Le Paige—Paris.

1640: "L'homme Apostolique en la vie de S. Norbert" by Camus. Caen.

1641: "Vita et gesta S. Norberti"—Vindelicae—by P. Schellenberg, S. J.

1650: "S. Norberti vita metro libera''—Duaci—by De Waghenare.

1656: "Vita S. Norberti"—Antverpiae—by Van der Sterre. This is the complete MS. life, known as "Vita B." We read in the Prologue: "Cum multi hujus vitam et gesta conscripserint, nullum omnino invenerim qui rem plenarie et ex ordine prosequatur. . . ."

1661: "Vita S. Norberti" in the "Monasticon Anglicum" T. II. p. 577 et seqq.—Londini.

1667: "Vida Apostolica, muerte y translacion di N. P. San Norbetto" by Francesco Dubail—Madrid.

1683: "Historia critica S. Norberti"—Ienae—by Gaspar Sagittarius (Protestant).

1695: "Vita S. Norberti" 6 Junii in Acta Sanctorum T. XX.

1704: "Histoire de Saint Norbert"—by Charles Louis Hugo—Luxemburg.

1732: "Vita S. Norberti"—by Daniel Schlinder— Pragae.

1738: "Vita S. Norberti recognita" vol. III of the Annales Ord. Praem. by Charles Louis Hugo.

1755: "Historia del gran Padre San Norberto"—Grand by Abad Illana.

1855: "De S. Norberto Ord. Praem. Conditore, commentatio

historica" by Tenckoff. Münster.

1859: "Vita S. Norberti" by Joseph Scholtz. Breslau.

1860: "Saint Norbert, Arch. de Magdebourg et Fondateur de l'Ordre de Prémontré. Lille.

1865: "Die Pramonstratenser der 12 Jahrh." Berlin– by Franz Winter. (Protestant.)

1866: "Histoire de S. Norbert"—Bruxelles—by P. Alphonse de Liguori.

1874: "Die altesten biographien des heiligen Norbertus" —Berlin—by Rosenmund.

1875: "Ienae Literaturzeitung"—Bernhardi.

1876: "Die streitige Papstwahl des Jahres 1130." Innsbruck.—Muhlbacher.

1877: "Svaty Norbert" by Dominic Cermak.—Prague.

1883: "Leben des heiligen Norbertus" by G. Hertel.—Leipsig.

1886: "Histoire de saint Norbert . . . d'apres les manuscrits et les documents originaux. " by G. Madelaine. Lille.

1886: "The Life of St. Norbert" by M. Geudens, London.

1890: "Het leven van den heiligen Norbertus" by G. VandenElsen.—Averbode, Belgium.

1898: "Vie de saint Norbert. Tableaux historiques du XII Siècle." by Ign. Van Spillbeeck. Bruxelles.

1900: "Der heilige Norbert" by Alphonse Zak. Wien.

1914: "Der Hl. Norbert" by Barth. Wozasek—Wien.

The above list shows how, especially since the discovery of Mr. Wilmans in 1856, the former interest in the history of St. Norbert has been revived in the different countries of Europe. And thus it has been a comparatively easy task for the present writer to compile this history. Whenever possible he has taken quotations from English authors and historians, but for the rest he has chiefly relied on "*Het leven van den H. Norbertus*" by G. VandenElsen, of whose accuracy the writer is fully convinced, and the "*Histoire de Saint Norbert*" by Madelaine, whose history of the Saint is said to be the most complete. Both these authors have relied on the "Vita B," the oldest life, and have used the "*Vita*" discovered by Mr. Wilmans as a secondary source of information.

It now remains to express sincere thanks to all those whose assistance has so greatly lightened the burden of the compiler. May the intercession of St. Norbert, in whose honor the work has been undertaken, be their constant reward.

The Author.

St. Norbert's College,
West Depere, Wis.
December, 1915.

FIRST PERIOD

FROM HIS BIRTH UNTIL HIS COMING TO PRÉMONTRÉ

1080-1119

ST. NORBERT (*second from the left*) AT THE COURT OF HENRY IV

❧

CHAPTER I
His Birth and Education

Pone metum Hadwigis: sic vox monet æthere lapsa:
Tam mundo Illustrem gignere digna Virum.[1]

A voice from heaven said:
"Be of good courage, Hadwigis, for you are found worthy to be the mother of a renowned servant of God."

O observant student, scanning the history of Christianity, can fail to see the Providence of God coming to her rescue, whenever special intervention seems necessary. As often as the powers of darkness and the intrigues of a corrupt world threatened to undermine the faith and morals of the multitude, so often did the Holy Spirit raise up men of learning and sanctity to counteract the evil influences of Satan's helpmates. Some of our most eminent Saints have lived in the times of moral corruption. They were sent by God to lead the army of the faithful against the legions of vice and heresy, and thus defend the honor of the Spouse of Christ.

The year of our Saint's conversion coincides with the death of Tankelin or Tanchelm, the heretic, who had shaken the faith and corrupted the morals of thousands. His followers were found in

[1] These Latin verses were composed by an unknown author and originally formed the inscriptions under thirty-five paintings representing scenes of the life of St Norbert. The paintings were executed by J. A. Pfeffel, 1674-1750. Cfr. "Iconographie Norbertine," by Ign. Van Spilbeeck, O. Praem. Vol. III, p. 51.

Flanders, on the banks of the Rhine, and had infested the diocese of Cologne. Norbert was the Angel of peace chosen to restore the true practices of religion, to defeat Abelard and Peter di Leone, and to raise a strong arm on the side of right in the conflict then raging between the temporal and the spiritual powers.

The traveler coming down the Rhine from Wesel towards Nymegen, beholds to his left—at the extreme border of an immense plain—the two rising spires of the collegiate church of Xanten. The town, situated near Wesel, has only about four thousand inhabitants, who are nearly all Catholic. Built at the foot of mount Fürstenberg, Xanten has a certain attractiveness, increased by an ancient venerableness difficult to define. Although the date of its exact origin is lost to history, local pride traces it back to the city of Troy—the Troy of the Franks. To the end of the third century its name was "Vetera Castra." However, since it became the scene of the martyrdom of a number of soldiers belonging to the illustrious Theban Legion, the name has been changed into Xanten, the town of Saints.[2]

In this historic little town Norbert was born in the year 1080,[3] of one of the most illustrious families of Germany's nobility. His father, whose name was Heribert, was related to the Imperial House itself, and his mother Hadwigis, was a descendant of the ancient House of Lorraine. His father bore the title of Count of Gennep, which he derived from his great castle, situated about seven miles from Xanten. The road leading from the castle to the village is called Norbert's road to this day, on which account there is a local tradition that the Saint was born in the castle. Most historians agree, however, that his cradle stood in his father's costly mansion at Xanten, where he also received his early education.

His parents, belonging to God's nobility as well as that of the

[2] Cfr. Acta SS. T. V., Octob., p. 14-30.

[3] This is the date on which most biographers agree. There are some who name 1084 and even 1086, but give no reason for it.

world, were both virtuous and God-fearing Christians. Besides Norbert, they had another son, Heribert by name, older than the Saint, and one younger, Erbert.[4] The Saint's mother especially was a very pious woman. Although history is quite silent about her, there is one very significant incident of her life related in all the biographies of Norbert. Shortly before the Saint was born, she heard very distinctly a voice from heaven, saying: "Be of good courage, Hadwigis, for you are found worthy to be the mother of a renowned servant of God, a future illustrious archbishop." Thus also were announced the great Samuel, St. John the Baptist, and other Saints. As the golden dawn heralds the sun which brings to the earth light and heat, so also were announced the approach of these saints, who were to spread the light of the Gospel and kindle the warmth of Jesus' love in the hearts of the people. Blessed indeed may we call the mother who receives such tidings from above. It was also said of the Precursor of Our Lord that he would be great before God, and it is remarkable that Norbert during his lifetime always considered the great Preacher of Penance his special patron and protector. He tried continually to model his own life after St. John's example.

When the new-born babe was baptized, it was not without reason that his name was called Norbert or Notbert, for this name means "Shield of the North." As history will prove, our Saint in reality did become a protector of Northern Europe against the invasions of Paganism, where his Order for centuries proved a mighty rampart.

Although we know very little about Norbert's early education, we have no doubt that his pious mother took charge of it herself and gave him a gentle and reverential training. She also must have imprinted upon that youthful soul that real piety, which, though dimmed for a time, shone forth in all its splendor immediately after his conversion. It must be further observed that Xanten had a collegiate church, formed in those days after the model of

[4] This younger brother is mentioned in the Necrology of Xanten and Floreffe. Cfr. further in the Acta SS. T. I. Junii Analecta C. III, p. 857.

cathedrals, and therefore had a grammar school attached, the duties of the Canons being such as did not occupy more than a few hours each day. Probably, therefore, the education of our youthful Saint was entrusted to the Canons of Xanten.[5] He quickly surpassed his fellow-students, and convinced his teachers of the fact that God had bestowed extraordinary gifts upon him. Before very long, the Canons advised Norbert's father to send his son to a university. Norbert went to Cologne, where he again so distinguished himself, that when he was twenty years of age, he was looked upon as a scholar. His contemporaries are unanimous in praising his profound knowledge of philosophy. This solid foundation served him admirably in his later life, when he was called upon to refute the heretical doctrine of the clever Abelard and expose the sophistry of the party of the antipope. He had moreover an inborn eloquence and a wide knowledge of literature, sacred and profane. When we add to all this his noble birth and genteel appearance, we can readily believe that the young Norbert was considered a veritable leader among the rising generation of his day. His biographers agree that he was tall in stature—in bearing, graceful and refined, quick and penetrating of intellect, tractable and tender of heart. Thus equipped at the age of twenty, our Saint faced the world at the time of its mediaeval crisis.

The two great powers of the civilized world had for years been at open war. The great Pope Hildebrand had died when Norbert was a child of four, and conditions were still very much unsettled. Although the right of lay-investiture had been taken away from the Crown—although the perfidious Henry had gone to Canossa, in Germany, the old simoniacal practices had long since been resumed.

---

[5] This is the opinion of G. VandenElsen "Het leven H. van den Norbertus," p. 6. Madelaine in his "Vie de Saint Norbert," p. 33, observes that it is more probable that Norbert had a private tutor at home, according to the custom of wealthy families in those days. Both agree about Norbert's going to the University of Cologne.

The war between the temporal and the spiritual powers, far from being settled, continued as a matter of fact, for more than fifty years, and the Saint himself took an active part in this great struggle and also beheld the triumph of the Church before his death.

It might be well to call the reader's attention to the fact that we are now at the beginning of the period of the Crusades. The zealous indignation over the insults and cruelties suffered at the hands of the Turks by Christians in the Holy Land, was just at its height. Great fears were being entertained as to the fate of that valiant army of over half a million warriors, many of whom were of the nobility, who had set out for Asia Minor. And if anywhere, it certainly must have been at the home of Norbert that the movements of the Crusaders were being watched with feverish excitement, since the leader himself, Godfrey of Bouillon, Duke of Lower-Lorraine, was a blood-relation of Norbert's mother. Although it is but insinuated in some biographies, it seems quite probable that, when on July 15th of that same year the news came from the Holy Land that Jerusalem was captured and that Godfrey had been proclaimed its King, Norbert's enthusiasm to join the army of the Crusaders was thoroughly aroused. How very natural to picture this accomplished young man, in the vigor of youth and full of ambition, pleading with his father and mother to be allowed to join the holy army and win fame by setting free the Holy Places and driving out the Turks. However, his virtuous parents, mindful of the heavenly warning given before his birth, had decided to lead Norbert into God's sanctuary. Not that they lacked the general enthusiasm, for his illustrious father, the Count, died a Crusader in the Holy Land. His younger brother Erbert, in a later expedition, is said to have lost his life under the walls of Tyre, in Palestine,[6] but Norbert was, in their opinion, destined to become a "Cleric." Whether or not his parents had selfish motives in this determination, it is impossible to say. Some biographers are inclined to think they had, first because

[6] Thus the Necrology of Xanten and Floreffe.

it was customary in those days to have at least one son a "Cleric secondly", on account of Norbert's subsequent behavior.

Norbert was ordained subdeacon by the Archbishop of Cologne, his Ordinary, and forthwith appointed to a Canonry in the Imperial Church at Xanten. It was not unusual in those days to meet canons who were not yet elevated to the dignity of the priesthood. Many clerics were given a canonry through the influence of some friend, or on account of their exalted station in life, and derived rich emoluments from it. We should not forget that we are in the beginning of the twelfth century, when, as Cardinal Newman says: "The Christian world was in a more melancholy state than it ever had been, either before or since." Any one acquainted with the struggle of lay-investiture will readily understand the truth of this statement.

Norbert did not remain very long a canon at Xanten. The Archbishop, hearing of his natural talents and learning, invited him to come to live at his Court in Cologne. Alas! our worldly-minded Norbert, blinded by ambition, obeyed with great eagerness. Soon misled by the flattery of the world, he allowed himself to be entirely carried away by its pleasures and allurements. He forgot the lessons of his pious mother and the obligations of his state in life, and became thoroughly worldly. True, he was living at the Court of an Archbishop, but as in those days bishops and abbots often filled the post of Chancellor or Ambassador at the various courts, so also worldly chancellors and ambassadors often filled episcopal sees, or were placed at the head of monasteries. Consequently a worldly spirit prevailed even at the court of many a Church dignitary. In regard to the Court of Cologne in particular, a panegyrist of Norbert has said that there especially the Church and the world made their display successively.

We can readily understand how well the young Count was received at the Court. His nobility, his learning and graceful bearing, made him a favorite with all, especially when he showed his eagerness to join in their amusements. Still, to do him justice, we feel obliged to add here, that however worldly he was, Norbert never gave himself over to the sinful excesses of those days. Even his greatest enemies, who after his conversion, did all in their power to counteract his influence, never accused him of having been guilty of any great sin or scandal. On the other hand, we cannot deny that at this time Norbert's eyes and ears were open only for things of the world, that he was ambitious and fond of honors. Says the author of the Office of St. Norbert:

Yet worldly glory wooed thy heart,
And thou, of noble race, didst turn
Away from thine eternal part
To seek the fair, false lights that burn
In royal halls of earth. ...[7]

Norbert succeeded in obtaining a second ecclesiastical preferment, a canonry in the cathedral of Cologne, besides other benefices, by which he was enabled to increase his income. But growing dissatisfied at the court of the Archbishop, he did all in his power to enter that of the Emperor, to whom he was related through his father. The Emperor was Henry V, who came to the throne, Dec. 25, 1105, having forced his father to abdicate. Henry was a bitter opponent of Pope Paschal II. Nevertheless, his gay court tempted our young canon, which fact alone shows sufficiently how far Norbert had drifted.

Cæsaris hinc juvenem favor allicit, inde Voluptas,
Addictum studiis dum tenet aula suis.[8]

By what intrigue he succeeded we do not know, but very soon Norbert was installed as chaplain and almoner of the Emperor

[7] Hymn at Matins. Cfr. Manual of Third Order of St. Norbert, p. 66.

[8] Royal favor and luxury attracted the youth who had tasted court life at the palace of the archbishop.

himself. In the capacity of almoner he was present at the Imperial Diets, and was one of the immediate councillors of His Majesty. Thus we read that at the Diet of Ratisbon, held on Epiphany day, 1110, Norbert spoke in the name of the King. He did this with such eloquence and conviction, that he was designated by the votes of the most prominent men of the kingdom, to accompany the Emperor on his expedition to Rome; truly a great honor, but by no means an enviable one, when we consider the Emperor's mission.

Pope Paschal II had refused to restore to Henry the right of Investiture. Henry's first object, therefore, in going to Rome was, as. his ambassadors themselves expressed it, to decide the question by the sword, if necessary. His second object was to receive the Imperial Crown from the hands of the Pope. Norbert's part in this woeful expedition was to assist Henry in coming to terms with the Pope. From Florence, where the Emperor spent Christmas, that year, the conditions of the Coronation were arranged by letter as follows:

> On the day of the coronation, Henry shall make in writing a renunciation of all right of Investiture of churches. He shall pledge himself by oath to the Pope, in the presence of the clergy and people, to its strict observance. He shall swear to leave the churches in the peaceful enjoyment of their property. He shall confirm the Holy See in the possession of its estates and fiefs, after the example of Charlemagne and other predecessors. On these conditions the Pope will crown Henry V and acknowledge him as Emperor. He will assist him to maintain his authority in Germany, and forbid the bishops to usurp the 'regales,' or do anything prejudicial to the rights of the prince.[9]

We have reason to fear that when these terms were duly drawn up and signed by both parties, Norbert prided himself on his

[9] Cfr. "General History of the Catholic Church," by J. E. Darras, Vol. III, p. 181. The same author also observes that what is here meant by "regales" are the temporal rights and fiefs, which flowed, as such from the suzerainty of the king.

successful diplomacy, not knowing the false character of Henry. At first everything pointed to real success. The king entered Rome, preceded by an immense multitude of people bearing green boughs, palms and flowers. However, when Henry was required to sign the document, he proved false, and boldly refused to give up the right of Investiture. It was on this occasion that one of the most shocking scenes related in history took place within the very walls of St. Peter's. The outcome of it all was that Henry was forced to flee from Rome, but he dragged the venerable Pontiff along as his prisoner, and for two months the Pope was subjected to fearful threats and cruel treatment.

Norbert, now realizing the baseness of the king's action, exerted his influence to obtain the release of the Pope and to restore peace between the two sovereigns, but all in vain. He visited the Pope in prison, consoled him in his distress and appeared greatly shocked at the king's violence and injustice. He is also said to have thrown himself at the feet of the august prisoner and implored his pardon. That this incident made Norbert turn seriously into himself, we know from his subsequent conduct. As yet, however, he was too ambitious, too much of a courtier to listen to the inner voice of his conscience and forsake the unjust cause of the king altogether; still we shall presently see signs of an inward struggle.

History informs us that, overcome by the entreaties of many bishops, and fearing a new schism in the Church, Pope Paschal II at last yielded, and signed a treaty by which he conceded to Henry the right of investing bishops by ring and crozier. On his return journey, Henry wanted to make use of his privilege at once, and offered the Archbishopric to his Chancellor, and the Bishopric of Cambray to his chaplain and almoner, Norbert. Strange to say, Norbert refused. The king's offer was tempting, for the Bishopric of Cambray was a very important see and yielded a large revenue; but Norbert had changed. Although he lacked the courage at the time to lead the life of an exemplary cleric, his upright character had been shocked by the late acts of the king, and thus at the risk of losing Henry's favor, he declined the honor. Attached to honors he was, but nothing could ever have induced him to accept the ring and the crozier from an excommunicated layman. On the other hand, it is strange that even after this event, Norbert does not entirely sever his connection with court-life. True, after returning from Italy, he left the Court of Henry, but returned to that of the Archbishop of Cologne. He had either offended the king by declining his offer, and thus lost his favor, or perhaps he no longer dared, even tacitly, approve of his perfidious conduct. At any rate the change did not affect his manner of living.

> But lo!
> These halls are trembling 'neath the power
> Of Him Who stoops to thee, to show
> Thou shalt be His. Alas! that hour
> Thou 'rt faltering still. The voice of fame,
> Its flattery, in thine ear is sweet.
>
> (Office of St. Norbert.)

Norbert plunged into society, took part in all amusements, and seemed to be leading a life even more worldly than before. He was so thoroughly enslaved by the world at this time, that nothing short of a miracle could change this ambitious Saul into a second Paul.

CHAPTER II
NORBERT'S CONVERSION

Ardeat ut Superis intus mens ardua flammis,
Corpus salvifico fulminis igne cadit.

Lo! the lightning flash is falling
And the voice that will not cease
Speaks in accents, richly calling:
"Turn to Me and seek for peace."

URING the summer of the year 1115,[1] Norbert, bent upon pleasure, was on his way to a village called Freden, situated a few miles from Xanten. He was riding a fiery steed richly caparisoned; his servant rode at his side. It was a beautiful summer day, and his silk cloak and costly ornaments glittered in the bright sunshine as he sped through the rich meadows. Suddenly the heavens darkened; a violent wind arose, and the next moment thunder and lightning followed each other in rapid succession. The rain fell in torrents, and unfortunately the nearest place of shelter was a good distance away. Norbert, though trembling with fear, insisted on continuing his journey. His servant, however, less courageous, stopped and exclaimed: "Sir Norbert, whither art thou going? Come back, for the hand of God is against thee!" Hardly had he spoken these words, when with a loud clap of thunder, a flash of lightning tore up the earth at the very feet of Norbert 's horse. The horse fell and threw its rider, who lay for a long time like one dead. When he regained

[1] According to Ch. Louis Hugo's MS. *Hagiolog. Ord. Praem.* Norbert's conversion took place on May 28.

consciousness, the last words his page had spoken, "The hand of God is against thee," were still ringing in his ears and were to him like a message from heaven. A most vivid picture of his past life flashed at that moment before his mind. Realizing the great danger he had just escaped, and thoroughly frightened at the condition of his soul, Norbert exclaimed with the Apostle: "Lord, what wilt Thou that I do?" At the same moment a voice from heaven sounded in his ear, saying: "Turn away from evil and do good; seek after peace and pursue it."[2] This was the turning point in Norbert's life. Humbled while in the full pursuit of pleasure, he became on the spot a sincere penitent.

Protinus ad sacras Tyro volat impiger ædes,
Deserit et lubricum, quod male trivit, iter.[3]

Norbert returned to Xanten and forthwith renounced all his appointments at Court. He locked himself in a room and there, prostrated before the Crucifix, shed an abundance of tears. This same room, where Norbert for three long years practiced the severest penances in expiation for his sins, is still pointed out to the visitor in the old chapel of St. Denis. Every year numerous pilgrims visit the place around which for eight hundred years the most authentic souvenirs of our Saint have centered.[4]

We may now picture Norbert alone with God. In solitude he began to realize the greatness of the event which a few hours before had taken place on the road to Freden; and, reflecting on the consequences of his sudden resolution to renounce all his court appointments, happiness filled his soul. Oh! how sincerely he must have thanked God for sending him this warning! The gifts which

[2] Cfr. Acta SS. T. XX, p. 802.

[3] At once the Novice turns away from the dangerous road which he has foolishly been treading, and flies eagerly to the sanctuary.

[4] Cfr. "Die Victorskirche zu Xanten," s. 167.

God so lavishly had bestowed upon him—his talents and scholarly education—his constant dealings with the great men of the age—all had predestined him to exercise immense influence. Until now he had served only the world and offered his talents to the idol of vanity. Almighty God, in His inscrutable wisdom, had allowed all this for reasons best known to Himself; but now His hour had come.

After spending days and nights in tears and prayers, asking God for guidance and strength in his good resolutions, Norbert calmly began to make plans for the future. He did not, as many of us would expect, lay aside his silks and costly adornments; but under them he began to wear a rough garment of hair-cloth, his penitential garment, as he called it, and from this time never passed a day without it. His reason for this was, no doubt, that he might still be able to associate with his former companions and bring them also back to God. This will become more clear in the study of his later life.

The sudden conversion of Norbert has been truly compared by all his biographers to the conversion of Saul of Tarsus. Certainly no one can fail to see the striking resemblance. The road to Freden was for Norbert what the road to Damascus was for Saul. The same words sounded in the ears of both, and while the Holy Spirit led Saul to Ananias for further instruction and direction, Norbert, as we shall see presently, was led by Providence to the school of a monk, well-known for deep learning and piety.

At a distance of about five miles from Cologne, on the other side of the Rhine, there was in those days the celebrated Benedictine Abbey of Siburg, founded by St. Annon, in 1066. Since the year 1105 it had been under the able management of a very distinguished and saintly abbot, by the name of Conon. He was known all over Germany, and it was chiefly through his personality that the abbey was considered at the time the centre of religious life. If the common saying be true, that a saint is needed to form another saint, Norbert, in going to Abbot Conon, undoubtedly went to the right school. The very first thing Norbert did upon his arrival, was to unburden his heart by a sincere and humble confession. Tears flowed freely while he related the whole story of his former life to his spiritual father; but the good and wise abbot greatly encouraged him, and spoke to him of the mercy of God. He advised him to spend some time in complete retirement from the world, meditating and studying the Scriptures, and meanwhile praying the Almighty with all confidence and fervor to complete in him the good work He had begun. Norbert followed this advice to the letter. He stayed for some time in the monastery, and although he did not join the Benedictine Order, he at once began to lead their life and to spend his days in solitude.

From our own knowledge of human nature we can easily infer how great was Norbert's struggle in this solitude. The chief obstacle to the carrying out of a good resolution is the reaction, which almost invariably comes after we have been touched by extraordinary graces. Satan and his helpmates did their very best to make Norbert change his good resolutions and go back to his former gay life. Like the great St. Augustine, he was tempted by his former friends, who continually tried to hold him up to ridicule and scorn, well knowing how deeply his proud nature had always resented this. It would have been contrary to human nature, had Norbert not felt these attacks keenly. However, he stood firm. Inexperienced soldier as he was in the great spiritual battle, he went with all his temptations and difficulties to his commander, Abbot Conon, asked his advice and followed his directions.

As often as he went to the abbot, as Norbert himself later testified, peace was restored to his soul. Days and weeks and months he passed, apparently dead to the world, but fighting a fierce battle with his former self. At other times his impetuous nature asserted itself; he then would hasten to Abbot Conon and beg to be allowed to plunge into the blind world, and preach by word and example, the vanity of earthly things. But the wise abbot checked his ardor and taught him how to control this impetuosity by studying the conduct of our Blessed Redeemer. He made clear to

Norbert that his hour had not yet come, but that it would be plainly revealed to him in God's appointed time. Thus did our Saint make great progress in self-denial and self-mastery under the prudent guidance of his spiritual father.

Meanwhile the time was drawing near when the Archbishop of Cologne was accustomed to hold his ordinations. We know that the Saint had long since been ordained subdeacon. He had refused to receive the higher orders that he might with more freedom lead a worldly life. Norbert, now realizing the greatness of the scandal he had thus given, was most anxious to make due reparation. When he spoke to Abbot Conon to this effect, he found to his great delight that the abbot also advised him to present himself for Orders. After some deliberation it was decided that Norbert should go in person to the Archbishop and request him, not only to admit him among the candidates for Holy Orders, but also to allow him to receive Deaconship and the Holy Priesthood on one and the same day. Thus we find Norbert after his long retreat, his soul filled with a heavenly joy, once more in the palace of the Archbishop of Cologne with an unexpected request.

Imagine the surprise of the Archbishop when made acquainted with the request of his former courtier. Informed of the great change which had taken place in Norbert, he called him into his presence and said: "Indeed, you greatly surprise me, so often have you refused Holy Orders when offered to you even by learned and virtuous men." Norbert felt the truth of the rebuke, and when pressed to account for the change in him, wished to tell all, but tears choked his voice. Unable to speak, he threw himself at the feet of the Archbishop, and begged him to forgive him his past life. This so touched His Grace, that he said: "Who am I, that I should dare to keep the gates of God's Sanctuary closed against you?"

Enter now, pious reader, the vast and venerable Cathedral of Cologne, dedicated to the Prince of the Apostles; it is the hour of the inspiring ceremony of solemn ordination. The church is richly decorated; the Ordinandi, carrying their sacred vestments, are taking their places in the sanctuary, and an immense crowd fills the spacious cathedral Many, no doubt, have come, led by devotion, but a large number also are there through mere curiosity. Norbert is to be ordained! Norbert, the son of the Count of Gennep; Norbert, the well-known, gay courtier! This rumor has spread through the city of Cologne and all who knew him had come to verify for themselves this incredible report. Note their disappointment as they vainly scrutinize the Ordinandi, for Norbert is not among them. They are questioning the truth of the report, and even giving expression to their doubts, when down the center aisle moves a stately figure, clad in silk, costly adorned with gold and jewels. It is Norbert in all his former glory. All heads are turned—all eyes are fixed on him. What does it all mean, they ask? Is he returning to his former gay life? Verily no! The break between himself and the world is to be completed, and the vast crowd is to witness it and to be convinced of his sincerity. As the sacristan offers him the sacred vestments, Norbert calls one of his servants who is near at hand. At last he thinks his hour is come—the hour in which he may repair, at least in part, the scandal he has given, and show his former friends how deeply he is in earnest. He wills to impress most vividly upon their minds that he is no longer the Norbert they have known —no longer the happy courtier and slave of the world, but the humble penitent of Jesus Christ renouncing the world and its pomp. Before the eyes of this vast multitude, he casts his princely garments on the floor, and replaces them by a penitential robe of sheepskin, tied around the waist with a rough cord. Then putting the liturgical vestments over this simple tunic, he goes to the altar and presents himself for Ordination.[5]

---

[5] Pellibus agninis gemmis auroque nitentem
Permutat populo Mysta stupente togam.
In the third chapter of the *Vita B* we read: "Notus, ut putabatur, omnibus; sed ignotus, ut rei veritas se habebat, universis ... innuit sibi praesentari pelliceum agninum ... videntibus universis consortibus ... pristinae levitatis ... etc."

> Thy robes of princely state are spurned;
> The court, its pomps, its gilded strife,
> Are thine no more, for higher love
> Has fortified thy glowing heart. ...
>
> (Office of St Norbert.)

The crowd, breathless, especially those who were ignorant of the happenings on the road to Freden, could not believe their own eyes. "Who would ever have thought it?" they said, "this is truly a miracle!" Meanwhile, in the sanctuary, the Holy Ceremony was proceeding. "Receive the power to consecrate the Body and Blood of our Lord Jesus Christ," was at last spoken to Norbert, and God alone knows the feelings which at that moment animated his noble soul, unworthy as he considered himself, to become the minister of God—a priest of the Most High. . . ! His sentiments on this sacred occasion are expressed, however imperfectly, in these his own words:

> O Sacerdos! tu non es tu, quia Deus es; tu non es tui, quia servus et minister Christi; tu non es tuus, quia sponsus Ecclesiae; tu non es tibi, quia mediator Dei et hominum; tu non es de te, quia nihil es. Tu quis ergo, O Sacerdos? nihil et omnia. O Sacerdos cave ne tibi, quod Christo patienti, dicatur: Alios salvos fecit, seipsum non potest salvum facere.

> O Priest! thou art not thyself, because thou art God; thou art not of thyself, because thou art the servant and minister of Christ; thou art not thine own, because thou art the spouse of the Church; thou art not for thyself, because thou art the mediator between God and man; thou art not from thyself, because thou art nothing. What then art thou, O Priest ? Nothing and everything. O Priest! take care lest what was said to Christ on the Cross be said to thee: He saved others, himself he cannot save.

In vain did the eager crowd look for Norbert when the solemn services were concluded. He had secretly left the cathedral and returned in haste to his spiritual father. In the monastery of Siburg, under the direction of the abbot, he at once began a retreat of forty days, fasting on bread and water, in order to prepare himself for a worthy exercise of his sacred calling. His time he divided between meditation and a study of the duties of the sacred ministry. It was his good fortune at this particular time to make the acquaintance of Abbot Rupert, a saintly man, and the learned author of a beautiful book on the ceremonial of the Mass. It was largely through his influence that our Saint conceived so profound a respect for the adorable Sacrifice, and that later he became a real champion of the august Sacrament of the Altar. Henceforth, love for the Holy Eucharist and a burning zeal for the salvation of souls were his characteristic virtues.

After his forty days retreat Norbert returned to Xanten, his native town, and again took his place among the Canons. With deep humility and devotion he joined in the recital of the divine Office and evinced great fervor in his efforts to serve God as perfectly as possible. The day after his arrival the members of the Chapter offered him the privilege of celebrating a Solemn High Mass on the following day, for it was customary thus to honor newly-ordained priests. Norbert gladly accepted the favor. "O day, forever memorable in the annals of religion!" exclaims one of the Saint's panegyrists,

> Overcome by a holy enthusiasm, Norbert suspended the sacred function and, burning with love for souls, mounted the pulpit and delivered a most powerful discourse on the fleeting pleasures of the world and the emptiness of its honors and promises. With an eloquence which foreshadowed the future great orator he warned his vast audience of the dangers of a worldly life, and urged them to reform, pointing to his own life as

an example.[6]

Norbert shared the zeal of all the Saints of his period for reform among clerics as well as among laymen. On the very next day he spoke to the Canons assembled in the chapter-house, of their lack of discipline. Holding in his hands the Rules of the Fathers, promulgated by the Council of Aix-la-Chapelle, in 816, for secular canons, he urged so fearlessly and forcefully the necessity of reforming their lives, that many of the older canons were deeply moved, and looked upon Norbert as one sent by heaven to restore discipline. But the younger canons, more attached to the pleasures of the world, became so exasperated on being rebuked, and especially by one like Norbert, that, not being able to bear his remonstrances nor to silence him, some left the chapter-house while others became most insulting. Instigated by the latter, a young cleric of low birth even spat in his face.[7] Norbert, however, excused him, and forgave him at once, thanking God for this occasion of doing penance for his sins. In this manner did God prepare His servant for his life-work, namely, the betterment of the people by the reformation of the clergy. Henceforth this is to be his constant aim as Missionary—as Founder of a new Religious Order—and especially as Archbishop of Magdeburg.

---

[6] Migne T. LIII, p. 347. Panegyric of St. Norbert, preached in Paris on the 11th and the 17th of July, 1763.

[7] Cfr. *Vita* A, Ch. II.

ST. NORBERT DIVESTS HIMSELF OF HIS FORMER LIFE

CHAPTER III
THE PENITENT

Argenti vilescit honos, nimiumque cupitas
Prodiga Norberti dextera spargit opes.

Despising worldly goods,
Norbert with a lavish hand
Bestows all he has upon the poor.

HE three years following his ordination were for the greater part spent in solitude on a high mountain, called "Fürstenberg," near Xanten. They are termed the formation-period of his religious life. As the shining marble of Paros and Carrara, the same in substance as common limestone, is fashioned in secret by the wonderworking hand of nature; as the sparkling diamond, identical in composition with charcoal, receives its marvelous crystalline structure in nature's own secret laboratory—so has it often pleased God, to form the saint from the sinner under His divine action in solitude, by prayer and meditation.

There was a little chapel on the Fürstenberg, which had long been entirely deserted. This Norbert arranged for his new dwelling. Here he mortified his body by fasting and discipline; here he offered daily the Holy Sacrifice, and spent most of his nights as well as days in prayer.

Then with fasts,
With scourges, and with iron chain,
Thou'lt seek to expiate the past,
And heal, with care, the former pain
Thy pride inflicted. . . .

Occasionally he would come down from his Thabor to preach to the people or to visit the Abbot of Siburg, who still continued to be his spiritual adviser. He had now become accustomed to rely on Abbot Conon for spiritual direction, and in the many trials sent by God at this time to arm him for the future battle, the abbot's help was indispensable to Norbert.

One of his greatest trials at this period must have been his inability to preach to the people in the church at Xanten. We are informed that on one occasion when Norbert was on his way to Siburg and wished to deliver a sermon to the people of Xanten, he was actually driven from the church by his former colleagues. Like all reformers, he was disliked by most of the canons, and even hated by some. At their instigation the enemies of Norbert, all former friends, had formed a party, a clique we might say, whose only object was to oppose and persecute in every way the innovator, as Norbert was called by them. However, though they prevented him from speaking to the people, he nevertheless continued fearlessly to address the canons themselves at every opportunity, in private as well as in public. Needless to say that he thus found numerous occasions for the practice of many virtues. When, for instance, they reproached him, calling him a newcomer, a convert of a day. . . . etc., he found therein a reason for increasing his spiritual and penitential exercises, hoping by these means and by the grace of God, to become a trained soldier in God's army in a short time. He was persuaded that his constant example and unwavering virtue would be more convincing than his preaching. Virtue, in fact, always triumphs even where the most powerful and eloquent sermons have miserably failed.

With this end in view he began to walk about barefooted, even in the midst of winter, wearing only his sheepskin tunic and penitential cape. In accordance with the strictest observance of earlier Christianity, he also began to observe, the whole year around, the fast and abstinence of the Lenten season. Except on Sundays, he took no meal till evening, and by his austerity became another St. John the Baptist. His daily life became a most powerful and continual sermon, which no one was able to prevent, and which, Norbert reasoned, was bound to succeed. But human nature is ever the same, and to see a man strictly perform duties in which we ourselves fail, is for us a constant rebuke. Soon, through real spite, did the enemies of Norbert look for an occasion to take their revenge.

But let us turn from them for the moment to follow Norbert on one of his excursions to Abbot Conon of Siburg. The monks of this abbey were very strict in the observance of their rule, and Norbert loved to listen to their singing the divine praises. He often joined them in their diligent study of Holy Scripture, and made great progress in the knowledge of God's Word. But his greatest attraction was the abbot, whose exemplary life always stimulated him to persevere in his good resolutions. To spend some time in his presence, and to be able to see him and to converse with him, worked like an inspiration on our Saint. After these visits, as he himself later testified, long fasts and severe discipline lost even their natural repugnance, and the nights spent in prayer were full of heavenly consolation.

> ... for higher love
> Has fortified thy glowing heart,
> And, barefoot, through the snow thou'lt move
> As one all heedless of the smart
> Of scorn and insult. . . .

His returns to the abbey were therefore quite frequent. Another pious diversion in his solitude was his frequenting a grotto near Rolduc, which he visited on his way to the Canons Regular of that place. He often spent some time in the abbey, where the clerics were still in their first fervor. The abbey had been founded in 1104 by St. Ailbert, of noble birth, who had for some time been connected with the cathedral chapter of Tournay, in Belgium. After his ordination, being anxious to lead a more perfect life, he had come to this place and founded a monastery. He, like Norbert, also went barefooted, and with his companions led a strictly apostolic life according to the rules of St. Augustine. These two Saints, in fact, became very much attached to each other, and as we shall see later, Norbert took St. Ailbert's abbey as a model, in founding his order.

Norbert loved especially to offer the Holy Sacrifice in the above-mentioned grotto. One day, at the moment of the Consecration of the Chalice, a large spider fell into the Precious Blood. In those days spiders were generally considered poisonous, as, in fact, the old English name: attercope, attyrcoppe, literally poison-cup, still indicates. The Saint knew perfectly well what the rubrics of the Mass allow on such occasions, but his biographers explain, such was his reverence for the Precious Blood, that at the time of the Communion, resigned to die at the foot of the altar, he consumed the Precious Blood containing the venomous insect. But God Who watched over his servant, rewarded his lively faith by instantly relieving him of the dangerous insect. "This fact," adds the contemporary author of the Life of St. Norbert, "shows how lively was his faith and how great God's goodness towards him." "Two special virtues," continues this same biographer, "were necessary to enable him to do the work for which God had destined him: patience and faith. Patience served as a shield, lest being unarmed he should yield; faith, for strength; lest being too weak, he should fail."[1] Doubtless at this time, he was endowed with other virtues, but faith was his characteristic virtue; by it he wrought many

[1] Cfr. *Vita B.* Ch. VI. Also Hugo, "Histoire de St. Norbert," p. 23, who quotes a manuscript history of the abbey of Kloster-Rath.

miracles, and it animated all he did. It was a common saying that faith excelled in Norbert, charity in Bernard and humility in Milo, Bishop of Therouanne and a disciple of Norbert.[2]

We now return to our Saint in the period of his spiritual formation. How admirably does divine Providence guide the future Founder of a religious Order! Thus far God has led him through the canonical life at Xanten—has made him acquainted with monasticism in the monastery of Abbot Conon—has directed him to St. Ailbert, who with his disciples was leading the life of the Apostles, and lastly, that Norbert might know the eremitical life, He leads him to the hermit Ludolph, a man of great sanctity and extreme austerity, who lived at Bedburg. Ludolph's object in life also was to reform the people by first reforming the clergy, and so, like Norbert, he must bear insults and injuries. We are not surprised to learn that Norbert and Ludolph became sincere friends, for like aims invariably draw souls close together.

There is surely no ground for the supposition that Norbert had at this time the faintest idea of founding a religious Order. Still, since his aim was "reform," he, being a Canon, must have felt himself drawn into the reform of canonical life, which at that time was taking place. History informs us that about the eleventh century canonical life was given up by the clergy in many churches, and thus we read of the distinction which henceforth was made between those clerics who lived by themselves in separate houses and others who still adhered to the old discipline. The former were called "Canonici saeculares," the latter "Canonici regulares," and these names have ever since distinguished them. We shall refer to this again in the second volume.

When we accompanied Norbert on his visits to Siburg and Rolduc, or found him in company with Ludolph, we saw him constantly exposed to the vilest abuse by his former colleagues of Xanten. His strict fasts and long vigils had emaciated his body, and

---

[2] Ibidem.

the study of the lives of saints added to constant prayer and meditation, had so spiritualized our Saint, that his mere appearance among his former friends was now a sufficient excuse for a new outbreak. It must be remarked, however, that they never reproached his former life. Worldly Norbert had been, but no one ever accused him of having led a scandalous life. What mostly roused his opponents was the fact that Norbert, only a short time before one with them, was now trying to be their reformer. They refused to believe that his conversion was sincere, notwithstanding the numerous proofs he constantly gave of his sincerity. Also his success in preaching made him a number of enemies. Norbert, as we know, was very anxious to preach. He lost no opportunity of ascending the pulpit, where he spoke with real eloquence. He was considered one of the most eloquent speakers of his day, and immense crowds gathered to listen to him. How much good he effected by his preaching we know from the Annals of those days, especially of the year 1117, when one calamity succeeded another, so that the end of the world was generally thought to be at hand. "The most learned men of the time," thus says Baronius in his Annals, "looked upon the enormities of sin and the calamities of the age as signs of the coming of the Antichrist and the end of the world."[3]

Norbert's success in preaching, added to his austere life, at last led his enemies, no longer satisfied with ill-usage, to discredit him in the eyes of his ecclesiastical superiors. The clique which had been formed some time previous, now began to work in earnest and systematically, trying to find evidence against him. Well may one of the early historians compare their work to a coming thunderstorm, when small and insignificant clouds are gathering together to darken a clear sky. The moment was near at hand when their petty accusations, heaped together, were to burst forth like the

---

[3] That Norbert shared this belief we know from one of the letters of St. Bernard. Cfr. Letter LVI, sent to Geoffrey, Bishop of Chartres. See also later, Second Period, Chapter X.

thunder and lightning of a heavy storm.

Apparently unconscious of what was going on around him, Norbert kept up his good work, preaching by word and example and bringing a number of sinners back to God. The Annals of Cleves give us an interesting detail of his missionary zeal at this very time. At Lunen, in Westphalia, there still existed a remnant of the old Saxon paganism, in the form of an idol dedicated to Venus, the evening star, and venerated by the inhabitants. In his holy zeal and enthusiasm, Norbert not only broke this idol, but even succeeded in having a church, dedicated to the Blessed Virgin, built in its place.[4]

At last the storm broke. On July 26th, in the year 1118, Cuno, Cardinal Archbishop of Preneste and Legate of Pope Gelasius II, had assembled an important National Council at Fritzlar in Lower-Hesse. The object of this Council was to find means to maintain the Pope's authority in Germany, where it was threatened by Henry V and his antipope, Maurice Bourdin. Present at the Council were a great number of archbishops and bishops, abbots and priests, also many of the most prominent laymen. Norbert's enemies considered this a fine opportunity for taking their long-planned revenge. Led by the Canons of Xanten, they appeared at Fritzlar and demanded that the Council should begin proceedings against the fanaticism of Norbert. The Council gave them a hearing; and, after considering the matter, judged it wise to have Norbert appear before them in person. His enemies lost no time in bringing him before this tribunal.[5]

Norbert, known to nearly all present as the gay courtier, the former chaplain of Henry, whose doings are being condemned, now stands before this distinguished assembly; he is accused of being a religious fanatic. His features are completely changed—his body, emaciated from fasting and discipline, is wrapped in a penitential robe of sheepskin. Calm and dignified, he faces his accusers, who

---

[4] Annales Cliviae, p. 217.

[5] Cfr. *Vita B*, Ch. VIII.

are shouting at him—calling him a hypocrite—one who cloaks evil designs under the pretext of religious zeal, etc. ... The Council asks for clear and detailed accusations. Ah! they have plenty, everything is ready. Their first reproach is for having taken unto himself the function of preaching. Who, they ask, has charged him with this mission? Secondly, they accuse him of attacking, in his sermons, the lives of clergymen, and even of prelates. Is he their ecclesiastical superior? Furthermore, why should he live like a anonk since he is not a member of a religious Order? Why has he put aside the traditional habit of the Canons, and clothed himself in sheepskin ?

The Saint, remembering his past sins, confessed that he deserved all manner of contempt and ill-treatment, and rejoiced at injuries and afflictions. Nevertheless, reflecting on what he owed to God's honor, he cleared himself of all their calumnies to the entire satisfaction of the judges.[6] Certainly, he might easily have been their accuser, and charged them not only with the neglect of their sacred duties, but with grievous interference in the apostolic labors of a zealous priest. But Norbert no longer knew of any revenge but the revenge of the Saints, namely to suffer and to forgive. Jesus, his Master, had also been falsely accused, ill-treated and even crucified, and he was trying to resemble that divine Master as closely as possible. "Calumny," he later repeatedly told his followers, "is the test of a patient and generous heart, which bears with it rather than to give up working for God."

At the close of this trial, we find that the most eminent men of the Council greatly admired Norbert. The Archbishops of Cologne, of Mainz, of Munich, and even the Legate himself, did not fail to see that the underlying cause of all these various accusations was the sting of rebuke caused by Norbert's virtuous life, and his zeal for bringing about a much-needed reform among the clergy. The Legate therefore advised Norbert to present himself to the Holy Father and

---

[6] It is expressly stated in the Acta SS. and also by Winter, Chron. Gratiae Dei, p. 327, that Norbert had received from his bishop proper jurisdiction to preach.

ask for general jurisdiction, in other words, permission to preach everywhere. That the Saint had privately spoken with the Legate after the Council, seems very probable from his subsequent conduct. From that time on Norbert put away his sheepskin and began to wear a woolen cassock. In this he is said to have acted on the advice of the Legate. Later we shall find Norbert introducing into his Order, customs which up to that time were new to Canons, excepting those whom Cuno had helped to found.[7]

Leaving Fritzlar, Norbert again returned to Xanten, but he was not to remain there long. Persecuted on all sides, and misunderstood by those for whose conversion he had sacrificed his life, the Saint sought his consolation at the foot of the Cross. There, after some days and nights alone with God, we find him taking a most unexpected resolution. He decides to leave his native country. Since the day of his ordination, he had done all in his power to change the conduct of clergy and people, but without great results. He fully realized that no prophet is acceptable in his own country. Instead of bringing about the reform he had hoped for, his preaching and mode of living seemed to make conditions worse. He therefore decided not to give up his work, but to change his field of labor, and after the example of St. Gregory of Nazianz, to satisfy the wishes of his enemies and to depart. "If on my account," he said, "the whole diocese is upset; if my words, instead of edifying, are but the cause of scandal and strife, for the welfare of my diocese I will go away."

He went to Cologne and resigned all his ecclesiastical preferments into the hands of his Archbishop. It was in vain that Archbishop Frederic endeavored to have him change his decision. As later events will abundantly prove, he was specially guided in this by divine Providence.

---

[7] Cfr. Bollandists, Jan. 13th, p. 112, 113.

Norbert then sold his estates and distributed the money among the poor. The chapel of the Fürstenberg, where he had spent nearly three years, and which he had gradually converted into something like a monastery, together with all the surrounding country belonging to himself and his brother Herbert, he donated to the Abbot of Siburg, his dearest friend.[8] All he reserved for himself were ten silver marks, a mule, and the sacred vestments and articles necessary for the celebration of the Holy Sacrifice of the Mass. His numerous servants he had dismissed long before, except two who had begged to be allowed to be near him, and now wanted to follow him.[9] One of these was the servant who had witnessed his miraculous conversion on the road to Freden, which event had made nearly as much impression on him as on Norbert himself. The other was probably the servant who had given him his penitential robes in the cathedral, the day of his ordination. Their names we do not know, but Camus observes that both were devoted to Norbert, and to be with him was all they desired.

After the Saint had disposed of all his earthly possessions, he went once more to his native town, now to say farewell to his people. It appears that his father had died before this event, but his pious mother was probably still alive, since there is nowhere any mention of her death before this. No doubt, the saintly woman made the sacrifice most willingly and even joyfully, convinced as she must have been of the saintliness of her son.

---

[8] The charter concerning this donation, which was drawn up the following year, is the only place where any mention is made of the family of Norbert. The name of his brother Herbert is herein mentioned. It must also be observed that in this same charter Norbert is praised by the Archbishop of Cologne as the "Vir ad omne opus bonum paratus." This saying of the Archbishop has been the "motto" of the Premonstratensians ever since.

[9] It would seem that these two servants had also been near him on the Fürstenberg, but whether they lived with him in his little convent or not is nowhere stated.

Finally, stripped of all earthly goods, Norbert, once the wealthy Lord of Gennep, now barefooted, begins his missionary career. This was towards the end of the year 1118. Not knowing whither to go, he abandoned all to divine Providence. Like Abraham he had heard the voice of God in his inner soul: "Go out from thy country and go to the land which I will show thee." He hearkened to that voice and thus became a willing, and hence a powerful, instrument in the hands of God for the welfare of souls and the good of the Church.

CHAPTER IV
THE MISSIONARY

Praeco, totum, Gelasius inquit, in orbem;
Fac, caleant flammis omnia regna tuis.

The Pope commissions Norbert to preach throughout the world and by his burning words to inflame the hearts of the people.

NORBERT, in appearance a second Peter the Hermit, set out preaching in that same country where, twenty-five years before, Peter had aroused the people by preaching the Crusades. As we know, he had been advised by the Papal Legate at the Council of Fritzlar, to present himself to the Holy Father, and this he intended to do at the outset. But where in those troubled days was the Pope to be found? A true missionary, Norbert relied entirely on Providence; he went from town to town preaching, hoping on his way, to learn of the Pope's whereabouts. He first arrived at the little town, Huy, situated between Liège and Namur, in Belgium. Naturally the people were much surprised to see this poor equipage enter their town; Norbert, barefooted, his two former servants, and a mule carrying their luggage. Though in appearance beggars, yet in reality they were not, for Norbert had still the ten silver marks which he had kept for himself. He began to realize that to have this money was not only against the spirit of poverty, which they outwardly professed, but also contrary to entire dependence on God's Providence. He reproached himself for lack of confidence in God, and forthwith distributed the ten marks among the poor.

He considered the mule also an unnecessary luxury, and gave it away. Henceforth he will have absolutely nothing but what is necessary for the celebration of the Holy Sacrifice, and that he is now obliged to carry wherever he goes. Barefooted and begging his daily bread—a worthy precursor of St. Francis—Norbert thus espouses the poverty of Jesus Christ. His lively faith and unlimited confidence in God are to be from this time his only riches.

Pope Paschal II, with whom Norbert, while at the court of Henry in Rome, had come in contact, died in the beginning of this same year. Fearing an interference on the part of Henry, the Cardinals hastily met, and seven days after the death of Paschal elected as his successor John of Gaeta, who took the name of Gelasius II. This happened on the 24th of January, 1118. On learning of the election, Cencio Frangipani, leader of the German faction, at once seized the new Pope and cast him into prison. Scarcely had the august prisoner been set free, in fact on the very day of his ordination, for the newly elected Pope was only deacon as yet—Henry V came to interfere, and Gelasius was obliged to escape under cover of darkness. He landed in Gaeta, his native city, and here he was consecrated. He then went back to Rome, but Cencio Frangipani for the second time laid his sacrilegious hands upon the Lord's anointed. Again the Pope escaped, and this time went to France, the country always devoted to the Papacy. On Nov. 7th, 1118, he stepped upon the shores of Provence, and for a time made his residence in St. Giles, in Languedoc, now in the department of Gard. Here the Holy Father was received with due honor and great enthusiasm by the good people.

In the beginning of the twelfth century news did not travel very fast, so it was some time before the tidings of the Holy Father reached the ears of Norbert. As soon as he had learned that the Pope was in the South of France, he decided to go thither. Winter had well set in at the time, and a most severe one it was. The country was thickly covered with snow and ice. But no obstacles could keep Norbert from fulfilling what he considered his mission, so with his two companions he set out at once.

It would be impossible for any one to give an adequate description of the hardships of this journey. Barefooted on cold winter days—in a strange country—and unacquainted with its language, begging their daily bread, the little party traveled on foot for seven long weeks.[1] The Saint offered to God the hardships he endured, in expiation of his sins, and his two companions were constantly encouraged by his example. At last they were kneeling greatly exhausted, before the relics of St. Giles, thanking God for His protection.

St. Giles was a famous shrine, and from all parts of the country pilgrimages were continually made to the venerable tomb of the illustrious solitary of the Flavian valley. Although it was mid-winter at the time of Norbert's arrival, the crowds were unusually large on account of the presence of the august Pontiff.

Not one of the vast multitude assembled there recognized our humble servant of God. The Saint rejoiced greatly in this, for ever since his conversion, his ambition was to be unknown and forgotten, except as penitent and missionary. Having satisfied his devotion at the shrine, Norbert proceeded to the Pope's residence and asked to be admitted into his presence. He had no difficulty in obtaining the great favor of a private audience, notwithstanding his beggarly appearance. With a heart full of gratitude to God for all His favors, he approached the Holy Father. Throwing himself at the feet of the Pope and shedding an abundance of tears, he made with the greatest humility a general confession of his whole life. He begged the Holy Father to absolve him, and offered to make any satisfaction which the Vicar of Christ might choose to impose on him.

When after a long interview Gelasius had come to the knowledge of Norbert's noble birth, his position at the court, his

---

[1] According to Vanden-Elsen, o. c., p. 31, it was at this time that Norbert, while in Lyons, spoke on the Immaculate Conception of the Blessed Virgin.

miraculous conversion, in fact his whole life's history, he expressed his desire to keep Norbert at his own court for the benefit of the Church.[2] Our poor Saint trembled at the very thought of resuming the life of a courtier, even with the Holy Father, and related how he had received the clearest signs from heaven to be a missionary and work for "Reform" among clergy and laity; at the same time he begged on his knees the Pope's leave and blessing to preach the Gospel. Pope Gelasius was anxious to assist the earnest missionary in his apostolic labors, and gave him full faculties to preach the Gospel wherever he judged proper. He gave him a document also, by which Norbert became a "Missionary Apostolic," which means that he could preach in any diocese.[3]

Imagine his immense joy on receiving this great favor. His vocation was thus recognized by the highest authority—all his desires were now gratified, and his happiness complete. It is not without reason that several writers consider this event as the beginning of Norbert's apostolic career. Thus, for instance, writes Anselm of Havelberg: "In the time of Pope Gelasius there arose a man, by the name of Norbert, who imitated the life of the Apostles, and on account of his zeal and holiness of life, received of the Roman Pope Gelasius, special recommendation to preach, in order to check the many abuses in the Western Church. He went preaching through the provinces and won a great number of followers..."

Burning with zeal for the salvation of souls, Norbert was anxious to make use of the power the Pope had granted him, and soon left St. Giles. Although spring was near, snow and ice still made the roads most difficult for travelers. Still, barefooted, Norbert

---

[2] Cfr. Madelaine, o. c., p. 91, where an extract is given of the tenth chapter of the *Vita B.*

[3] Ibidem., p. 92, where further is quoted the "Chronic, de Mailros," apud Fell. S. S. Rerum Angl., p. 164. An. 1118: Dominus Norbertus papam Gelasium adiens officium ab eo praedicationis accepit. Also *Vita A*, p. 448, An. 1118.

returned to the North. In many places he was obliged to wade knee-deep through the snow, nevertheless he refused to make a stop even for a day, except for the purpose of preaching. Speaking of this truly heroic journey, the earliest biographer says: "His burning love of God rendered him insensible to cold, and his thirsting after souls made him forget his lack of nourishment and fatigue." At this time he still kept up his earlier practice, except on Sundays, of not taking food until evening. When not actually traveling he was preaching, and many of his nights were spent entirely in prayer.

Passing through Orleans in the beginning of Lent, he was joined by a new disciple, who asked to remain with him and assist in his missionary labors. Thus Norbert, with his two former servants and his new disciple, who was a subdeacon, journeyed on as far as Valenciennes. Here they arrived on the 22d of May, that year the eve of Palm Sunday. The time was, doubtless, very favorable for the zeal of our apostle, but he was not well conversant with the French language. What, then, should he do? That he knew some French, we may safely infer from the fact that he had been preaching on the way, but he had not that mastery of it which this solemn occasion seemed to demand. At first he was quite disheartened, but soon we see him in the church, and while there, praying most fervently; the thought came to him that the Holy Ghost had bestowed upon the Apostles the gift of languages. He thus asked God for the sake of the apostolate and for the benefit of the people, to make them understand his words. Full of confidence in God's mercies, and with that lively faith so characteristic of him, he fearlessly mounted the pulpit, and, carried away by holy enthusiasm, preached a most eloquent sermon in his own language. "And oh! wonder," says the biographer of Brandenburg,[4] "his words were received by the people with delight and listened to with the closest attention."

Some historians, relating this incident, say that his appearance and gestures spoke more eloquently than words, and conveyed his

---

[4] Acc. to Madelaine, o. c., p. 94, two codices (Morinensis et Knechtstedenensis) of the *Vita B* relate here the miracle of "tongues."

meaning. Others, however, and among these his earliest biographers, ascribe the fact to a great miracle, which recalls the first great Pentecost at Jerusalem. This miracle is also affirmed by so reliable an authority as Bl. Hugh, at that time chaplain of Bishop Burchard, and later Norbert's best beloved disciple and successor. Moreover, it is a most remarkable fact, that the inhabitants of Valenciennes continued coming in large crowds to listen to him, and begged him to spend some time with them. He succeeded in bringing about a number of conversions, and the people honored him as a truly apostolic missionary. But Norbert had not intended to stay among them. He thought merely to pass through their town on his way to the North, and so did not wish to delay his journey thither. However, it soon appeared to be the will of God that he should remain here longer, where a great trial awaited him.

His three companions suddenly became ill, and Norbert was obliged to accept the generous offer of hospitality which he had previously declined. It is very probable that the illness was caused by privation, fatigue and exposure during their long and tedious journey. This must have been the case at least in regard to his two former servants. Their illness showed from the start disquieting symptoms as the fever ran high, and soon Norbert realized that it was question of life and death. "He attended them faithfully," relates a manuscript of the abbey of Vicogne; "he cleansed and nursed their sore and emaciated bodies, their feet bruised by ice and frozen snow; he prepared their food which he himself begged from the charity of the faithful, and he waited on them constantly."[5] But his affectionate care could not stay the hand of death, and during the Octave of Easter, after two weeks of suffering, the three helpers of our zealous missionary passed to where suffering is unknown. Norbert himself had administered to them the rites of Holy Church; and aided by him they died fully resigned to the will of God, though they were far from home and in a strange and unknown country.

---

[5] Cfr. Charles Louis Hugo, "Annales Ordinis Praem." Book I. p. 34.

Broken-hearted and worn out by fatigue, Norbert accompanied their bodies to their last resting place. This trial was all the greater for Norbert, coming at the very outset of his missionary career. Still his confidence in God was unshaken. With Job he exclaimed: "The Lord hath given, the Lord hath taken, praised be the name of the Lord." Consoled by this thought, he had the bodies of his faithful companions buried with great honor amidst a large concourse of people.

During these weeks of suffering and anxiety, while Norbert had been busy nursing his sick companions, a most providential circumstance occurred. Burchard, the Bishop of Cambray, a sincere friend of Norbert, had made his entrance into the village. Burchard had, for the past three years, been Bishop of Cambray, which see, as we remember, had been offered first to Norbert by the Emperor Henry, on his return journey from Rome, but which Norbert at the time declined to accept. Burchard and Norbert had known each other a long time at the court of Henry, and had always been sincere friends. Feeling at this time the special need of a trusted friend, our Saint went to pay his respects to the Bishop.

He arrived at the Bishop's residence, met one of the chaplains, and asked him to arrange an interview with His Lordship. This cleric, not knowing Norbert, announced to the Bishop that a beggarly looking pilgrim wanted an audience. No doubt the chaplain thought that this poor man had come to beg for alms, and hoped to spare the Bishop the trouble of seeing him personally. The good Bishop, however, asked to see that poor pilgrim, and Norbert was admitted into his presence. Entering the room, Norbert greeted his former companion familiarly, and in German, which greatly surprised the Bishop who thereupon looked at him intently for a few minutes. He saw his bare feet—bruised and swollen—his beggarly appearance—he scrutinized his emaciated features, until suddenly overcome by emotion and greatly astonished, he exclaimed: "Is it you, is it really you, master Norbert? But who would ever believe this?" Then recalling Norbert's former greatness, his wealth and high position, and at the same time realizing that he had forsaken all this for God, Burchard burst into tears and embraced his noble friend, dearer to him now than ever before; for a long time neither was able to say a word.

At last the silence was broken by Hugh, the Bishop's chaplain, who had been present all the while and who was greatly astonished at the tears and marks of friendship between the Bishop and this beggar. Since he could not understand German, he could only surmise the meaning of it all, and said to the Bishop: "But who, my lord, is this stranger? "Ah," the Bishop replied,

> if you only knew who he is and what he has been, you would undoubtedly share my surprise and admiration. This poorly-clad beggar is the son of the illustrious Count of Gennep, and is related to the highest nobility in Germany. We spent several years together at the Court, and he was always a great favorite of the Emperor, and one of the most elegant courtiers. And what is more, it is to this man that I owe my bishopric. The Emperor offered me the see of Cambray, only after Norbert had refused it ... and to meet him now in this state ... a barefooted beggar seeking God in poverty and sacrifice!"[6]

A flood of tears prevented the good Bishop from saying more, but he had said enough to further God's designs over his chaplain, for his words together with the sight of Norbert so touched the heart of the chaplain, that at once he took a generous resolve. He beheld in Norbert no common man, but a true saint, and the grace of God revived in his heart that desire for the religious life which he had felt for a long time. Should he not also be able to say farewell to the world and its allurements, and consecrate himself to God forever? Oh! may we not here again admire the all-guiding Providence of God, for this chaplain, as we shall see later, will be

[6] Cfr. Madelaine, o. c., p. 97, quoting Acta SS. XX, p. 853. Analecta Norbertina: Si scires quis fuerit, etc.

one of Norbert's most illustrious disciples.

Norbert and the Bishop spent a long time conversing together, unconscious of the change that was taking place in the heart of the chaplain. Burchard was at once convinced of Norbert's absolute sincerity and holiness, and gave him every token of the deepest respect. Their old friendship was renewed and they met frequently.

But illness soon prostrated Norbert. The nursing of his sick companions, following upon his long and tedious journey, had overtaxed his bodily strength. Utterly exhausted, his mortified frame at last gave way, and he was forced once more to prolong his stay at Valenciennes. Soon his condition became so alarming that the good Bishop postponed his own departure in order to be of assistance to Norbert, whenever possible. Every day the Prelate came to inquire after his condition, either in person or by one of his clerics, usually his chaplain Hugh. The latter especially was very anxious to spend a good deal of time with the Saint, in order to imbibe his spirit and maxims. The oftener he saw Norbert the more he admired his patience and entire resignation to the will of God, and he felt himself strongly drawn to him. So this illness was in the unscrutable designs of God, a great blessing for both. When Norbert was at last well on in the way of convalescence, Hugh opened to him his mind and heart, and told him the story of his life. He emphasized especially the feelings he had experienced at their first meeting, and when he begged Norbert as a great favor to allow him to join in his apostolic work, our dear Saint was beside himself with joy. "Lord," he exclaimed, "Thou art my witness that even on this day have I asked Thee for a companion. Behold here he is. Thanks, my heavenly Father, I thank Thee with my whole heart."[7]

These events occurred in April, 1119. The following month Norbert's health was so far restored that he felt able to travel to Cambray and visit his dear friend, Bishop Burchard, as we read in the annals of the diocese of Cambray: "In the year 1119, during

[7] Cfr. Madelaine, o. c., p. 98.

Rogation week, master Norbert came to this town for the first time." We mention this fact to show how highly our saint was esteemed, since even his visit to the place is mentioned in the annals. Hugh, meanwhile, had gone to Fosse, his native town, to put his estates in order and say farewell to his kinsfolk. He actually joined Norbert for good after the latter's return from Cambray to Valenciennnes, in the month of June, 1119. This same Hugh is to play a very important part in the early formation of the Premonstratensian Order. When Norbert is raised to the Archiepiscopal See of Magdeburg, Hugh succeeds him and takes the management of the whole Order.

CHAPTER V
THE PEACEMAKER

Saepius armatae coeunt in foedera dextrae,
Norberto hostiles pacificante globos.

Angel of peace, at thy command
Fierce discord vanished from the land,
And hearts by thee to Jesus given
Brought forth abundant fruit for Heaven. (Office.)

ORBERT had intended returning to Cologne but, for some unknown reason, at this time changed his former plan. During his illness he had devoted a great deal of time to the study of French, and talented as he was, we may safely presume that he soon became able to express himself with ease in that language. This may account for his change of plan. At any rate when Hugh returned, Norbert at once resumed his missionary career. Accompanied by Hugh, he went through Hainault, Brabant, and the principality of Liège, preaching the importance of salvation at every opportunity on his way. "What will it profit a man if he gain the whole world and suffer the loss of his soul?" How convincingly could Norbert dwell on these words of St. Matthew! Had he not seen the vanity of it all? Little wonder, therefore, that God's choicest blessings rested visibly on his missionary work. Wherever he went the people crowded to hear him. His powerful sermons, strengthened and illustrated by his own evangelical life, and spoken with the strength of conviction, made numerous conversions even among the most hardened sinners. God seemed to have given our Saint the special grace of reconciling the most relentless enemies, and this gift, as events will presently show, did not remain hidden in him.

We know also that Norbert, zealous as he was for the salvation of souls, absolutely refused any remuneration for his missionary labor. He, as well as Hugh—true beggars of Christ—depended entirely on God's Providence for life's necessities. As the early historian remarks, it seemed to Norbert to be unworthy of their state to take any earthly remuneration, since they, for the sake of Christ, had given up and even despised their own earthly goods.[1] Strangers and pilgrims on earth, they wished nothing that might prevent them from continually raising their aspirations and thoughts to heaven.

It is quite natural that this total disinterestedness in earthly things deeply touched the hearts and minds of the people. The name of the great missionary Norbert, was soon on the lips of all.

> ... And with amaze
> The Gallic nation stood to hear
> Thy matchless accents, rich and clear.
>
> (Office of St. Norbert.)

The enthusiasm with which he was received in many places goes far beyond description. He was hailed as the great Apostle from heaven, and when he left one place, says Madelaine, shepherds even left their flocks to announce his coming to a neighboring village. Upon his arrival the bells rang out and all the people assembled in the church. Then Norbert at once mounted the pulpit; after him Hugh addressed the people and the exercises often lasted for hours. Happily, historians have not failed to tell us what subjects our Saint most frequently chose for his sermons. The frequentation of the Sacraments, the necessity of doing penance, restitution, the obligations of people about to be married, and the duties of the rich,

[1] *Vita B*, Ch. XIII.

were his usual themes.[2]

Every night, when the services were over, our missionaries retired to the dwelling-place of some family in the neighborhood. Even the most prominent people, governors of the provinces as well as lords of the castles, urged our poor beggars to come to spend the night with them. Norbert passed his nights mostly in prayer and in instructing his companion, for his great zeal for the salvation of souls, did not make him forget the spiritual education of Hugh, his first disciple. Any spare moments he could find, by day or by night, were spent in this important work. He urged him to the practice of the virtues of patience, humility and especially of poverty, saying:

> My brother, let this virtue of poverty not discourage you. Jesus Christ has borne all the burdens of it; be not disheartened, but embrace what your Redeemer first practiced. St. Lawrence poured the treasures of the Church into the hands of the poor; imitate his example in the disposal of your property. This generous sacrifice, which I advise you to make, is not according to the liking of a covetous heart, but the spirit of poverty is necessary in order to preach the Gospel successfully. If it costs much to nature, a man truly poor in spirit is already rewarded in this world by the unction of God's grace and by the solicitude of His Holy Providence. Be not ashamed of humiliations; they are the germ of glory. Be attentive to the custody of your chastity, this virtue will transform you into an angel. Be prompt to comply with the orders of obedience; it is by this virtue that you will raise yourself to an understanding of God's greatness. Arm yourself with patience in the time of adversities; these are the portions of the elect. Do not expect a better lot than that of the Apostles; you are heir to their ministry, you will be heir to their suffering.
>
> (*Vita B*, Ch. XIV.)

By this and similar exhortations did Norbert succeed in inflaming the heart of Hugh. He, moreover, continually practiced

[2] Ibidem.

what he taught, and thus made his counsels more easy to follow. Above all, Hugh was eager to study the life of his master, for whom he had the greatest admiration.

We note some change about this time in Norbert's manner of traveling. Until now he had journeyed on foot, but hereafter we shall see him at times make use of a modest equipage. Dr. Winter observes: "Sometimes also when the fatigue of an excessive journey prevented Norbert from walking, he would ride a donkey so as not to be obliged to interrupt his missionary labors."[3] Still, whenever able, Norbert always walked, carrying with him the articles necessary for the celebration of the Holy Sacrifice.

Without doubt this constant self-denial and sincere humility, added to his forceful preaching, made his apostolic work doubly effective. He never allowed the people even to set a table for him, but whenever he could do so without giving offense, took his meager repast sitting on the floor. When, however, he was the guest of an Archbishop or of an Abbot, he would conform himself to the rules of the house in deference to his distinguished host.[4]

In order to appreciate rightly Norbert's great mission as peacemaker, we must consider some conditions peculiar to the times. We shall find in them an explanation of Norbert's frequent preaching on the subject of restitution. At no period were bloody fights between princes, landlords, and even common people, more general. These were the reconstruction days of the ecclesiastical government, the beginning of the twelfth century. The great political power acquired by churchmen under the feudal system, as well as the assumption of ecclesiastical power by secular princes, had opened the way to abuses and scandals of all kinds. The vice of simony especially had made deplorable progress. St. Peter Damian draws a most gloomy picture of this period which, as is known to the student of history, is unfortunately no exaggeration. The great

---

[3] Winter, "Die Praemonstratenser," p. 327.

[4] *Vita B*, Ch. XIII.

Pope Hildebrand, Gregory VII, had been raised by God to bring about a much needed reform; and he proved himself equal to the task. In the year 1075, in a Synod held in Rome, he struck the evil at its root, realizing that deep-seated abuses can be eliminated only by drastic measures. He prohibited under pain of excommunication the practice of lay-investiture, and deprived secular princes of their assumed ecclesiastical power.

As was to be expected, this sweeping enactment became the cause of bitter strife. Although the preaching of the Crusades, some years later, had, to a great extent, diverted the attention of the people, and re-established peace and concord in mlany places, yet history shows that many of these petty sovereigns, feudal lords, became bitter and revengeful after their power had been thus curtailed by Gregory, and their influence lessened. Feeling themselves powerless against Pope Gregory, they often looked elsewhere for revenge, and this explains in part the hard-heartedness—inveterate enmities—frequent quarrels and bloody fights of those days. Great tact, no doubt, was required to do real missionary work among this class of people. As Thomas à Kempis rightly observes: "First keep thyself in peace and then shalt thou be able to bring others to peace." (Imit. II.8.)

Norbert, who by constant prayer and mortification had become entire master of himself, was on that account eminently fitted for this arduous task. After leaving the diocese of Cambray, he and his companion went to Fosse, Hugh's native place, situated about seven miles S. W. of Namur, in Belgium. Since Norbert's austere life and the success of his preaching were well known in that place, he was received as a man from God. Both clergy and laity came out in great numbers to hear him. In the record of this mission there is an instance given of Norbert's great power as peacemaker.

After the usual mission exercises were over, the people came to the Saint requesting him to reconcile two families, for a long time separated by deadly hatred. Already more than sixty persons had been killed, they said, in consequence of family feuds, and neither priest nor magistrate had been able to restore peace. While they were thus entreating Norbert, there appeared upon the scene a brother of one, who that very same week had been killed by a person of the opposite camp. "Behold," they exclaimed, "there comes one of the very persons of whom we are speaking!"

Uttering a silent prayer, Norbert went at once to meet the young man, embraced him and then said: "My dear friend, I, a stranger in this place, a mere passer-by, should like to speak to you. Since my arrival I have not as yet asked a favor of any one, neither have I received one. It would be a great pleasure for me to receive from you the very first favor I ask for in this village. God will reward you abundantly if you grant me what I ask."[5] The young man, touched by these gentle words, and still more by the grace of God which had come over him in answer to Norbert's prayer, wonderingly said: "Speak, Father." "I beg of you," answered the Saint, "as a great favor, that you forgive from your heart the murderer of your brother." That the young man not only promised to forgive the murderer, but at the same time gave his word to do all in his power to reconcile the two parties at enmity and help Norbert to put a stop to these hateful feuds, may be considered truly miraculous.

On the following Saturday a meeting of the hostile parties was arranged for, to be held at Moustier, not far from Fosse. An immense crowd from the surrounding country was assembled in the village, when on the appointed day Norbert arrived. As this work of reconciliation was most delicate and required heavenly wisdom, Norbert prepared for it by long and fervent prayers, that God might bless the undertaking. The Saint must have arrived early in the morning, for we are informed that by 9 o'clock the people had grown tired waiting, and that the crowd began to murmur. At their request Hugh sought Norbert, and asked him to come to speak to the impatient crowd. "As from a profound ecstacy," says the early biographer, "Norbert arose and answered that his time had not yet

[5] *Vita B*, Ch. XV. "Dilecte mi, peregrinus ego sum pertransiens ... placet mihi primum munus quaerere a te ..."

come." Then he went back to pray, and only some hours later he returned, entered the church and began to celebrate the Holy Sacrifice. As it was Saturday, he offered first, according to his custom, one Mass in honor of Our Lady; a second was then offered for the repose of the souls of those whose death had been caused by these family feuds.[6]

When Norbert at last mounted the pulpit it was 3 o'clock in the afternoon. Most of the people had left, but Norbert spoke with equal ease and eloquence to a small as to a large assembly. His voice, however, was soon heard afar, and a great many returned to listen to his discourse. Thus Norbert began:

> My dearly beloved brethren, when Our Lord Jesus Christ sent out His disciples to preach the Gospel, He ordered them to say wherever they came: 'Peace be to this house,' promising that the inmates of that house would receive God's peace. We, who are not by our merits but by a gratuitous gift of God, successors of the Apostles in the ministry, we bring you this same peace. You will not refuse to accept this gift of God, my brethren, since this peace will lead you to the eternal peace of heaven. You all know what has brought me to you. I did not come here in my own name; I am but a stranger, a pilgrim, but through me does Almighty God ask you to forgive your enemy, and if you are Christians, you are bound to obey your Master.

Norbert's discourse on this occasion was long, but when at last it was finished, the whole crowd was deeply moved, and the parties agreed to put their cause into the hands of Norbert, willing to abide

[6] There is nothing new or extraordinary in celebrating these two Masses, as the rules of the Church were not then what they are now. Pope Leo III often offered as many as seven Masses in one day. Saint Ulderic, Bishop of Augsburg, often said three; and also in England, S. Elphege and S. Anselm, Archbishop of Canterbury, often said two. Cfr. Ch. Hugo, o. c., T. I., p. 44, who quotes Card. Bona (Rer. Liturg. lib. I, cap. 18) and Martene (de antiq. Eccles. rit. a. 3, c. 3).

by his decision. The cause was won. On the relics of St. Frederic, the Patron Saint of the place, the old enemies swore a lasting friendship.

From Fosse and Moustier, Norbert proceeded to Gembloux, a small town in Brabant. Wherever he went, he was hailed as an angel of peace. Convinced that God could never enter a heart possessed by the demon of hatred and envy, he always prepared sinners for the grace of a true conversion by first inducing them to forgive their enemies. People knew this and thus as soon as he came to Gembloux, he was begged to reconcile two lords who were sworn enemies, and from whose enmity all the people in that place suffered greatly. Norbert went in person to them and won from one of them a solemn promise to forgive everything. The other was obstinate and unyielding. A few days later the latter died a miserable death, as Norbert had foretold when he refused to forgive his enemy.[7]

> Filled with Faith's spirit, prophecies were thine,
> And thy skilled lips interpreted each sign
> Of heavenly dealings. Thou didst banish far
> The phantoms of hell's spiritual war. ...

At Corroy near Gembloux the Saint also restored peace in numerous families; however, most of the details of his missionary work here are lacking. As the contemporary biographer observes, the above instances are only a few of the many reconciliations he effected.[8]

While the Saint was thus busily engaged in Belgium preaching missions and reconciling enemies, he learned to his great sorrow that Pope Gelasius had died in Cluny, while in exile. Norbert felt this loss keenly, first because the generous efforts of this Pope to

---

[7] Vita B, Ch. XVI. In hoc etiam vir Dei spiritum prophetiae habuisse credatur. ...

[8] Ibidem., Ch. XVII. Sunt enim cuncta quae premissa sunt, ex multis pauca, quae gessit; nunc autem plurima restant. . . .

reform abuses and to restore peace to the Church, gave promise of a glorious and useful reign; secondly, because he had been Norbert's first real protector. By making him "Missionary Apostolic", His Holiness had attached to Norbert's work the broad seal of Rome, and thus most effectively silenced his enemies. The coming of a new Pope, however, could be, and according to Rupertus, actually was, in the eyes of Norbert's enemies an occasion for them to try once more to put a stop to his preaching. "For," he continues, "they were ever bent on opposition." No doubt, their defeat at Fritzlar had greatly embittered them. Norbert therefore resolved to visit the new Pope as soon as possible.

While Maurice Bourdin, favored by Henry, but excommunicated by Pope Paschal, was residing in Rome as antipope under the title of Gregory VIII, the Cardinals who had followed Gelasius into exile, held the election in Cluny for a successor, and elected Guy, Archbishop of Vienna, who took the title of Calixtus II. His election was soon recognized by Catholic Europe; and in Rome, even under the very eyes of the antipope, the Bishop of Porto, Vicar of His Holiness, asked the people as usual for their acclamation to ratify the election. One of the first acts of the new Pontiff was to assemble a great Council at Rheims, which in reality, his predecessor had already called. This came to the knowledge of our Saint and he decided to go at once to Rheims.

It was in the month of October, 1119, and all the roads leading to the old city of St. Remigius were crowded with the most distinguished travelers. Louis, King of France, was on his way to summon justice against the King of England, who had seized upon Normandy, and moreover was holding in captivity Robert, the brother of Louis. Then there was the Countess of Poitiers who had come to ask protection against her adulterous husband, the Duke of Aquitaine. Besides, more than four hundred Archbishops, Bishops and Abbots were arriving from all parts of the world, to be present at this important and solemn assembly. Picture to yourself, dear reader, our poor beggarly looking Saint in the midst of all this pomp and splendor. No wonder that little attention was paid to the barefooted pilgrim with no distinction save his singular life. But he had come, determined to see the Holy Father and to ask a renewal of his apostolic faculties to preach the Gospel everywhere. For three days he remained at Rheims, begging for an audience, but was unsuccessful. At last, sick at heart and very much disappointed, he decided to leave, and await a more favorable opportunity. But presently divine Providence came to his rescue.

Accompanied by Hugh and another disciple, who meanwhile had joined him, he had gone but a few miles and was approaching the Benedictine Abbey of St. Thierry, when, deciding to rest for a while, the three sat down by the roadside. While there conversing together, they distinctly heard a voice, a mysterious voice, saying: "Behold Norbert and his companions," and another like an echo to the first: "Behold Norbert and his companion."[9] All three felt embarrassed; first, because no one could be seen near at hand; and, secondly, as to the meaning of these words. But, adds the biographer, they were soon to be enlightened, for Hugh alone proved to be a real companion; the other soon left them.

While Norbert was still considering the meaning of these mysterious words, Bartholomew, Bishop of Laon, happened to pass our three wayfarers. The Prelate, who was on his way to Rheims, to be present at the Council, noticed the three strangers; and, moved by curiosity, or rather by divine inspiration, addressed them and inquired the purpose of their journey. "Who are you?" the Bishop asked. Norbert replied candidly that they were strangers, who had left their country in order to lead an apostolic life. They had come there, Norbert further explained, to obtain from the new Pontiff a renewal of the faculties and privileges granted to them by his predecessor; but, after waiting for three days, they failed to obtain an audience. "My only ambition," pleaded our Saint to the good

---

[9] Pertz. Script. XII. Hermanni de miraculis S. Mariae Laudunensis lib. III, p. 653-660. Quomodo domnus Bartholomeus Episcopus domnum Norbertum invenerit.

Bishop, "is to obtain the right to evangelize the people everywhere."

The Bishop was touched by this simplicity of manner, and greatly admired these poor apostles. It seems he realized at the moment that jewels of sanctity were hidden under their poor exterior. On learning the cause of their sorrow, he expressed his sympathy and requested them to return with him, promised to speak in their behalf to Pope Calixtus and to obtain for them an audience. It is impossible to describe the feelings of joy Norbert experienced at this happy turn of affairs. Clearly God was on his side, and a fervent prayer of thanks rose to his lips. The Bishop furthermore ordered some of his men to dismount and he placed Norbert and his companions on their horses. On the way back to Rheims, the Bishop took Hugh aside and inquired into the life of Norbert; he appeared very anxious to learn all details of his work and life. Assuredly Hugh took great pleasure in relating all he had heard from the Bishop of Cambray in regard to his beloved master. He informed him of his noble birth, his life at the court of the Archbishop of Cologne, his intimate relations with the German Emperor, and finally of his conversion and the miracles of grace his words had produced during the last six months in Hainault, Brabant and Liège. The good Bishop listened very attentively and from that moment became Norbert's best friend and greatest admirer.[10]

As this same Bartholomew is to play a great and important part in Norbert's life, and especially in the later foundation of the Premonstratensian Order, we would here make the reader more acquainted with this noble character. He was about the same age as Norbert, and was born of a very illustrious family, in France. His father's name was Falcon de Vir, and his mother was Adèle de Roucy. When quite young, he had been entrusted to the care of his uncle, the Archbishop of Rheims. At the latter's palace he had received his elementary education from private tutors, but later he attended the well-known school of Rheims. When ordained

[10] Cfr. Madelaine, o. c., p. 114.

subdeacon he received a canonry at the Metropolitan church. He is described as a modest, loving character, of a firm mind. His face had an ascetic expression, and he lived frugally in the midst of opulence. Prudent as he was, he lived with his fellow-canons but never was really one of them. In the beginning of 1113 he had been unanimously chosen by the Chapter of Laon to be their Bishop. He would have refused the great honor, had it not been that this diocese was desolate; and, from a worldly standpoint, it held out to him nothing but ruin and poverty, together with the disfavor of the French King. Such was the character of the noble Bishop in whose company Norbert now entered Rheims for the second time.[11]

The Council was to open on the next day, the 20th of October, in the church of Notre-Dame. Upon their arrival, Bartholomew went directly to the Pope where he was well received, especially so since he was the Pope's cousin. As soon as he had paid his respects, the good Bishop lost no time in pleading Norbert's cause. He told His Holiness that, as the Father of all Christians, he should try to be in reality a father to all, good and bad, rich and poor. He even went so far, in his own gentle way, as to reproach the Pope for having refused an audience to a man like Norbert. At once the Holy Father gave orders to introduce our Saint and his companions. In his great happiness our zealous apostle spoke frankly to the Pope of his missionary labors and the good he, with the grace of God, was doing everywhere. He then begged of the Pontiff to renew the letters granted by his predecessor. In answer to this request Calixtus blessed Norbert's noble undertaking and most willingly gave him a fresh grant of the faculties previously received from Pope Gelasius.

While the Council lasted Norbert stayed at Rheims and was constantly at the side of Bartholomew who asked his advice on matters of great importance. He also met here his great friend Burchard, the Bishop of Cambray, and many other real friends. That he also preached here on some occasions, must be inferred from the

[11] Cfr. De Florival. Étude historique sur le XIIe siècle. Bathélemy de Vir, évêque de Laon, p. 31.

fact that the historian observes: "All the Prelates were charmed with his eloquence, wisdom and piety, and amazed at the austere way of living which some advised him to moderate."[12] But the Saint, mindful of the words of the Savior: "He who hates his life in this world shall find it," would not hear of mitigation until the Pope himself insisted on it. In deference to the wish of the Holy Father, hereafter he will not go barefooted.

[12] Pertz. Script. XII. Sigeb. contin. Praem., p. 448.

THE ABBEY AT PRÉMONTRÉ TODAY

CHAPTER VI
PRÉMONTRÉ

Norberto niveas vestes, ceu Signa pudoris,
Offert Angelica Virgo Maria manu.

In token of her constant love
The Angels' Queen of Heaven above
Clothes thee in white. . . .

FTER the Council of Rheims, Norbert and Hugh were for a time separated. Hugh with the full consent of Norbert, accompanied his Bishop, Burchard, whom he had met at the Council, back to Cambray, while Norbert went to Laon. Pope Calixtus decided to spend the winter with his cousin, Bishop Bartholomew, at Laon, and in order to learn more about the character of our Saint, His Holiness requested the Bishop to invite Norbert also. The Bishop did so most willingly, for he saw in Norbert the very man who could be of great assistance to him in bringing about a reform in his poor and neglected diocese. Madelaine gives us a second reason, namely, that Norbert's relatives who lived in the diocese of Laon, had requested the Bishop to bring the Saint thither, for they feared for his health.[1] Norbert, on his part, was very eager to go to Laon, since this would give him the opportunity to unfold his plans in detail to the Holy Father, to ask his advice and get his approval on the carrying out of the great work of reform.

[1] Madelaine, o. c., who quotes from *Vita B*, Ch. XIX: Habens in progenie matris suae quosdam in eodem episcopatu et civitate propinquos. Cfr. Maurit. du Pré, *Annales breves Ord. Praem.* (Namurci, 1886), p. 1.

Thus all three went to Laon. Here the Pope soon greatly admired Norbert and his noble aim, and gave him constant encouragement. It is not without reason then, that one of the early chroniclers observes, that the Premonstratensian Order owes its origin to the conference between Norbert and the Pope at this time.[2] A sincere and lasting friendship sprung up also between Norbert and the Bishop. Bartholomew will one day be considered the second Founder, so to speak, of Prémontré. Before he died, he had established no less than five monasteries for Norbert and his brethren, first having enabled Norbert to found Prémontré. The following are the words of Bartholomew, written twenty-four years after this first meeting:

> "We want it to be known to our people and to posterity that in the year of Our Lord, 1119, a man of wonderful piety, by the name of Norbert, happened to come to our diocese; that we, seeing his holiness and admiring his learning and eloquence, forced him by our entreaties to remain over winter. The more we associated with him, and the oftener we heard him speak, the more we were refreshed by the sweet odor of his holy life. Winter being over, he was anxious to depart, but many of the clergy and nobles begged us to retain him in our diocese, which we also desired most earnestly. By the grace of God we at last with great difficulty succeeded in obtaining this favor . . .[3]

At this time there was in the diocese of Laon an abbey in which were great and numerous abuses, which the Pope as well as the Bishop was anxious to see reformed. For this reason the canons of St. Martin, such was the abbey called, at the suggestion of both Pope and Bishop, elected Norbert as their abbot. At first the Saint strenuously opposed this plan and refused the honor. He said to the

---

[2] Pertz XII Chron. de Mailros. an. 1119.

[3] Barthélemy de Vir by M. A. de Florival., p, 260. Cfr. also Le Paige, Bibliot. Ord. Praem., p. 373.

Bishop: "If I have given up wealth and opulence at Cologne, was it to come here to find wealth at the Chapter of Laon?" The good Bishop had recourse to the Pontiff, and when the Pope himself expressed his desire that Norbert should take charge of the abbey, the Saint replied:

> O Most Holy Father, you remember, that I have been twice commissioned to preach the Word of God, first by the authority of your predecessor, and secondly by Your Holiness. However, as I do not wish to follow my own will, I am ready to undertake this responsible work, but I cannot break my solemn engagement without great detriment to my soul. It is known to Your Holiness that this my solemn engagement is, that I have chosen to lead with God's help a strictly evangelical and apostolic life. But since You command me, I do not refuse the task, provided the canons are willing to live according to my principles and follow my maxims.

To this the Holy Father replied that, in case the canons should refuse to do so, Norbert would be entirely free to leave them. Upon this condition, then, Norbert undertook the reform of the abbey of St. Martin of Tours.

We already know that our Saint had received from God a special gift for bringing about peace even where discord reigned supreme. However, it is not always in the power of the physician to heal. Nothing is more difficult than to reform an institution, whatever its nature, where laxity in regard to the observance of the rules has crept in. According to the words of Peter the Venerable, it is even far easier to found a new monastery than to reform one where the rules are not observed. Norbert undoubtedly knew this, but acting under obedience, he went to the abbey.

Being duly installed, he began his reform by trying to re-establish canonical life among the clerics, and by showing them daily by word and example how to observe the duties of their state of life. Holding up to them the Gospel and their own Constitutions, he explained how their eternal salvation depended on the faithful observance of both. At first the canons listened to him respectfully, but when Norbert attempted to carry his words into action, they said: "Nolumus hunc super nos" . . . "We do not want such a master," and they refused to change their manner of living. After a stay of three months Norbert saw conditions to be hopeless, and begged the Bishop to release him from his office. He was determined to leave not only the abbey of St. Martin but also the diocese of Laon. However, Bishop Bartholomew prevailed on him to change the latter plan. In the old MS. Life we read that the Bishop actually begged the Saint to stay, and offered him all possible inducements.[4] First he asked him to come to live with him in his palace, but by this time Norbert had a particular horror of palaces. When the Saint further explained his desire for solitude, the good Bishop answered: "In the diocese of Laon there are many deserts and solitudes, which I will show you. Choose the one that pleases you, and it will be yours.'' Here again we see divine Providence leading Norbert to the place where be was to found a new Religious Order. As we have seen, Norbert had really failed in his efforts to reform existing conditions, first among the canons of Xanten and now among those of Laon. Still determined to carry out his work of reform, there was only one way open to him, namely, to create new canons according to his own ideals.

As the Bishop had promised, as soon as the weather permitted, he daily accompanied Norbert in search of a quiet and suitable place. They first visited Foigny, a charming and delightful spot. When Bartholomew asked Norbert's opinion of it, he replied, that having consulted not his own judgment but God in prayer, he knew that Foigny was not the place that God had destined for him. Neither was Thénailles, nor several other places which they visited. Finally they came into the forest of Coucy. Here they reached a deep marshy valley, named Prémontré, covered with thorns and

[4] *Vita B*, Ch. XIX.

brush, where the waters from the mountains gathered. There was in this retreat a little chapel built by the Benedictine monks of St. Vincent's Abbey of Laon, and dedicated to St. John the Baptist; but it had fallen into ruin. Still in this little chapel the Bishop and Norbert entered to pray.

Norbert was at once seized by the spirit of God, and when after a long time the Bishop wished to tell him that night was drawing near, he found him in ecstasy, entirely lost to the world around him. When the Saint did come to himself, the Bishop asked him if this, at last, was the place. "Lord and Father," replied Norbert, "let us praise the Almighty. I have found a solitude according to my heart. This is the place which it has pleased God to prepare for me from all eternity." He further begged the Bishop to be allowed to spend the night there in prayer, and Bartholomew returned alone to Anizy, a castle about nine miles from Laon.

Once alone in the poor little chapel of St. John the Baptist, far away from the noise of the world and in the darkness of the night, our Saint poured forth his heartfelt thanks to God. Oh! how fervently he must have prayed, for during the night the heavens were opened to him, and the Blessed Virgin, surrounded by angels, appeared to him, illuminating the poor chapel with a heavenly light! In very truth she came to direct him in the founding of his Order and to tell him that his prayers were heard. She indicated the place where the first house of the Order should be built; and, showing him a white habit, said to him: "Receive my son, the white habit." The Queen of heaven then disappeared.[5]

The Saint, with glowing heart, beheld
The radiant Queen who said:
"Take thou this sign of grace, my child,"

---

[5] Thus Le Paige Biblioth. Ord. Praem., p. 372.—Hanegravius, p. 15—and many others. In 1625 Theod. Galleus reproduced this Apparition in a beautiful picture; and besides, this scene is often referred to in different official documents concerning the Order.

As o'er his bending head
She held the snowy habit. ...

Thus the night passed quickly, and before Norbert was aware of it, Bartholomew stood at his side, anxious to know how God had inspired him in that long night of prayer. Radiant with joy, Norbert exclaimed,

> This is the place of my rest and the haven of my salvation. Here I must sing the praises of the Lord, together with faithful companions, whom God will send me. I have seen during my prayer a multitude of pilgrims, clothed in white robes, carrying in their hands silver crosses and censers, pointing out to me the place where God wishes to have a church built in His honor.

The good Bishop was greatly pleased with all that Norbert related, and gladly promised to procure for him the possession of Prémontré from the abbot of St. Vincent, to whom it belonged. They then returned to Laon. Norbert had, since the Council of Fritzlar, worn a gray woolen habit, but at this time he took the white habit, which he received from the hands of Bishop Bartholomew.[6]

It was not without a special design on the part of divine Providence that, among so many solitary places in the diocese of Laon, the Saint should have selected the desert of Prémontré as the cradle of the Order. Heaven, which had inspired him in this first choice, showed hereby that the Order, which was to have penance for its portion and preaching for its occupation, would most fittingly take its birth in a solitude dedicated to St. John the Baptist, the model-preacher of penance. Again, the very name Prémontré—Præmonstratum—Pratum Monstratum, means a place foreshown. Many of the historians seem inclined to think that the

[6] Le Paige, ibidem. Cfr. also De Waghenaere, "Vita Sancti Norberti metro libera.," p. 19. Both relate this event, adding that it took place on the feast of the Conversion of St. Paul—Jan. 25—in the year 1120.

Saint himself originated this name in remembrance of his vision.

Others, and among them Blessed Hugh himself, affirm that the place was thus popularly called long before Norbert's coming. Some even give us the origin of the name in relating the following story, which, however, Bl. Hugh, in his "Vita," considers a fable.

They tell us that at one time there was a lion doing considerable damage in that part of the country. In vain had the people tried to kill him, when Enguerrand I, of Coucy, resolved to find him and free the country of this dangerous intruder. He inquired of a hermit where the lion was. All at once he saw him very close by, and exclaimed: "De par saint Jean, tu me l'as de près montré." Hence, they say, the name Prémontré.[7]

At any rate, ever since the time of St. Norbert, his canons have been distinguished from others by this name of Prémontré. In history they are sometimes referred to as Norbertines, as for instance, in the life of St. Otho of Bamberg, but the more common historic name is Premonstratensians. In England, however, until the time of their suppression by Henry VIII, they were generally known by the name of "White Canons."

Norbert actually took possession of his dear solitude in the year 1120. His community was small, to be sure, but the Saint knew he was carrying out the will of God, and abandoned the future entirely to divine Providence. As St. Ignatius observes, the foundation of a Religious Order is too sublime to be a human work.

And no doubt this is why God has shown to nearly all Founders of Religious Orders the very spot where the first house of the order was to be built. Read, for instance, the lives of St. Romuald—St. Robert of Citeaux—Bl. Bernard of Tiron,—all these had visions in which God pointed out to them the very place of their first foundation. Then we must not overlook the part God's Mother also

[7] There are MSS. kept in the archives of the department of Aisne, according to which this story is no fable. They tell that Enguerrand, to perpetuate the memory of this dangerous hunt, established in his domains the Order of the Lion. Cfr. Madelaine.

took in the foundation of Norbert's Order, as related above.

The chapel and the surrounding country, of which Norbert had now taken possession, had at one time belonged to the Bishop of Laon. One of Bartholomew's predecessors had donated it to the Benedictine monks of St. Vincent's Abbey.[8] These monks had tried for years to cultivate the valley, but without success. So when the Bishop asked the Abbot and his monks for the property, they very willingly returned it, especially since the Bishop offered them in exchange the altar of Berry-au-Brac and a half bushel of wheat from the mill of Bancourt. These details we know from a charter given by the Bishop to Prémontré nearly a year later.[9] The first agreement therefore must have been a verbal one.

After Norbert and his two companions were established in Prémontré, they came in contact with a priest by the name of Guy, Guido or Wido, who was leading in that vicinity the life of a hermit.[10] He had led for some years a dissipated life, but now wore a religious habit and lived hidden in this desert to do penance for his sins. After meeting our Saint he went deeper into the forests in the direction of Valenciennes, and for three years lived all alone. One day, however, he is to be the founder of the illustrious Norbertine abbey of Vicogne.

The question is discussed by different historians as to whether

---

[8] St. Bernard says in one of his letters (253) that he himself is the giver of the land of Prémontré. S. J. Eales, in his "Life and Works of St. Bernard," observes in a footnote to this letter: "What St. Bernard says here about the ground being given by him seems at variance with the letters of foundation of Prémontré given in the name of Bartholomew, Bishop of Laon, in which the place in question is said to have belonged to the monks of St. Vincent, and to have been given by Bartholomew to Norbert. However, this seeming contradiction is explained when we remember that Hugh, in rebuilding the monastery of Prémontré, had transferred it to the other side of a mountain. The first site may thus have been given by the monks of St. Vincent and the second by Bernard."

[9] Cfr. next chapter where Charter is given.

[10] St. Bernard refers to this priest in the letter quoted above (253).

St. Norbert at this time had really any definite idea as to the kind of life and the work of the new Order he was now bringing into existence. Most of them agree that he did not, and this seems very likely. Ever since the day of his conversion his object had been "Reform." His aim in going to live at Prémontré was beyond doubt that he and his disciples might lead a life of penance, and make this their center of true missionary labors. The exact means and ways of attaining his object he left to Divine Providence.

God had thus far led him out of his own country and brought him among strangers. When Norbert had come to Prémontré, God had made known to him that this was the place destined for him, prepared from all eternity. We may therefore say that Norbert at this time was simply awaiting further developments of his providential mission.

SECOND PERIOD

From the time the Order is founded until Norbert becomes Archbishop of Magdeburg

1120-1126

CORPVS DOMINI IESV CHRISTI

❧

CHAPTER I
THE FOUNDER

Praemonstratensem radiis Crux fulgida monstrat,
Et peregrinorum plurima turba locum.

... And robed in light,
The Savior meets the raptured sight,
To show, by seven-fold rays, the place
Where Norbert's band—a chosen race,
Shall dwell. ...

LIFE at Prémontré was begun by a most fervent retreat, at the end of which Norbert left to go in search of disciples. No doubt it seems strange to us for the Saint to go out begging recruits for his new foundation. Such, however, was not unusual in those days, for history tells us that, at the time Norbert was trying to find disciples, St. Bernard was preaching at the University of Paris with the same purpose in view.

By the advice of Bishop Bartholomew Norbert went first to the celebrated school of Ralph of Laon. Here he spoke with his usual eloquence on the vanity of the world, and drew a vivid picture of the greatness of the religious life, urging his hearers to follow him. His words so touched the hearts of his audience that seven young men—all sons of the best families of Lorraine decided at once to yield to him, and become his disciples at Prémontré.[1]

This first unexpected success greatly encouraged Norbert, who considered it an unmistakable sign of God's blessing on his work.

[1] Pertz. Script. XII, p. 657—de Mirac. S. Mariae Laudun.

The seven new disciples were all sons of wealthy families, and their wealth would certainly be a great help in the erection of a monastery and church. How truly providential it all was! In spirit Norbert already beheld the realization of his vision on the first night in the little chapel of Prémontré. Who could describe his feelings of gratitude when he knelt once more in this same poor chapel, to spend another night in fervent prayer! A great trial, however, awaited him. The reader will perhaps remember the mysterious words Norbert had heard on his way from Rheims. Although two disciples were with him at the time, a voice was heard distinctly saying: "Behold Norbert and his companion!" None of the three then understood the meaning, but all will be very clear now, as one of the first two disciples is about to prove false.

Upon returning from Laon, Norbert had placed all the money of the new postulants behind the altar in the little chapel. What reason Norbert had for suspecting a certain young novice we do not know, but it is certain that the Saint mistrusted him. Norbert said to him: "Is there anything wrong, my brother? What evil plan has entered your heart? Tell me what you are hiding from me. If it is God you seek, remember that there can be nothing hidden before His eyes." Norbert clearly hinted here at some crime. But the young disciple persevered in his evil design, and one night, after taking all the money, fled from the abbey, leaving the brethren penniless.[2] We can imagine the surprise of all next morning, when everything was found out. Still, instead of discouraging the young community, this event only served to make them more dependent on Divine Providence. Norbert even reproached himself for having entertained any feelings of joy at the acquisition of wealth. Had they not in fact

[2] Such is the version of this incident as found in *Vita B*, Ch. XXVI, "De quodam novitio qui viro Dei fraudulenter adhaeserat." Also in Acta SS. T. XX, p. 851, note 1.—Hermann and other historians tell us that St. Norbert had entrusted the money to the young man, who on the very first night fled with it; therefore they do not mention the warning the Saint had given him.

renounced all their earthly possessions? "God will provide" became, from now on, their watchword, and their peace remained undisturbed.

Norbert spent the rest of the winter in Prémontré, daily instructing the new disciples in the practice of monastic virtues, and trying at the same time to awaken in their hearts a desire for the apostolic life. In early spring, however, he entrusted the young community to the care of Hugh, and he himself resumed his apostolic labors, with the view of again gathering more disciples.

He first went to Cambray, the episcopal see of his dear friend, Bishop Burchard. Having explained the purpose of his visit, he asked and obtained the good Bishop's permission to speak in the cathedral. Here also some young men decided to renounce the world and follow him to Prémontré. Among these was a young man, Evermode by name, of about twenty years of age. "He thought," says the early biographer, "that, when he was listening to the sermon of Norbert, he heard the voice of Jesus Christ Himself inviting him to the religious life." This same young man is to be Norbert's constant companion and most beloved disciple; he is the future saintly Bishop of Ratzeburg, who will receive in Norbert's dying hour the last words of our Saint.

Leaving Cambray, Norbert passed once more through Hainault and Brabant, following the same road he had passed nearly two years before, preaching by word and example, and converting many hardened sinners. When he came to Nivelles, a small village known from the life and tomb of St. Gertrude, another young man named Anthony, offered himself to follow Norbert. One day he will be Provost of Ilbenstadt. The three thus far named—Hugh, Evermode and Anthony, are, as later events will prove, to be real cornerstones of the spiritual structure Norbert is now raising for God's glory.

The Saint returned to Prémontré during Passion week of the year 1121, and celebrated Easter, surrounded by thirteen disciples. Besides the three already mentioned, there was Gualterus or Gautier, who is yet to be abbot of St. Martin at Laon, where Norbert himself had been for three months; later he will be bishop of the diocese. Then there was Milo, a true model of humility, who one day will be abbot of Saint-Josse-au-Bois, or Dommartin, and later bishop of Thérouanne. Richard will be the first abbot of the illustratious abbey of Floreffe. Gerardus, one of the Lorraine converts, will be prior of Prémontré and later abbot of Clairefontaine. Adam, who was born at Metz, also one of the seven students of Laon, will succeed Milo as abbot of Dommartin. Then there was another Richard, who is to be the first abbot of Sainte-Marie-au-Bois. Waltman will go with Norbert to Antwerp as an apostle of the Blessed Sacrament, and be the first abbot of St. Michael in that place. One by the name of Guarin will one day govern the abbey of Vicogne, and later the abbey of St. Martin at Laon.

Henry will die as abbot of Viviers, later Valsery, in the diocese of Soissons; the last, Luc by name, will be abbot of Mount Cornillon at Liège.

This little community in its first fervor was full of the spirit of Norbert. Milo is known to have excelled in humility, Adam was known for his great zeal to do honor to the Blessed Virgin, Guarin was called the servant of the poor, and of Luc we read that he was a strong promoter of devotion to the Guardian Angel. Henry, who like Norbert was also of a noble family, followed our Saint most closely in the practice of every virtue.

On Norbert's return all began a fervent retreat to prepare themselves for the solemn reception of the habit on Easter Sunday. The good Bishop Bartholomew came in person to Prémontré to assist at the solemnities. "Bishop Bartholomew had first brought them to Prémontré, and now they all received from his hands the white habit, like the one Our Lady had shown to St. Norbert; thus they began their pious exercise on the feast of Easter."[3]

On the glorious Easter morning of the year 1121, the Bishop, St.

[3] Cfr. Camus. L'homme apostolique, p. 109.

Norbert, and his thirteen disciples entered the poor little chapel of St. John the Baptist. The birthday of the Order had arrived. What must have been Norbert's inner joy as he watched his spiritual children approach the good Bishop one by one, and receive from his hands the white habit! Simple as the ceremony must have been, we dare say, that never afterwards, even amidst the splendor of costly decorations, was the reception of the habit more solemn and impressive than on that memorable morning. His Bishop, the Holy Father, and as we have seen, the Lord Himself, seemed crowning his efforts with great success.

When the glorious ceremony was over, Bishop Bartholomew had a surprise in store for Norbert, and calling the brethren together he handed over to the Saint the solemn deed of the property at Prémontré. As this deed might be considered the foundation Charter of the Order, we shall give here a translation of it:

> In the name of the Holy and Indivisible Trinity. To all, present and to come, we wish to have it known, that I, Bartholomew, Bishop of Laon, have given to Norbert, a man worthy of all respect, whose religious fervor is known to all, and also to his successors, who will live in their holy vocation, our territory of Hubertpont whole and entire, free from all rent, from the place which is called Halierpré to the valley Rohard, with the three valleys bordering on the latter, to begin at the river from the side of Vois, all as freehold. We give them this territory to build thereon a church and a monastery in honor of God and the Holy Mother of God. The pastures and meadows, from Hubertpont to Molnantvoisin, on both sides of the river, will at all times be, in common with the people of the village, for the use of their cattle. The farmers of the neighborhood shall have the right to cut on the mountains all the wood necessary for ploughs and wheels. The brethren shall be exempted in all the above-mentioned places from all rights of tenths or feudal rights, and from all parochial jurisdiction; and the hermits of the forests will be subjected to them. ...
>
> We also wish it known to all, that the church of Prémontré with the surrounding territory was given by my predecessor, Hélinand, to

the church of St. Vincent; but since in these latter days all this was in a state of ruin, the Abbot Siegfried and the convent of St. Vincent have thought it well to return this property to us; and this they did. We, not knowing what better we could do, have given the whole property, free forever from all extortions, to the venerable Norbert and his successors, faithful in their holy vocation, on condition that they will not have with them any lay-man, but only persons leading the religious life. We also give forever and as a freehold to the same brethren living religiously, the hills which surround the valley of Prémontré. All this is done with the consent of Thomas de Mare, who for the ransom of his soul has renounced his claims to two parts of the tenths on the above mentioned immovable property, and all his rights and the rights of his foresters, Girelme de Vauscillon, Raoul de Quincy and Raoul of Coucy-la-Ville. This same Thomas has given to the brethren a piece of land at Rosières, for cultivation. Besides, we have with the consent of all, closed up the road by which the neighbors passed through the valley of Prémontré to go to church.

We have furthermore given to the brethren three pieces of land, one at Anizy, near our "villa," one at Versigny, and the third on the mountain of Chrevregny on the other side of Aillette. Whosoever shall try to violate this Charter, let him be anathema, and may he incur the wrath of the Most High on the day of Judgment.

Given in the year of the Incarnation, 1121.

Following this are:

The seal of the church of St. Mary at Laon.

The seal of Abbot Siegfried of St. Vincent's. Further, the seals of Simon, Abbot of St. Nicolas-au-Bois; Dean Guy; Doctor Raoul, Archdeacon; Robert, Provost of St. Martin, and numerous other illustrious persons.[4]

When the solemnities were over and the Bishop had left Prémontré, Norbert began at once to establish regular monastic life in his community. Around the little chapel of St. John huts or tents

[4] Cfr. Madelaine, o. c., p. 153, who further quotes Hugo, Annales Ord. Praem. I Probat., col. VI. The document is preserved in the Library of Soissons.

were built as temporary quarters, and the singing of the Divine Office began on that very day. The strictest fast was observed by all, and when not occupied in the recital of the Office, the brethren spent nearly all their time in manual labor. This was necessary not only to make the place habitable but also as a means of support, for since the day they had been robbed, they had depended entirely on the liberality of Bishop Bartholomew.

To enable his young disciples to suffer all kinds of hardships and privations, Norbert himself led the way in everything. Every morning and evening he assembled the brethren in the little chapel and gave them fatherly advice. After the morning instruction all went to work on the "huts" or "tents," with Norbert always the hardest worker among them; thus he encouraged all by word and example. Inexperienced as these young novices were in the ways of religious life, they had a good will and a childlike confidence in the superior wisdom of their spiritual father.

Written rules there were none at the time; the will of Norbert was the rule of life for all. The Saint fully realized that without a written constitution his Order could not be lasting, therefore he warned his disciples repeatedly that the Evangelical Counsels needed an interpretation to make uniform religious life possible. But as the Saint said, he mistrusted himself in this all important matter of selecting a Rule. The wise and pious men to whom Norbert went for advice, did not agree. Some advised him to follow the Rule of the Carthusians, others that of the Benedictines; again, others spoke to him of the Cistercian Rule. But none of these Rules wholly satisfied our Saint. Norbert himself was a "Canon" and he wanted his followers to be "Canons." And since the clerical state was at that time only accidental to the monastic Orders, he refused to follow their rule of life because incompatible with his ideals. How often had he on his missionary tours realized the crying need of good and holy priests; consequently he wished his Order to be an Order of good priests, not of monks. He wished his disciples, like himself, to go out preaching. They were often to live in the world yet not be of the world. Again, they were to perform parochial work outside their monasteries, and all this was at that time contrary to the rules of monks.

Besides, as we have remarked, canonical life was at this particular time undergoing a great reform. A separation had come between those canons who lived in common and others who lived in separate houses. St. Augustine had in his time made rules regulating this condition in his own diocese, and in the ninth century at the Council of Aachen, the common life for canons had been recommended. There were places, to be sure, where St. Augustine's Rule was partly observed by canons, but nowhere, it seems, in all its strictness. Norbert therefore made a thorough study of this Rule and thought very seriously at this time of adopting it, and of adding the monastic customs as far as they were helpful, and did not interfere with the performance of priestly duties. Yet he remained undecided, and after fervent prayers resolved to open his mind on this point with great frankness to his disciples. He told them that he had consulted learned bishops and holy abbots; that by some he had been advised to lead an eremitical life, by others a monastic life, or else to join the Cistercian Order. He added that if he knew it to be the will of God, he should follow his own inclination and lead the canonical life of the Apostles. In order to know then the Holy Will of God, he asked them to redouble their prayers and acts of mortification, and to implore the guidance of the Holy Ghost in this so important a matter. For the present Norbert's will, directed by the Holy Spirit, was to remain their daily rule of life.

Meanwhile a Synod was being held at Soissons over which Cuno, Bishop of Preneste and Papal Legate, presided. The reader has already made his acquaintance at the Council of Fritzlar. The principal question to be considered at this Synod was the orthodoxy of Peter Abelard.

Peter was a highly gifted scholar and had a host of followers, but he was also proud and haughty, and his novel views, especially on the Blessed Trinity, had brought him in conflict with the authorities of the Church. St. Bernard, who has the well-deserved distinction of having been Abelard's ablest opponent, does not seem to have been present at this Synod,[5] and it fell to Norbert to use his deep learning in exposing this clever heretic. How well the Saint succeeded in this we may safely judge from the amount of abuse, which after the Synod, Abelard began to heap on our Saint and his followers.

Abelard complains bitterly in his subsequent sermons and writings of all he has to suffer from Norbert. The certain "new apostles," of whom he speaks in the "Story of my Calamities," are Norbert and Bernard. We shall quote a passage from "Peter Abelard," by Jos. McCabe, to give the reader an idea of the deep hatred of Abelard for Norbert, and the contemptible means he used to lessen Norbert's influence with the people. We read:

> "The other new Apostle was St. Norbert, the founder of the Premonstratensian Canons. He had fruitlessly endeavored to reform the existing order of Canons, and had then withdrawn to form a kind of monastery of Canons at Prémontré, not far from Laon where he occasionally visited Anselm. His disciples entered zealously into the task of policing the country. No disorder in faith or morals escaped their notice; and although Norbert was far behind Bernard in political ability, the man who incurred his pious wrath was in an unenviable position. He had influence with the prelates of the Church, on account of his reforms and the sanctity of his life; he had a profound influence over the common people, not only through his stirring sermons, but also through the miracles he wrought. Abelard frequently bases his rationalistic work on the fact, which he always assumes to be uncontroverted, that the age of miracles is over. Norbert, on the contrary, let it be distinctly understood that he was a thaumaturgus of large practice. Abelard ridiculed his pretensions and the stories told of him. Even

[5] Cfr. "The Works of St. Bernard," edited by S. J. Eales, D. C. L.—General Preface, p. 49: "First, we will commence by observing that long before the collision with Bernard, he (Abelard) had been cited by Conon ... to the Council of Soissons, in 1121."

in his later sermons we find him scornfully 'exposing' the miracles of Norbert and his companions. They used to slip medicament unobserved into the food of the sick, he says, and accept the glory of the miracle if the fever was cured. They even attempted to raise the dead to life; and when the corpse retained its hideous rigidity, after they had lain long hours in prayer in the sanctuary, they would turn around on the simple folk in the church and upbraid them for their little faith. This poor trickery was the chief source of the power of the Premonstratensian Canons over the people. Abelard could not expose and ridicule it with impunity . . . etc."[6]

We have quoted at length because these invectives of Abelard against Norbert show incidentally that Norbert was truly the Saint of his age and very popular with the people, while Abelard feared him and sought to injure his reputation. But all his abuse had the very opposite effect from what he expected, as will be clearly seen later from some extracts from contemporary writers, concerning Norbert.

At the Synod of Soissons Norbert learned of the sad ravages the Catharist heresy was making everywhere, and took the firm resolutions to oppose these heretics with all his might. Soon we shall find him in Belgium carrying out this resolution by fighting the heresy of Tanchelm, whose teachings were based on the Catharist doctrine.

After the Synod Norbert intended to return at once to his brethren at Prémontré. However, he was detained by the Bishop to exercise his favorite missionary work, that of peacemaker. Not far from Soissons was the abbey of Viviers, whose Abbot Henry had placed himself under the direction of Norbert with the intention of introducing into his abbey the Saint's reforms.[7] At the time there was a certain Hugh, Lord of La Ferte-Milon, who had laid a

---

[6] "Peter Abélard," by Jos. McCabe, p. 219, et seq.

[7] Thus says Le Paige, o. c., p. 454. According to other writers this Abbot Henry did not join the Premonstratensian Order till about three years later.

sacrilegious hand on the property of the abbey, and though a married layman, had proclaimed himself abbot. Norbert's aid was invoked by the Bishop and Abbot to induce Hugh to terminate this scandalous state of things. After asking God's help in fervent prayer, the Saint set out on this his favorite mission. Having won Hugh's confidence by his usual kindness, Norbert fearlessly showed him the consequences of his perfidious conduct, and actually succeeded in bringing him to sign an act of restitution, a copy of which is still preserved.[8] In it we read: "Lisiard, Bishop of Soissons, wishes it to be known to all that the quasi-abbot Hugh and his wife . . . upon the advice of master Norbert, a man well known for his piety, have returned to Abbot Henry and his brethren the church of Viviers and all the possessions belonging to it." When Hugh had signed the document the Saint restored him to God's friendship. One more splendid proof of Norbert's power over the hearts of sinners! For if it is always a very difficult task to convert public sinners, it must be more so when there is question of restitution.

It is truly regrettable that so few instances of this kind in his life have come down to us. Only here and there we find a few scattered details recorded by the early biographer. Yet nothing surely could be more edifying than some of the life-stories of his numerous converts. We can form some idea of their number when we consider, that during the next six years Norbert is able to build monasteries seemingly everywhere, while the required funds are forthcoming without difficulty. This financial aid he must have received from the numerous wealthy lords whom he brought back to the practice of their religion. The following chapters will show that among them Norbert found a great number of recruits for these monasteries.

---

[8] Thus Fath. G. Vanden-Elsen O. Praem. in his "Het leven van den H. Norbertus," p. 64.

CHAPTER II
TRIALS

Obsesso stygias e Corpore saepe Cohortes,
Orci Norbertus Caeca sub antra fugat.

... Then
The demon fled the tortured souls of men
At thy desire.

NORBERT was very anxious to find followers for his new foundations, and so whenever anyone offered himself, expressing the wish to lead a more perfect life, the invariable practice of our Saint was to give him a trial. Old and young, poor and wealthy, men as well as women, had thus in great numbers become his disciples. In fact, very shortly after founding a house for the training of priests, Norbert also made provisions for a house for Sisters. Apostolic men at the end of the eleventh and the beginning of the twelfth century, while establishing abbeys for religious, did not think it proper to deprive women of the blessings of religious life. They opened houses for them, and these places were then called "double monasteries." The most celebrated among these was the house of Fontevrault, founded by Robert d'Abrissel, where the abbess exercised authority not only over the Sisters but also over the men of the Institute. These double monasteries usually consisted of two distinct monasteries separated by walls, but within one enclosure. The religious were in reality but neighbors and their church and house, as all else, were entirely distinct, so that there was a complete separation.[1]

The first woman who placed herself under Norbert's spiritual direction was a noble lady of Vermandois, Ricvere by name, the widow of Raymond of Clastres.[2] She had given part of her property for the sustenance of Norbert's brethren, and she herself lived in a poor little hut near-by to care for the sick. In due time Norbert gave her the white habit and the veil, and thus her little hut became the cradle of the Second Order of St. Norbert, which flourished for centuries, and exists to this day in different parts of the world.

In consequence of Norbert's practice of allowing one to enter his monastery to try himself, several unworthy members, that is, without a vocation, had entered the young community. Hence it cannot cause great surprise to find that, during the Saint's absence at the Synod of Soissons, the evil spirit had caused disturbances among the brethren. As soon as Norbert, on his return, reached his beloved valley there arose a great tempest during which God revealed to him the pitiful state in which the community was at Prémontré. He learned that some of the disciples, who had come with him from Nivelles where he had also found his beloved Anthony, had become dissatisfied and left. They had now returned to that place, and still under Satan's influence, were trying to justify their own conduct by calumniating Norbert and the brethren. They spread false rumors about them and even accused Norbert of being a deceiver.

Besides, at Prémontré, there was a young religious named Gerard, who had been a model of piety and obedience, but now, having listened to the suggestions of Satan, to the great scandal of all the brethren, publicly broke the Lenten fast and abstinence, which at all times was strictly observed. Upon his return Norbert

---

[1] Madelaine, p. 159-160, who further quotes A. Lenoir, "Architecture monast." 1861, p. 474-478. Monast. double.

[2] Cfr. Acta Sanctorum T. CXI, p. 52: "Eo tempore ... quaedam nobilis mulier Rycwera nomine, uxor Raymondi de Clastris, in praedictum locum, conversionis gratia, se contulit ...

went at once to this young religious, embraced him with the affection of a father, but at the same time punished him with the severity of a judge. Gerard willingly accepted the penance Norbert imposed on him, overcame the enemy, and again became a model of virtue, and worthy to be one day, the first abbot of Claire-Fontaine. Further, with the Saint's return rest and quiet was at once restored to the community. Norbert then remained for some time at Prémontré instructing, and encouraging his spiritual children in the constant practice of virtue. His favorite topic was the confidence in God one ought to have in his struggles with the evil spirit. "Qui Deum habet pro se, turbatur in nulla re," "One who has God on his side will never be disturbed by anything," was one of his most frequent sayings. Knowing that Satan would do all in his power to frustrate the good work at Prémontré, Norbert greatly insisted on childlike confidence in God.

Towards the end of April he considered the young community strong enough to be left alone, and decided on another missionary journey. He went towards Nivelles, and on the road thither had the happiness of reconciling not only two inveterate enemies, but numerous sinners with God. The people at Nivelles, however, seemed quite hostile to him, as a result of the calumnies spread by his former disciples, and some reproached him bitterly. But, accustomed to all kinds of insults, the Saint did not even attempt to justify himself. He bore the results of these calumnies with great patience and resignation, and left his vindication entirely to Divine Providence, in Whose fields he labored. Since he came not to gain the favor of the people but to lead their souls to God, he inwardly rejoiced to be found worthy to suffer for the sake of Jesus Christ. And God, Who constantly watched over the Saint, soon found means to restore Norbert to honor and good name, and to bring his calumniators to shame.

There was a young girl in Nivelles who for years had been possessed by the evil one. She often became so unmanageable that they had to tie her with ropes and lock her in a room by herself. She then would get into a fury, abuse all those around, and become really dangerous. The young girl was brought to the Saint, who in all simplicity and full of the liveliest faith, read over her the exorcisms as found in the Roman Ritual, but seemingly without avail. Ascribing his ill success to his own unworthiness, he promised God to make himself less unworthy by fasting and prayer. After passing the whole night in fervent prayer, he sent word in the morning to the parents of the unfortunate girl to bring her to assist at his Mass. In the middle of the Mass, in fact, at the moment of the Elevation, the devil cried out in a loud voice: "See how he holds his God in his hands."[3] The early biographers observe here that devils are forced to confess what heretics deny. The prayer of the saintly priest increased in fervor meanwhile, and Satan exclaimed: "I burn, I burn, let me go," and the unclean spirit with loud protestations left his victim, and the poor girl remained lying on the floor like one dead. This happened publicly before a large crowd of people.[4] When at the end of the Holy Sacrifice she had regained consciousness, Norbert restored the girl to her parents, who were full of gratitude to him, and the people, in the highest admiration for the man of God, proclaimed anew his power and holiness of life. This event is thus narrated in all its details in the earliest biography of the Saint. That it took place under the very eyes of a great multitude, who in their enthusiasm sang the "Te Deum" to thank God for His goodness manifested through Norbert, was clearly the work of Divine Providence, for Norbert's reputation was at once vindicated, and his calumniators put to shame.

But Satan, conquered by Norbert at Nivelles, began to use all his power to cause disturbances in the young community at Prémontré. He worked on the natural pride and self-will of some and frequently succeeded in making the life of the young novice very trying. Soon

[3] *Vita B*, Ch. XXII: "Videte, videte; ecce iste deiculum suum inter manus suas tenet." Cfr. also Camus, p. 118.

[4] Ibidem. Hoc ita publice factum est, teste omni populo. Cfr. Pertz Sigeb. contin. Praem. T. VI, p. 448.

after the event at Nivelles we read in the Annals of Prémontré, that a poor boy, whose father was a lay-brother in the monastery, became possessed. As the boy was quite violent at times, the brethren were greatly disturbed, and knew not what to do. After holding council, they decided to lock him in a room and await the return of their Father Norbert. But the Prior took great pity on the boy and commanded all to pray fervently. He then took his Ritual, read the prayers given, and commanded the evil one to depart in the name of Jesus Christ. To their great consternation they all heard distinctly these words: "Cursed be the hour that that white dog (meaning Norbert) was born." Still Satan refused to give up his prey. At last a young and saintly novice, who acted only in virtue of holy obedience, succeeded in putting the evil one to flight.

Soon Norbert returned and with him came once more happiness and rest to the small community. The Saint's very presence was more than Satan could bear. Every one was happy and contented whenever Norbert was around; and, following his wise directions, all made rapid progress in virtue. Before long, however, another difficulty of a more serious nature presented itself.

Their number had kept on increasing, and soon the little chapel could no longer suffice for so many religious. All were anxious to erect a beautiful church, and to build it on the spot pointed out to Norbert in his first vision, by the Blessed Virgin herself. Though the brethren had been able to erect their own little tents, the building of a church, worthy of the name, was beyond them. There was no lack of material all around them, but where find able builders? Norbert counted on help from above. He had always had a special devotion to relics, and he reasoned that if he could only procure relics of Saints, whom he and his brethren would venerate, these Saints would undoubtedly assist him. He knew that Cologne, the city of his youth, possessed an abundance of relics, and that a number of artists and builders were also to be found within its walls. Further, he could rely entirely on the assistance of the Archbishop of Cologne; and, therefore, he decided once more to leave Prémontré, and to undertake the journey to Cologne. As was his wont, he turned the journey into a real missionary tour, and found numerous opportunities of converting sinners, and winning new disciples. He was so grateful to God for his own happiness that he was anxious to have others share in it.

The good Archbishop Frederic was delighted indeed to see his former courtier again, however much he was changed; and he received him with all kindness. His presence soon became known among the people, and the name of Norbert was once more on the lips of all. Never was there a greater concourse of people present than when he spoke in the old and venerable cathedral. Since a great many remembered him only as the young and gay courtier, a son of the nobility, his words, strengthened by his appearance, made a very deep impression when in his eloquent way he spoke on the vanity of the world and the necessity of doing penance. His confessional was crowded all day, as the early biographer informs us, and no less than thirty young men renounced the world and begged to become his followers.[5]

However, the first object of his journey was to procure the relics of saints. Now in attaining this object God helped Norbert in a most remarkable way. When he first made known his object to the Archbishop, His Grace as well as his clergy and the people were happy to be able to assist the man of God as a kind of remuneration for his inestimable services. As was known to everyone, the relics of numerous martyrs were hidden somewhere in the city of Cologne.[6]

Norbert was then given not only full permission to search for them, but even men to help him in his work, and if he succeeded, he had leave to take the relics with him to Prémontré. The Saint soon had his plans formed. He prescribed for his new brethren a day of

[5] Madelaine, o. c., who quotes *Vita*, Ch. XXIII, calls here attention to the fact of auricular confession, a century before the fourth Lateran Council. See p. 166.

[6] *Vita* (Pertz), Ch. XII.

strict fast; he himself doubled on that day his austerities, and all prayed with extraordinary fervor that heaven would guide them in their diligent search. And, wonderful to relate! the night which followed the fast, our Saint had an apparition of St. Ursula, who indicated to him her own burial place, hitherto entirely unknown.[7] This happened during the night between the tenth and the eleventh of October, in the year 1121, nearly a thousand years after St. Ursula and her holy Virgins had suffered martyrdom. Early the next morning a search was made in the place indicated by the apparition, and in reality the body was found in its integrity. With what a transport of joy did our Saint receive this precious treasure! Surely the blessing of Almighty God was seen once more to rest visibly on Norbert's undertaking. During the singing of religious hymns the precious remains were put in a costly urn, and then given over to the Saint. He further received two reliquaries containing notable parts of the bodies of the other virgins.[8]

Acting on divine inspiration, Norbert went the next day to the church of St. Gereon, whose Provost at the time was Hermannus. He begged that he be allowed to dig under the monastery; because the Saint seemed to know that there were buried numerous martyrs of the Theban Legion of the third century, and among them St. Gereon himself, their leader. However much surprised the superiors were, since Norbert was known to them as "an illustrious preacher and a great servant of God," they gave him their full permission. According to his invariable custom, before any work of importance, the Saint recommended himself to God and spent the whole night in fervent prayer. Meanwhile men were digging the whole night in the presence of Rudolph, Abbot of St. Panthaleon, (who had been

[7] Ibidem: Reliquiarum patrocinia quibus ab antiquo repleta et dotata erat Sancta Colonia. ... Virgo ex undecim millium ... et nomen virginis et locus mausolei ... per visionem cuidam designatus est. ...

[8] Cfr. Madelaine, o. c., p. 167. See also Cath. Encyclop., Vol. V, p. 672c, where this visit of St. Norbert to Cologne is mentioned in connection with the relics of the sainted Ewalds.

delegated by the Archbishop himself), and of a great many clerics and the most prominent people of Cologne. But during the whole night they found nothing in any way remarkable. At daybreak Norbert himself came upon the scene, and at once gave orders to the men to dig near a certain pillar on the south side of the church. Although there was no trace of any sepulchre there, the men began digging anew, simply because Norbert told them to do so. And behold! before long they came upon a precious slab of marble. All present were in great admiration, and when at last the sarcophagus was opened and they saw before their eyes a corpse bearing all the signs of a martyr of the Theban Legion, their enthusiasm knew no bounds, and they freely shouted for joy.[9]

The upper part of the head was missing, and hereby they knew that it was the body of St. Gereon himself, for in suffering martyrdom, the upper part of his head had been cut off, which part in fact had been venerated for centuries. When it became known in the city that the body of St. Gereon had actually been found, clergy as well as laity came hurrying in great numbers to the monastery, and, deeply touched, all joined in loudly praising and thanking God for His goodness. Then it was whispered by someone that Norbert was to take the body with him to Prémontré, and their joy was at once changed to anger. Loud protestations were heard from all sides, until the Provost of St. Mary's mounted the pulpit, and to calm the uproar, promised the people that the Archbishop was to decide that question.[10] This announcement quieted the people, and

---

[9] Vita (Pertz), Ch. XII. "Ubi nullum alicujus sepulchri patebat vestigium effodi praecepit. Ubi corpus integrum absque capite repertum est... Cfr. also Acta SS. Tom. V. Oct., p. 58. Rudolphi epistola: "Petente quodam Dei servo et praedicatore magno Norberto ... inter quos et ego peccator affui ... inventum est in eo corpus magnum ... indutum chlamide militari coloris purpurei ... ut conjicere verius potuimus, sic casu pertransierat inter caput et mentum persecutoris gladius. ..."

[10] Acta SS. L. c. Tota civitas statim infremuit . . . contradicebaturque ob omnibus domino Norberto ... differendum promittente usque ad praesentiam domini archiepiscopi.

it was then decided to leave, meanwhile, near the tomb a guard to watch day and night. Thus the tomb was guarded from the 13th of October until the 24th of November. "On that day, November 24th," continues Rudolph,

> in the presence of Frederic, the Archbishop of Cologne, of abbots, provosts and of all the religious of the city, and of an innumerable multitude of the laity, the tomb was again opened with great solemnity, and the body shown to the people. Abbots and priests, vested in alb and stole, lifted the body, and collecting all the precious relics in a linen cloth, went in solemn procession around the church and monastery. Returning to the church, Rudolph chanted a solemn High Mass in "honor of the martyrs of the Theban Legion.

Norbert did not assist at these solemnities, for he was no longer in Cologne. The Archbishop, to whom, as we remarked above, the case had been referred, had decided to give Norbert not the whole body but part of the relics, and thus the Saint had left the city in the latter part of October.[11] How happy he was on this return journey to Prémontré, we can easily imagine. He had gone out in search of relics of the saints, and had obtained far more than he had ever dared hope for; besides, he had gone in search of new disciples, and there he was returning with a community larger than the original. Wherever he went, people ran out of their houses to greet the man of God. Everywhere he was received with the greatest honor, and his journey was truly one succession of miracles. Wherever the precious relics rested, God poured out His divine blessing in abundance. And the people said: "These truly are the relics of Saints in the hand of a Saint."[12]

When Norbert arrived in the city of Namur, Count Godfrey and his wife Ermensinde, daughter of Conrad I, Count of Luxemburg,

---

[11] *Vita B*, Ch. XXIII.

[12] Illana, p. 69.

came in all haste to meet him and to venerate the relics which the Saint carried with him. They had heard, they said, that Norbert intended to pass through their estates, and they had therefore come to express their most ardent desire to receive him and his saintly disciples under their roof. Norbert consented. The Countess was so much impressed during a conversation which she held with the Saint, that she offered him her manor-house at Floreffe for the establishment of a second abbey.[13] Norbert accepted the offer and remained some days to regulate conditions for this second foundation, and at the same time to satisfy the piety of his distinguished hosts. In the course of time Godfrey, the Count, will really renounce the world and all his possessions and become a humble lay-brother in this abbey, which he is now about to found; his wife also will one day become a religious. As expressly stated in the memorable deed, they donated their property to give satisfaction to God for their sins. Literally it reads: "In the name of the Holy and Indivisible Trinity, the Father, the Son and the Holy Ghost. I, Godfrey, Count of Namur, and the Countess Ermensinde, having understood by the inspiration of the angel of good counsel, that we could expiate our sins in no better way than by giving alms . . ." etc.[14]

After this prolonged stay with Count Godfrey, Norbert hastened to continue his journey to Prémontré, where he knew that the brethren were anxiously awaiting his return. But before leaving Floreffe he entered the church and placed there on the altar, part of the relics of St. Gereon. In consequence of this act the religious of Floreffe have until this last century, chanted every year a solemn

---

[13] *Vita*, l. c. Obnixe deprecans ut quandam ecclesiolam suam in villa Floreffiae vellet suscipere. . . . Cfr. Cath. Encycl. VI, 105.

[14] Hugo Annales Ord. Praem. I. Prob., col. XLIX. Madelaine, from whom this quotation is taken, further observes that the bodies of Godfrey and Ermensinde still rest in the church at Laon, under a marble slab, with the following inscription: Godefridus—Ermensindis. See Madelaine, o. c., p. 225.

Mass of thanksgiving for the intention of the Canons of St. Gereon's church at Cologne, in return for their liberality in parting with these precious relics. The remainder of his treasure Norbert carried with him to Prémontré, where they have since been kept in great honor and constant veneration. In memory of the event related in this chapter, all Premontratensians the world over celebrate the feast of St. Gereon with special solemnity, and also the feast of St. Ursula and her holy virgins.

ST. AUGUSTINE PRESENTS ST. NORBERT WITH HIS RULE

CHAPTER III
Solemn Profession

Dans legem Aurelius vitae morumque Magistram,
Morigeros maneant praemia quanta docet.

St. Austin gives his hallowed Rule
To train thy followers in that school
Of holy life. ...

WHEN finally Norbert arrived in Prémontré, accompanied by his thirty new disciples, the joy of the brethren was exceedingly great. One could better imagine than describe their happiness when Norbert showed them the priceless relics he brought with him, and spoke to them of God's goodness, and of how His blessing in a visible manner had rested on his undertaking. Was not this an unmistakable sign from heaven that the time had come for the building of the church they had planned? Their numerous trials and hardships during the Saint's absence were at once forgotten, and, weeping for joy, they thanked God for His goodness. Norbert told the brethren of the meeting with Count Godfrey; he then sent a little band of religious to the new foundation. At their head was Richard, one of the earliest disciples, whom he appointed over the young fraters Luc, Emericus and Theodoricus. They received instructions to build at once near the little church of Floreffe a small convent, which, since that time, has been known by the name of "Salve."

The first thing now to be done at Prémontré was to make provision for the new disciples. Under Norbert's direction they began immediately to build more huts and tents of wood and clay, and Prémontré took on the aspect of a busy camp. All were diligently engaged in building, and the huts were arranged around the little chapel of St. John. At this time there were over forty religious studying for the holy priesthood, besides lay-brothers, whose number is unknown. Although all had a certain amount of appointed work, and were constantly and busily occupied, yet for their number, it became evident that a fixed rule of life was indispensable. Still, as heretofore mentioned, it was most difficult for Norbert to decide which rule to adopt. All had been praying for light from above, and as to Norbert, even in the midst of his missionary labors, the thought had been foremost in his mind, but thus far he had come to no decision. God, however, is soon to manifest His Will on this cardinal point of religious life.

One night, while absorbed in prayer, St. Augustine appeared to Norbert in a vision and advised the Saint to adopt his Rule. Listen to Norbert himself relating this vision, some years later, to the brethren of Floreffe assembled in their chapter-room. "I know," he said,

> "that St. Augustine has appeared to one of the brethren, who had been ordered to investigate with the greatest care concerning his Rule; it was not on account of our brother's own merits, but in answer to the prayers of all. St. Augustine took from his right side his Golden Rule, and handing it to the brother, said very distinctly: 'I am Augustine, Bishop of Hippo. Behold here the Rule which I have written; if your fellow-brethren, my sons, shall have observed it well, they shall stand without fear in the presence of Christ on the terrible day of the last Judgment.' Norbert tried thus, no doubt through humility, to make his disciples believe that some other religious had had this vision. The brethren, however, understood at once that no other than himself was the privileged person."[1]

Thus the uncertainty of the brethren in regard to a fixed rule

[1] Cfr. Acta SS. T. XX, p. 846.

had finally come to an end. To the Rule of St. Augustine statutes were added for the regulation of their daily life. These of course were required, for the Rule of St. Augustine was only as a framework, and regulations regarding the special character and object of this Order in particular, had to be filled in to make the structure complete. They now had at least a constitution on which to base the laws and rules regulating their daily life. From that time St. Augustine has been considered by the Premonstratensians as a second Founder, and held in great honor by them.[2]

The solemn feast of Christmas being near at hand, Norbert considered the time to have come for the religious to make their Profession. They, on their part, were very anxious to consecrate themselves more entirely to God by the religious vows, since for this they had left the world. The Saint himself preached the retreat in preparation for the solemn occasion, and by his heavenly eloquence so enraptured the brethren, observes the oldest biographer, that they forgot their earthly existence, and seemed to dwell in celestial spheres.[3]

It is the solemn Christmas night of the year 1121. Let us picture the young community consecrating itself to God, in the poor chapel of Prémontré, by the religious vows of Poverty, Chastity and Obedience. Listen to the words of Norbert as he addresses the brethren prostrated before God's altar. Sweet and consoling are his accents when, after speaking of the strict obligations they are about to take upon themselves, he reminds them of the reward

---

[2] Much has been written about this Rule of St. Augustine which is followed by many religious Orders. Did the Saint really write this Rule? Is it perhaps his famous letter of the year 423 to the Sisters of Hippo? That it was first intended for women seems beyond doubt. Cfr. Poujoulat. "Histoire de Saint Augustin," Paris, 1852, p. 381-382. Also S. Aurel. Augustini opera omnia edidit Migne. T. II, col. 958-965. Epist. CCXI.

[3] *Vita B*, Ch. XII. Velut equila operibus praemonstrabat plerumque mentis excessu raptus . . . Ch. XXVI. In tanto mentis excessu rapti sunt. . . . (*Vita A.*) Cfr. further Camus, L'homme apostolique, p. 130.

"exceedingly great" which awaits them in heaven. One by one they approach and all sign the following document, after having first read it aloud:

> "I, Frater N . offer and give myself to the church of N. . and promise to change my morals, better my life, and remain attached to this church. I also promise Poverty, Chastity and perfect Obedience in Christ, according to the Gospel of Christ and the Rule of St. Augustine, to you, Father . . . and your successors, whom the Convent of this church, according to the form of the Order, will canonically elect or receive."[4]

Dec. 25, 1121, was thus the real birthday of the Premonstratensian Order, and from the bosom of the Church militant, rent by schism and internal strife, sprung a new religious family destined to defend and protect her. "Do not overlook," one of the early writers observes, "the part Almighty God had in the birth of this Order. Heaven determined the very place where the center of the Order was to be, the habit the brethren were to wear, the rule which was to regulate their life."[5]

Here the reader may wish to become acquainted with the real object and the distinctive character of the Premonstratensian Order. Its first and main aim is the formation of canons regular, that is, monastic priests. In his "Tableau des Institutions et les Moeurs de l'Èglise au moyen age," the historian Hurter gives us in a few words the exact idea of the Holy Founder, saying:

> His aim was to unite both the active and the contemplative life; for it was less his intention to found a religious order than to institute canons of a more regular life . . . they were to explain to the ignorant the articles of faith, preach penance, refute heretics,

[4] This formula is used at present. One from the thirteenth century found in the Archives of the abbey of Grimberghen (Belgium) differs slightly as follows: ... Successors canonically elected by the sanest part of the community. Cfr. Madelaine, p. 177.

[5] Cfr. De Hertoghe "Religio canonicorum Ordinis Praemonstratensis, p. 87, et seq.

> and fulfill pastoral duties when imposed on them. ... Still, the cenobitical and conventual life was the foundation of their institution. Norbert flattered himself that his successors would acquire in retreat the force and necessary knowledge to work with greater vigor and success in the Lord's vineyard. Then from time to time they were to come back to the solitude of the monastery, and leave it again armed with new forces.[6]

Norbert's disciples, consequently, were to be neither secular canons nor monks. As a religious order,[7] the Premonstratensian Order has this in common with all other Orders, that it places its members by the profession of the three vows, in a state of perfection. As a canonical order, it adds to the religious state the clerical dignity, and attaches its members to a particular church (*stabilitas in loco*). Almost from the very beginning the Order included the three following classes or branches: 1) Priests or Clerics under an Abbot or Provost. These are, in the strict sense, the canons regular. 2) Sisters who embrace the rule of life as laid down by Norbert; and 3) People living in the world who wear the white scapular underneath their secular dress, and conform themselves to the spirit of the Order. Both clerics and nuns pass through a novitiate of two years before taking the simple perpetual vows; and, three years later, they take the solemn vows. In the monasteries of the priests as well as of the nuns, there were from the very beginning lay-brothers and lay-sisters, who also made perpetual vows. As to the Oblates or Donates, who offer themselves to the Order, they make only temporary vows. We quote here a modern writer on the Premonstratensian Order:

> St. Norbert, by the institution of the canons regular, enkindled in the heart of the Catholic Church a furnace of uninterrupted prayers and an everlasting apostolate. By the institution of

[6] Hurter "Tableau," etc. T. II, p. 468. Paris, 1843. Cfr. also Hugo "La Vie de Saint Norbert," liv., II, p. 99.

[7] "Life of St. Norbert," by Geudens. See Introduction.

> Norbertine Nuns, he opened to weak women a living source of devotedness and self-sacrifice. And lastly, by the institution of the Third Order in the midst of the stream of temporal anxieties, he has introduced the religious life into the circle of the family . . ." etc.[8]

Besides these objects, there is the particular one which at all times has distinguished the Premonstratensian Order from other Canonical Orders, as e. g., the Canons Regular of the Lateran, of St. Rufus, of the Holy Cross, etc., and that is, 1. To spread and increase devotion to the Blessed Sacrament; and 2, a filial devotion to God's Immaculate Mother. These special characteristics of the Norbertine Order are, first of all, vividly illustrated in the life of its holy Founder. St. Norbert is usually represented in engravings, painting and statues, holding in his hand a Monstrance, while the heretic Tanchelm lies prostrate at his feet. The Monstrance is the emblem of his devotion to the Holy Eucharist, and the prostrate heretic points to Norbert's great victory over the Sacramentarian heresy in Antwerp. Norbert moreover constantly inculcated the all important precept of great cleanliness about the altar, especially in the celebration of the divine mysteries; "for, on the altar," said he, "we show our faith, as also our love of God." He, himself, never undertook any important work without first offering up the holy sacrifice of the Mass, and spending hours in prayer, prostrate before the altar. The very first chapter of the Constitution of the Order has for its title "De tremendo altaris Sacramento," and explains how to derive from the Blessed Eucharist true zeal for the salvation of souls.

In regard to devotion to Our Lady, we read in the Preface to the Statutes of the Order: "This was the true spirit of our most holy Father Norbert, and in order that his disciples should be filled with

---

[8] See Ferdinand Duhayon, S. J., in "La mine d'Or" Ch. 5—Tiers Ordre de St. Norbert.—The first member of the Third Order of St. Norbert was Theobald, of whom we shall speak in a later chapter. There we shall also more fully explain the origin and the meaning of this Third Order.

the same spirit, he wished them to honor and venerate in the most devout manner the Blessed Virgin Mary, the most Holy Mother of God, the Patroness and Protectress of the whole Order."

We remember also that whilst Norbert was praying fervently in the chapel of Prémontré on his first visit, the Queen of Angels appeared to him and told him that his prayers had been granted. She it was who indicated the place where the first church of the Order was to be built, and she herself showed him the white habit. The Roman Martyrology commemorates this apparition on the 5th of August, saying: "Eodem die apparitio ejusdem Beatissimae Virginis quae S. P. Norberto canonicum Instituti habitum in capella S. Joannis Baptistae Praemonstrati ostendit."[9]

Furthermore, Norbert himself composed an Office in honor of the Blessed Virgin, from which the following words are taken: "I hail thee, O Virgin, who, preserved by the Holy Ghost, hast triumphed over the formidable sin of our first parents, without being tainted by it." In the "Monita Spiritualia" or Spiritual Counsels, which are said to be extracts from the writings of St. Norbert, we read: "The intention of the Mother of fair love in adorning us with the white habit—a symbol of purity—was no other than to teach us a true devotion to her Immaculate Conception." Never did a Saturday go by without Norbert's offering up the Holy Sacrifice in honor of the Bl. Virgin; to the Queen of Heaven he also dedicated the first foundation at Prémontré.

> Ever silently repeating,
> "Love for Thee, and Thee alone;"
> Ever, 'mid dark shadows, meeting
> Starlight from Our Lady's throne;

[9] On the same day is commemorated the apparition of the Blessed Virgin who, in the chapel of St. John the Baptist at Prémontré, showed our holy Father Norbert the canonical habit of his Institute.

Ever on her Aves dwelling
When the foes grew loud and strong;
Ever from his heart was swelling
Mary's praise in one sweet song.

O St. Norbert, may thy spirit
Live in us till Mary's hand
Lead thy children home—for ever
Sheltered in the changeless land.[10]

It is not surprising, therefore, to find devotion to Our Lady, and especially to her Immaculate Conception, a distinguishing miark of the Order. Far the greatest number of its churches are dedicated to the Mother of God, and the lives of many of its members have been remarkable for their tender devotion to Our Lady.[11] Moreover, ever since the time of its foundation all the religious of the Order have recited daily the Office of the Blessed Virgin in addition to the Canonical Office, and every day one Mass in each abbey, called "De Beata," is offered in her honor. In the early writings, we read that the Premonstratensian Order was sometimes referred to as the Order of Mary.

Although these particular characteristics of the Order of St. Norbert are greatly emphasized in the Constitutions, yet they do not lose sight of the first and most important object, the one great aim of Norbert's whole life, the salvation of souls. In fact, the above-named characteristics are but means to this end. "To reform the

[10] Hymn in honor of St. Norbert, by S. G., taken from "Manual of the Third Order of St. Norbert," p. 76.

[11] Special mention in this regard is merited by Bl. Herman Joseph, the chosen playmate of Our Lord and St. John, who is known the world over as the great servant of the Bl. Virgin. He was a Premonstratensian in the abbey of Steinfeld, in Germany, and died in the thirteenth century. His wonderful life, truly one act of devotion to his heavenly Mother, was written in English by Wilfrid Galway and published in 1878. (Burns & Oates.)

people by reforming the clergy," had been the Saint's watchword from the very day of his conversion. He therefore fully realized how necessary it was to give his young disciples a solid clerical training and to endow them, as future parish priests, with both learning and piety. In this, too, Norbert succeeded so well that he has been often spoken of as the Charles Borromeo of his day, and in later years his abbeys have been called by popes and bishops "seminaries of missionaries and parish priests."

The Premonstratensian Order had from the beginning a great number of parishes cared for by her own priests. Colleges were and are still attached to many of her abbeys, to prepare young men for parochial and missionary work. In the Austrian Province to-day more than seventy Fathers are professors in different colleges; in South America three seminaries are entrusted to the care of the Norbertines. Almost one of the first things the Fathers did on coming into the United States was to build a college in Wisconsin, to prepare worthy priests according to the heart of Norbert. In fact during the eight hundred years of its existence, the Premonstratensian Order has always been engaged in parish work, the teaching of youth and the preaching of missions, the very works to which our Saint devoted himself in the beginning of the twelfth century.

When the Order was still in its infancy, we read, that Norbert and his followers were reproached because, having left the world and retired to a monastery, they again returned to it, took charge of parishes and even became bishops. As we have observed, nearly all the first members of the community of Prémontré became bishops, and we shall yet find Norbert himself as Archbishop of Magdeburg and Chancellor of the German Emperor Lothaire. Moreover, they were all seen to leave the monastery, and to go out preaching. These fault-finders were silenced, however, first, by the edifying and religious conduct of the Fathers while away from the monastery; and, secondly, because their conduct was approved by the most learned and saintly men of those days.[12] Thus writes A. Miraeus:

"With the Norbertines, almost every abbey has some parishes in charge of priests of their own monastery. This is entirely proper for that Order, and is of great benefit to the Church, especially when there is such a dearth of good priests. Therefore are the Norbertine monasteries rightly called seminaries of pastors of souls.[13]

And Anselm of Havelberg, a great admirer of Norbert and for many years closely associated with him, writes: "You hold that Canons Regular ought not to have parishes, and the care of souls among the people ... every one knows that according to the Church, no monk can be called to any dignity or ministry; so also, according to the Church, no Canon Regular can be excluded from either."[14] He further shows how a true religious, even in the midst of the world, can keep the religious spirit, and that he does not necessarily give up religious life when he takes part in the active ministry. Here we find an exact reflection of the mind of Norbert. The union of the contemplative and the active life, was to be the life of his followers. Whenever not actively engaged in the missions, they were, to use the words of the Saint, to come to the monastery "like bees to gather honey," that is, to lay by treasures of spirituality to be spent in the active ministry.

We may add here a few words about the white habit of the Premonstratensians. We have seen that, since the Council of Fritzlar, Norbert had constantly worn a gray woolen habit. This was the habit of penance proper to monks, while canons wore a white linen habit. Since Norbert's aim was to combine the life of the monk and the canon, and since the Bl. Virgin herself had shown him the white habit, he and his disciples wore white woolen habits, wearing their linen habits only around the altar. He thus combined the wool of the monk's habit with the color special to the canons. This

[12] Fath. VandenElsen, o. c.

[13] A. Miraeus Chronicon Praem., p. 2. Also Crusenius, p. 427.

[14] Cfr. Dr. Winter "Die Praemonstratenser ...," Ch. IV. Also Thesaur. Anecd.

innovation, as many were pleased to call it, caused a great deal of disturbance among the monks as well as among the canons, as is clearly shown in different letters of St. Bernard to various monks. There seem even to have been disputes among the early disciples themselves about the shape and color of the habit. In his gentle way the Saint rebuked the latter, saying: "If you have disputes about the color of your habit, or the kind of cloth . . . must therefore the rule of charity be broken?" (*Vita B.* Ch. XXV). He also gave them the reasons, quoted above, for adopting the white woolen habit and showed them how their habit, being the outward sign of their inward vocation, distinguished them as canons of a monastic order.

The Blessed Virgin appears to St. Norbert at Prémontré

CHAPTER IV
THE MONASTERY

Pratum monstratum Septena luce coruscum
Ordinis esse caput coepit ut octo boni.

The meadow shown to Norbert by seven-fold rays of heavenly light becomes the center of the Premonstratensian Order.

AVING described in the last chapter the general object and character of the Premonstratensian Order, we shall now proceed to study the organization, or the means which Norbert employed to attain his object. After his return from Cologne there were about forty brethren, without counting the lay-brothers, in the primitive convent. All were animated with one desire, that of serving God in the most perfect manner; and they had adopted the Rule of St. Augustine as a basis on which to regulate their daily life. The actual regulation was entirely left to the Saint. Norbert was at the head, but not in the ordinary capacity of Superior; he was the very life and soul of the community; his will was law and his authority absolute. Although one of the earliest chroniclers of the Order speaks of Norbert as Abbot, it is quite certain that the Saint firmly refused this title for himself. He is never mentioned as such in the early documents, and the monk Hermann observes that Norbert refused this title even in the monastery of Prémontré.[1]

The great responsibility of forming the early novices rested on

[1] Pertz VI, p. 459—Ao. 1121. Bartholomeus Laudunensis Episcopus et Norbertus Abbas Praemonstratam ecclesiam fundant. . . . Acta SS. T. XX. p. 852: Etiam in Praem. ecclesia Dominus Norbertus Abbas esse noluit.

the shoulders of Norbert alone. As new disciples were constantly arriving at Prémontré, unworthy as well as worthy, the Saint was quite strict with the young religious. All his time he devoted to the study of their character and to the testing of their religious vocation. No records are left to show how many young men the Saint sent back to the world, but the different biographers agree that Norbert was constantly sifting the wheat from the cockle. How well he succeeded in this may be inferred from the fact that the zeal of the brethren became such, that Norbert, austere as he was, found himself obliged to moderate their fervor.

The Saint never tired recommending to the brethren his three favorite counsels:

> Cleanliness about the altar, for on the altar one proves the liveliness of his faith and the fervor of his love; a humble confession of all their faults and negligences, daily made in the chapter-house, for this would render their consciences purer, and make them more watchful over themselves; thirdly, love for the poor and hospitality towards strangers, by which they were to prove their charity towards their neighbor. A house where these three practices are observed, he used to say in conclusion, will never be in want.[2]

And here we may add that Prémontré soon experienced the truth of this prediction. This abbey has ever been the refuge of the poor, and the alms thus given brought God's abundant blessings in return.

Norbert instructed his disciples daily, both in the morning and in the evening, initiating them in the secrets of mystic theology and Christian perfection. A few of his ascetic maxims have come down to us, and are, in a way, a reflection of his own noble soul. Thus he often spoke of the dignity of the Priesthood in the words quoted above. He repeatedly told the story of his life and miraculous

---

[2] *Vita B.* Ch. XXV.

conversion, saying:

> At Court I was never satisfied; in the monastery I have never been dissatisfied. I was frequently at the courts of princes, I possessed abundant wealth, I did not deny myself the pleasures of the world; nevertheless, believe me, dearest brethren, an abundance of worldly goods is real poverty. Never was it better for me than when I was without them, because entire freedom from these worldly possessions gave me the fullness of heavenly goods which are more pleasant for their sweetness, more lasting for their constancy, better constituted for the satisfaction they give to the heart of man.

Under Norbert's direction all proceeded daily with great order, and soon a monastic regularity was observed by these inexperienced religious. The Saint now considered the time to have come, when one of the brethren might share with him the great responsibility of preparing worthy ministers of God. He chose his first disciple Hugh for this work, and gave over to him the entire interior government of the monastery. It was Hugh's duty to see that all rules were daily observed, and also to look after the material welfare of the religious. As their number constantly increased, the duties and responsibilities of Hugh became so great that after a short time Norbert gave him assistants. Although no record is kept of their names, we know some of these had charge of the clerics, while others looked after the welfare of the lay-brothers.[3] In Norbert's absence Hugh had absolute authority, and thus his office was that of a present-day Prior. Although Norbert refused the title of Abbot, de facto he certainly was the Abbot of Prémontré; the present government of the Premonstratensian abbeys is based on this same old plan of organization. The Fathers elect their Abbot, who, in his turn appoints a Prior and the Prior's assistants—Subprior, Novicemaster, Circator.

As to the daily life of the early religious, none was more occupied than theirs. The Constitution has from the earliest times

[3] Madelaine, o. c., p. 187.

prescribed how to perform the important duty of singing the Divine Office: "Since by our religious profession we are consecrated to sing night and day God's praises, and since by virtue of holy obedience we have been charged by the Church to sing the Divine Office with devotion, attention and reverence, all must take the greatest care to prepare themselves, in order to sing it with the necessary reverence and devotion." (Stat., Ch. IV.) At midnight, then, the monastic bell called all the religious to the chapel to sing Matins; the rest of the Office was sung at stated hours during the day. The intervening time was spent in study and manual labor. Norbert failed not to impress on the minds of his disciples the necessity of the constant and diligent study of Sacred Letters and the Scriptures. The young religious were all destined to go out to preach the Gospel—to teach the people their religion—to argue with heretics and unbelievers; therefore only a most diligent study could fit them for the apostolic duties of their sublime vocation. "The study of Theology is so indispensable for a Premonstratensian religious, that he who ignores it is a bastard and ought to be ejected as an illegitimate son of St. Norbert."[4] A book was written in the eighteenth century by a German Premonstratensian[5] in which the great learning of Norbert and of eight of the ten first disciples is proved historically. This author further shows that the love for study, inspired by Norbert, has always signalized the Order. To this subject we hope to return in the second volume.

It is beyond doubt that the first clerics were also obliged by the Saint to perform some daily manual labor. According to some historians it must have been Norbert's first idea to provide by manual labor for the material necessities of the brethren. In fact a Charter of the Bishop of Laon, of the year 1125, leaves hardly any room for doubt on this point. Therein we read:

---

[4] Abad Illana. Vida de San Norberto. Lib. I. Ch. IV, pp. 57-62.

[5] Spiritus Literarius Norbertinus. Augustae Vindelicorum, 1771.

> It is part of the virtue of religion to love the holy life of religious men, and with a pious devotedness to assist them in their material necessities. It behooves one to praise and venerate in others, that which, on account of human frailty, he himself is not able to imitate. Thus in our days a new Order, deep hidden in the woods of Voas at Prémontré, has been founded in our diocese with our consent and the help of pious people, by the zeal of brother Norbert, a most illustrious man, and as far as one is able to judge, with the approbation of God. Serving the Lord according to the Rule of St. Augustine and wearing the habit of clerics, the brethren proposed to lead an eremitical life for the sake of providing themselves with life's necessities. We, however, anxious to recommend our weakness to their sanctity, and desirous of being sustained during the storms of the present life, and after death, by the help of their prayers, have added to all that we have previously given them, our new mill of Barantel, lately built at our expense, for the use of the brethren of this convent.[6]

Yet we read that even after this Norbert prescribed for the brethren some hours for manual labor. Although their material welfare seemed to be provided for, the Saint insisted on this, no doubt, as part of the monastic discipline, since the Order was both Canonical and Monastic. It was especially in harvest-time that one saw the brethren leave the monastery, and in strict silence begin their work in the fields. They then even took their noon-meal there, sang Vespers and returned only at night. The sick and the Officials alone were dispensed from manual labor. Charles Louis Hugo, the historian of the Order, says: "As the penance, which Norbert had embraced after his conversion, was greater than the mild rule of Canons exacted, so he added to his Order the austerities of monasticism that his Order might not be wanting in that which was found in Canonical and Monastic Orders."

Mindful of the words of St. Augustine's Rule "Subdue your flesh

[6] Dr. Winter. Die Praemonstratenser. . . . Ch. IV. Also Pez. Thesaurus Anadectorum. IV.

by fasting and abstinence from food and drink as much as your health permits," Norbert prescribed for his Order a continual abstinence from flesh meat and an almost continual Lenten fast. His first regulations, however, were so strict that Norbert himself mitigated them later. Thus we read in the oldest Statutes, composed by Blessed Hugh and approved by Norbert, that from Easter until the feast of the Exaltation of the Cross, the brethren were allowed to take two meals a day. Entire abstinence from fleshmeat was kept for a much longer time, but gradually certain relaxations in regard to this were granted. Thus at present the Fathers abstain from fleshmeat during the whole of Lent and Advent, from the feast of St. Luke to the feast of All Saints, on the vigils of certain feasts, and on all Wednesdays and Saturdays of the year. Fasting is still observed during Lent and Advent, on all Fridays and the Vigils of the feasts of Our Lord and Our Lady.[7]

The rule of silence was rigorously observed almost continually, not only in the monastery but even on journeys. These the religious were obliged to make on foot, except when the distance was more than four miles. However, we must not forget that Norbert himself was their constant exemplar, for while trying to make his disciples true religious, he was always the first to lead the way in everything. We read that he was in the habit of choosing for himself the poorest clothing in the house, and when away from the monastery never looked after his own welfare, but was very solicitous for others.

Thus the first Norbertines learned to observe the Evangelical Counsels and to follow Christ, and to them Prémontré was a Paradise on earth. Well may we apply to them the beautiful description of monastic life in those days, written by Guibert of Gemblours. After spending eight months at Marmoutiers, he writes: "Hatred, jealousy and ill-feeling are unknown in these peaceful dwellings; they are forever banished by the law of silence, observed with exactness and guarded with a fatherly prudence. A glance from

[7] The above description about fasting, abstinence, silence, etc., is based on Chapter XXX of the *Vita B.*

the Abbot suffices to recall the rule and insure its observance. . . . Where shall we find deeper recollection at the Divine Office, greater piety in the celebration of the Holy Mysteries? ... Every countenance beams with modesty, mildness, and the inward peace of a good conscience; all breathes the true peace of Jesus Christ. ... Every thought of the world has been left at the gate of the monastery; no one boasts of his lineage ... the only soldiery acknowledged here, is that devoted to the service of Jesus Christ. Labor, fast, and watching, tame the passions and bring the body into subjection. ... The Divine Presence controls the whole course of their life and animates their every action. Strict necessity alone measures the rest granted to nature; all the remaining hours are given to God. During meals the religious receive also spiritual food from pious reading, and they are more desirous of this heavenly nourishment than of that of the body. A great number of them are daily occupied in transcribing manuscripts.[8] These are the treasures from which they draw stores of learning and virtue. I have heard those pious solitaries mutually urge one another on in the path of virtue, consoling one another by thoughts of their journey heavenward. Holy walls! Saintly citizens! With what grief shall I quit you! ..."[9]

As we noticed above, Norbert's foundation was not for clerics only, but in imitation of monastic establishments, it had also a large number of lay-brothers. These occupied special quarters in the monastery, and their habit differed slightly from that of the clerics. They rose at the same hour as did the clerics, and during the singing of the Divine Office, they recited a prescribed number of "Paters" and "Aves." They were also required to assist at the Conventual Mass. The daily work of some was the work of servants in the house, others labored in the field or exercised their trade. Thus there were tailors, bakers, etc., among them. Their penitential

---

[8] Madelaine (193) speaks of the scriptorium of Prémontré, a room reserved for copyists.

[9] This description is taken from Darras "General History," III, 433.

exercises were the same as those of the other religious, and many prominent men were found among them.[10]

In order to have a complete idea of this first foundation of St. Norbert at Prémontré, we now leave the monastery of the Fathers to see the convent of the first Norbertine Sisters. Norbert, mindful of the poor of Christ, had, from his arrival at Prémontré, thought of a means to provide for sick and poor people. When the religious were building their huts around the chapel, he made them erect also a structure called a "Xenodochium," which served both as an infirmary and an almonry. In those days no religious house was complete without a place where the poor could come every day and receive alms in the name of Christ. The charge of this place Norbert entrusted to Blessed Ricvere, widow of Raymond de Clastres. She had given her possessions to Norbert, and now lived in a little hut near by. Following the example of both Martha and Mary, this valiant woman was constantly occupied with the sick and the poor; nevertheless she always found time for prayer and meditation.[11] Performing her daily duties in the spirit of recollection and prayer, according to the instructions she received from the Saint, she was constantly united with God, and advanced rapidly on the road to perfection. A legend informs us, that when one day her poorhouse had taken fire, she extinguished the flames by a single sign of the cross. Being of noble birth, her humble occupation and saintly life were the more edifying, and before long other noble ladies followed her; thus originated the Second Order of St. Norbert.

Among those that joined the Order at this time we find: Ermengardis, Countess of Roussi; Agnes, Countess of Braine; Fredisindis, Foundress of Mount St. Martin; Gude, Countess of Bonneburg; Beatrix, Viscountess of Amiens; Anastasia, Duchess of Pomerania; Hadwigis, Countess of Cleves, and Gertrude, her

---

[10] These lay-brothers are called "Conversi"—the fratres "Donati" take only temporary vows.

[11] Acta SS. T. CXI. 13 Oct. De B. Rycwera, moniali Praemonstratensi. Also die 29 Oct.

daughter; Adèle, of Montmorency, daughter of Bouchard, High Constable of France, and a number of others of equal nobility and virtue.[12] Many daughters of the best families of France and Germany seemed anxious to leave the luxuries of their own palaces to join the new Order. The first abbey thus became a double monastery.

The rules which Norbert prescribed for these Sisters seemed beyond the strength of their sex; however, they were far below the height of their courage. It must be observed that this Second Order developed in its infancy into a strictly Contemplative Order. The Nuns might never leave the cloister, and they cut themselves off entirely from all commerce with the world. They were not permitted to speak, even to their nearest relatives, except through a grating, and then always in the presence of two other religious. They never ate meat and kept an almost unbroken Lenten fast the whole year round. At midnight they rose to sing the Divine Office, which practice is kept up by them to this day. In their early foundation they were required by Norbert to sew and spin when they were not occupied in the recitation of the Office. They were called Canonesses, and their habit is still like that of the Canons, except for the black veil. Though their rule of life was most severe, it seems to have been very attractive in those days, for such was their numerical growth, that in less than fifteen years there were over ten thousand Norbertine Nuns in the various countries of Europe.[13]

Besides the Choir-sisters, as the Canonesses were also called, there were lay-sisters, whose duties and position in the convent corresponded with those of the lay-brothers in the monastery. Further there were the Oblates, Sorores Donatæ, as they are still called. These were free to communicate with the outside world, and their vows were only temporary. As to their government, from the beginning the Sisters have had practically the same as the Canons.

---

[12] Hugo. La Vie de Saint Norbert. Liv. II, p. 112.

[13] Acta SS. T. XX. p. 853 . . . plus quam decem milia feminarum. . . .

The Superior is called "Abbess;" she has absolute authority in the community.

Like the abbot, she also bears the Crozier as the symbol of her office and rank. She is assisted by a Prioress, a Subprioress and other officers.

Bl. Ricvere, the eldest spiritual daughter of the Saint, who next to him might be considered the Foundress of the Norbertine Canonesses, died in the odor of sanctity in the year 1136. Although a Countess, she was buried according to her own wish in the cemetery of the poor, in order to proclaim to the world, even after her death, her great love for poverty. There is a pious tradition that wonderful occurrences have taken place on her grave, and that for years beautiful roses bloomed miraculously over her tomb at Prémontré.[14]

[14] Acta SS. T. XIII, Oct., p. 53.

❧

CHAPTER V
THE CHURCH AT PRÉMONTRÉ

Quum Nivigellae Satanam de corde puellae
Propulsas, album te vocat canem.
Tartareum dum nempe lupum mordesque fugasque
Ipse fuga Domini Te probat esse canem.

When at Nivelles St. Norbert drove out the evil spirit from a young girl, Satan called him a white dog. His continued chasing of Satan proves Norbert in reality the dog of the Lord.

ITH the marvelous growth and development of the spiritual edifice at Prémontré, the necessity of material expansion had become more and more urgent. There were still the poor little huts, made of wood and clay, and arranged camp-like around the chapel. These thus far had served as temporary quarters, and had given to the brethren shelter and protection against the chilly fall weather. However, as is evident, this could be only a provisionary arrangement, and the building of a spacious house had now become imperative. Further, there was the small chapel of St. John the Baptist, where we found our Saint in ecstasy on his first visit to Prémontré, and which at this time proved entirely inadequate for the community. For lack of space the canons were even unable to observe the proper ceremonial of the Church in the chanting of the Office. In a word, the young community had entirely outgrown its primitive monastery, and lack of accommodation must interfere with the regularity of religious life. Now it was with the intention of soon building a church, that Norbert had undertaken a journey to Cologne the year before, to procure the relics of saints, in order that by their intercession the brethren might be enabled to erect a church worthy of the name. It is not recorded in what manner these saints came to Norbert's assistance; however, in the beginning of the year 1122 the brethren decided to erect both a church and a monastery.

Humanly speaking, every one will admit that the marshy valley of Prémontré was by no means a favorable location for the establishment of the center of an institution such as Norbert had planned. Neither can we be surprised that some of the brethren, reasoning from a natural standpoint, expressed their disapprobation of the plan, saying that the valley was neither a place for a church nor a monastery. The Saint, however, rebuked them, and told them of his determination to build both a church and a monastery on the place pointed out to him in his vision.[1] Why should they rely on human wisdom when God Himself had pointed out the place ?

As was his wont, Norbert took refuge in prayer, and was soon more than ever convinced of help from on high. He asked the brethren likewise to pray, urging that faith and confidence in God know of no obstacles, but often accomplish things which, humanly speaking, seem utterly impossible.

> It is an incontestable fact, dearest brethren, he said, that Jesus our Master did not come into this world to lead a life of ease, but to suffer and die on the wood of the Cross. He knew full well that Jerusalem was preparing for Him a gibbet; nevertheless, He looked upon the city with compassion, and when His hour had come, He did not take one step to avoid the place. Thus, brethren, must one live in religion; the true religious lives only for Christ. He who would attain this sublime ideal, must first of all put aside all worldly conveniences; the world must be dead for him. Has not St. Paul, our model, said: "I live, now not I, but Christ liveth in me?" If we pretend to be truly poor, we should not preoccupy ourselves with our way of living; to desire presents and to look

[1] *Vita B*, Ch. XXVII.

> for the comforts of life, is degenerating for true disciples of Jesus Christ. Assuredly anxiety for this earthly home should not disturb the life of those who have come to the monastery to die to the world. Only those are truly living who live, not for themselves, but in whom lives the poor Christ. (*Vita B*, l. c.)

Thus far two revelations had indicated the place where the new church was to be erected. Now whilst Norbert and the brethren were earnestly engaged in prayer, God's will was made manifest to them a third time, and the exact location pointed out. This happened in the following manner: in the center of the valley, the very spot where the church was eventually built, there appeared to Bl. Hugh, Our Lord full of glory, hanging upon the Cross. "Thabor and Golgotha at the same time!" as one of the biographers remarks. Seven sunbeams of marvelous brightness shone upon our Crucified Redeemer. There was a multitude of white-robed pilgrims, holding staffs in their hands, and wallets strung across their shoulders, coming from the four quarters of the earth, and they paid homage to the Cross on their knees, kissed the feet of their Savior, and then went back to spread the glory of His Holy Name over the whole world. (*Vita B*, l. c.)

Norbert, to whom Hugh had related this vision, understood at once that the church had to be built on the exact spot where the Cross had appeared. Though the Saint himself had not the honor of the vision, heaven revealed to him its import. Full of gratitude, he first humbly knelt before God's altar, and poured forth his heart in an ecstasy of joy. He then went to the brethren and, in the fullness of his prophetic spirit, explained to them the future events foreshadowed by this miraculous Cross.

> Courage, brethren, he said, prepare yourself for battle and have courage! Visible and invisible enemies will try your virtue, and seek to disturb the calm of our dear solitude. The Cross is the symbol which at once announces war and foretells victory. New soldiers will join, and persevere unto the end in the warfare which you have undertaken. (*Vita B*, Ch. XXVII.)

The brethren were deeply moved by this visible intervention from on high, and at once work on the new church was begun. The shadow of the Cross seen by Hugh in the vision, formed the outline of the walls. A capable builder from France was put at the head of Norbert's little army of volunteers, and when these were joined by a number of workmen from Cologne, the excavations were soon well under way. But alas! the soil was so wet and marshy that soon even the most experienced workmen despaired of ever being able to build a solid foundation. But Norbert's faith and confidence in God could not he shaken. Prospects looked very discouraging to every one except Norbert. He told the brethren to go out and gather all the stones they could find in the neighboring country, and cast them into the ditches as the men were making them.[2] Meanwhile, he was so convinced of his ultimate success, that he even went ahead and fixed the day for the solemn blessing and laying of the cornerstone, and invited for this occasion Bartholomew, Bishop of Laon. The day soon arrived, and what at first seemed to all impossible, had now been accomplished, and everything was in readiness for the ceremony.

How great a day this must have been for Norbert! When the good bishop arrived, thus we read in the Acta Sanctorum,[3] a whole army of religious went out to meet His Lordship. Clothed as they all were in the white habit, and chanting joyful hymns, the Prelate was vividly reminded of Norbert's first vision in this same place two years before, and appeared very much affected. His Lordship was accompanied by Lisiard, Bishop of Soissons and by several very prominent persons. There was also present on this occasion Thomas de Marle, Lord of Coucy, very unfavorably known for his wild life.

---

[2] Vita B, Ch. XXVIII. Pars coementariorum Teutonici ... pars nostrates, amici jam Praemonstratensium ... tanta namque ibi palus erat quod vix sorberi poterat, cum etiam multa lapidum congeries projiceretur.

[3] Acta SS. XX. "Analecta Norbertina," p. 854. Venienti Episcopo totus ille Dei exercitus. ... Quod Norbertus in visu viderat, hoc idem Episcopus revera corporaliter nunc fieri cernebat.

A man, says Guibert of Nogent, who had absolutely no regard for human life, but treated his men like cattle, and killed them like wild animals. He was present because, strange to say, he stood in great awe of Norbert, whom he feared, knowing him to be a man of God. He had come with his young son Enguerrand, who is to become one of the greatest benefactors of Prémontré, and whose body will one day be buried in the church of the monastery.[4] According to some, St. Bernard was also present on this occasion, but this seems doubtful. It is certain, however, that there was a great number of people and clergy.

Many were of the opinion that Norbert would never be able to carry out his plans in the marshy valley at Prémontré, and a certain feeling of compassion for Norbert had no doubt increased the number of those present. We read (*Vita B*, Ch. XXVIII) that some treated the whole enterprise as something most unpracticable, shook their heads and tried to prevail on Norbert still to change his location. Others, however, who knew him to be a Saint who was doing this work under divine inspiration praised his work highly. It is even related that after the ceremony of the blessing was finished, a woman present became so enthusiastic, that she applied to Norbert these words of the Gospel: "Blessed is the womb that bore thee." On hearing it, the Saint became really indignant and exclaimed: "Cursed be the evil one who inspired thee with this thought, to give me the honor which is due to God."

As soon as the solemnities were over, the workmen resumed their task with renewed ardor. Norbert was more than ever strengthened in his confidence in God; and, leaving the supervision of the work to his disciple, Hugh, without the least anxiety as to the future, he resumed again his missionary labor. He first went to Floreffe where, as we have observed, a new foundation had been made on his return journey from Cologne. We can imagine how great his solicitude must have been for this second foundation under

[4] De Florival. Barthélemy de Vir. Ch. IV, p. 65, et seq.

the direction of Richard, since he felt that his presence was necessary at least for some time, in order to perfect the work he had begun. No mention is made as to whether or not Norbert assisted at the solemn inauguration of the new monastery, which, according to the Annals of Floreffe, took place on the 25th of January, 1122. There certainly is every reason to suppose that he did. But of this we are assured, that Norbert by his example at Floreffe grafted the true spirit upon this new foundation, and that this abbey was as dear to him as Prémontré.

During his stay at the abbey, a singular event occurred which is chronicled by different biographers. While offering up the Holy Sacrifice with his usual piety and deep faith, Norbert remarked upon his paten, just before the Communion of the Mass, a large drop of the Precious Blood, all red and surrounded by rays of light which came from the Sacred Host. Turning towards Ludolph, his deacon, he said: "Brother, do you see what I see?" The deacon replied: "I do, Father!" whereupon Norbert, shedding abundant tears, continued his Mass.[5] The altarstone on which the Saint celebrated this Holy Sacrifice has been kept ever since in the main altar of the abbey church at Floreffe.

A brilliant and great future awaited the monastery of Floreffe, so happily inaugurated. The Bishop of Liège, Albéron, favored it in every way, and approved and confirmed the foundation by a solemn charter, dated May 20th, 1124. He exempted the abbey from all diocesan rights, asked from the brethren a filial submission, and gave to the abbot the right to appoint the pastor for Floreffe.[6] When the saintly Abbot Richard died in the year 1131 (Dec. 30th), the abbey was firmly established, and continued its good work until the days of the French Revolution.

Having seen the monastery placed on a solid foundation,

---

[5] Acta SS. XX, p. 846 "Videsne," inquit, "Frater, quod ego video?" "Video," ait, "Domine." Coepitque pro tantae rei magnitudine uberius flere.

[6] Cfr. Hugo. "La vie de saint Norbert," p. 149. Also Barbier "Histoire de l'Abbaye de Floreffe," p. 39.

Norbert resumed his preaching, going to Namur, Huy, Liège, Tongres, and probably as far as Louvain, for thus we read in the Annals of the Abbey of Parc, near Louvain: "In 1122 Norbert began to preach in Brabant" (p. 598). Although no details have come down to us describing this missionary tour in particular, we have reason to believe that his journey was one series of triumphs over sin and Satan.

In the beginning of May the Saint arrived at Maestricht, in the South of Holland. The people were just celebrating the patronal feast of their city, the feast of St. Servace. This Saint had been a bishop of Tongres in the fourth century. Acting upon a warning from heaven, he had moved his episcopal throne to Maestricht, where ever since his death, the people honored his memory every year with great solemnity, and invoked him as their special protector. Here also his sacred remains rested in the cathedral church.

Norbert at once expressed his great desire to venerate the relics of St. Servace, which were kept in a silk veil. According to popular tradition this veil had been brought down from heaven by angels at the time of the holy bishop's death, to envelop his sacred remains. In the presence of Norbert and at his urgent request, the reliquary was opened with the greatest respect. No sooner had this been done than the veil was by some invisible power lifted up in the air, and after moving about in the basilica remained suspended from the ceiling. The people were struck with awe and admiration, but some began lamenting the loss of the veil, and a general commotion ensued. Meanwhile Norbert, who in silence had been admiring the prodigy, now inspired from above, prepared himself for the celebration of the Holy Sacrifice. And behold! when at the beginning of the Canon he stretched out his arms in the form of a cross, as is prescribed by the rubrics, the veil miraculously returned, resting on the arms of Norbert, who then replaced it with great reverence in the reliquary.[7]

Whatever heaven's design was in this most wonderful event, it is certain that all the people were filled with the greatest admiration and reverence for Norbert, and that his missionary labors became thereby all the more effective. It is impossible to estimate all the good he accomplished at this time at Maestricht. A great number of sinners were brought to repentance, peace was restored between enemies, and the more virtuous were reanimated in the practice of their religion. Leaving Maestricht the Saint crossed the Rhine and, going into Westphalia, went from town to town preaching the gospel of penance. At his prayer the sick were healed, and they who were possessed were delivered from the evil one. Many of these events were recorded, but the records were mostly destroyed in the fire of Magdeburg, of which we shall speak in a later chapter. That Norbert did perform a great many miracles we know positively, both from contemporary writers who befriended the Saint, and also from his enemies who made them a subject of reproach to him, as for instance, Abelard.

> "As all great and saintly enterprises are exposed to the most violent attacks, it ought not to surprise us that religious Orders, especially in their infancy, are a constant target for the fury of Satan, for he naturally does all in his power to prevent the raising of establishments which he knows to be fatal to his empire. Thus the Patriarch of the Monks of the West had no sooner formed his great project of founding that grand Order, which throughout the course of its history has done so much for the good of religion, than Satan came to declare war and to frustrate his plans. Many times did he frighten the masons and even break down the walls they had built. . . ."[8]

Thus also at Prémontré, especially during the absence of Norbert, Satan never ceased in his endeavors to disturb the young

---

[7] *Vita B.* Appendix Can. Cappenb., Ch. VIII, where a detailed description is given of this occurrence. Cfr. also Acta S.S. T. XV, pp. 208-230.

[8] Hugo "La Vie de saint Norbert" preface.

community. Their holy lives aroused his anger, and the progress of their new building seemed to make him desperate. Sometimes he appeared with a number of his satellites to attack Prémontré as a band of armed soldiers attacks a stronghold. The religious as well as the other workmen felt plainly on these occasions the presence of some invisible enemy preventing them from working until they sprinkled holy water all over the place. On one occasion especially, all were greatly disturbed and felt obliged to call the Prior. Blessed Hugh came and banished the evil one by the sign of the Cross. At other times Hugh commanded Satan in the name of Norbert to depart, and the evil one obeyed. It happened on one occasion when Bl. Hugh was exorcising one of the laybrothers, that the devil confessed openly that he was that same spirit whom Norbert—"that white dog whose birth should be cursed forever"—had expelled from the girl at Nivelles. He left his present victim under loud protestations, showing incidentally Norbert's great power over evil spirits. (*Vita B*, Ch. XXIX-XXX.)

However, in spite of all the annoyances of Satan the building at Prémontré progressed marvelously, and in less than nine months a truly magnificent church had been erected. Even before it was entirely completed, the foundations had also been laid for a spacious house, as the early historian says, "large enough to accommodate two hundred brethren." When both were finished, there were assembled once more clergy and laity for the solemn dedication.

In November of the same year we again see the good Bishop of Laon, Bartholomew, Bishop Lisiard of Soissons, and a large number of clergy and laity, preceded by white-robed canons, move in stately procession through the marshy valley of Prémontré towards the new church. The precious relics which Norbert had brought over from Cologne the year before, were placed in costly reliquaries and exposed for veneration; the church, beautifully decorated for this impressive occasion, could hardly contain the great number, who came for the solemn ceremony. A truly great day for Norbert, whose faith and unshaken confidence in God were thus rewarded, and a day of triumph for the brethren who at last saw their holy desires realized! But alas! a singular event changed their joy into real sadness. The consecration of the new altar had hardly taken place when all of a sudden the altar gave way, owing to the great pressure of the crowd, and leaned over to one side; with a crash the newly consecrated stone broke in two, invalidating the consecration.[9]

For a moment even the Saint himself was greatly disturbed, but at once checking this impulse of nature, he remained unshaken in his confidence in God. In his prophetic spirit he then saw in this sad occurrence a foretoken of the future history of his Order, which though once almost annihilated, would again rise to a new life; of this he spoke to his disciples. We may add that later events have proved the truth of this prophecy. At the time of the French Revolution the Order became almost extinct not only in France but also in other parts of Europe, but since that crisis it has been steadily rising to a new life. In the year 1805 Pope Pius VII, while at Paris, said these remarkable words to the Abbot-General of the Order: "God will, no doubt, bring back to life an Order which has rendered such excellent services to the Church.[10]

At last the church and the monastery at Prémontré were completed; and, when to-day we read the historical description of these buildings, we ask ourselves how was it possible for those men to erect such beautiful buildings in the short time of nine months, and that under the most trying conditions. The monk Hermannus wrote, in regard to the foundation of Prémontré: "All travelers come to see the church and the monastery at Prémontré, and also the great wall built around the whole by Blessed Hugh. I do not believe that one can find anything similar even in the wealthiest and most

---

[9] *Vita B*, Ch. XXVIII. Sub tempore novem mensium . . . cum multitudo innumera . . . currerent, motum est altare majus, et lapis dissolutus, consecratioque cassata est ... ! In the same chapter, however it is also related, that the consecration was done over privately one week later, on the feast of St. Martin.

[10] Cfr. G. VandenElsen "Het Leven van den H. Norbertus " p. 94.

ancient monasteries of France. Every visitor is forced to exclaim that this is not the work of man but of God."[11]

After the church and the monastery were built at both Prémontré and Floreffe, and the daily routine of monastic life was resumed with new vigor, Norbert did not rest; but, to make new foundations, and thus work a reform of all canons, now became his ambition. The marvelous growth of the new Order from now until the Saint's death is nothing short of miraculous. New foundations sprang up as if from the ground, and wherever Norbert found a lax community of religious, he always tried to induce them to affiliate with one of his abbeys. This he effected in the following manner: Two or more of these religious came to a Premonstratensian abbey, studied for a while the customs and manner of living of the Fathers, and then were sent back by Norbert to their own house to introduce the same discipline. Thus Norbert was rapidly attaining his object, "Reform," for even at this time his numerous disciples were bringing about a notable change in existing conditions. In the first five years new foundations were made by Norbert in Floreffe, Viviers, St. Josse, Ardenne, Cuissy, Laon, Liège, Antwerp, Varlar, Cappenberg, and thirty years after the founding of Prémontré, over one hundred abbots were present at the General Chapter of the Order.[12]

---

[11] Cfr. Pertz. Script. XII.

[12] Cfr. VandenElsen, o. c., p. 96.

ST. NORBERT WITH GODFREY OF CAPPENBERG

CHAPTER VI
GODFREY OF CAPPENBERG

Godefridus Comes hic, comitis cum conjuge,
Frater Nomina Militiae dant pretiosa novae.

Godfrey, Count of Cappenberg, with his wife and brother, enter the Order of St. Norbert.

E here deviate from the chronological order of events, to devote some time to the Counts of Cappenberg on account of their great liberality towards the young Order. It might be well to recall, that we are writing of the ages of faith, when eminent virtue was admired and honored, even as in our times, great learning and affluence are. Norbert's austerity, his manifest power over Satan, his powerful preaching—all these had aroused the admiration of the people and inflamed their hearts with a holy enthusiasm. His advent was hailed like that of a great conqueror. Thus we read in the life of Bl. Godfrey, written by a contemporary: "In those days there appeared in Westphalia that brilliant light of the Church, Norbert, the famous preacher. He was a man graceful in appearance, eloquent in speech. He reformed the clergy and propagated the Order of Canons Regular by founding numerous monasteries . . .!"[1]

Large crowds ever followed him and the number that offered to become his disciples, sometimes surpasses the belief of even the most credulous. Among the many nobles who at this time were

[1] Acta SS. T. II. *Vita B.* Godefridi, Ch. II, p. 129: Apparuit . . . exium quoddam jubar ecclesiae, memorabilis ille Dei praeco Norbertus. . . .

deeply influenced by the Saints preaching and manner of living, was a young Count, by the name of Godfrey. Although quite young, (he was born in the year 1097, and thus was only in his 26th year) he was considered one of the most powerful princes of Westphalia, and when in the army of Henry V, had distinguished himself on several occasions. He lived in the splendid castle of Cappenberg, in the diocese of Munster. Situated on a high mountain, the castle was famed for its picturesque surroundings, and was also considered an impenetrable stronghold.

Godfrey was a descendant of a very illustrious family. He had married a daughter of the noble and wealthy house of Arensberg. Her name was Jutta. Since the death of his father, Godfrey as eldest son, governed the large estates of Cappenberg and was greatly beloved by his subjects. Different historians disagree as to the time and place where Count Godfrey first became acquainted with our Saint. Some say they had first met while Norbert was at the Court of the Emperor. Others assign Xanten as their first meeting place, since Godfrey owned large estates near the birthplace of our Saint. Tenkoff observes that Godfrey had heard Norbert's sermons while the latter was at Cologne procuring relics.[2] At any rate it appears certain that the Count knew Norbert, for before the Saint arrived, Godfrey had made all necessary preparations to become his disciple.

Since their meeting, at whatever place it was, Godfrey had felt himself strongly drawn towards Norbert, and had even mentioned to others his intention of dedicating himself entirely to God.[3] Divine Providence then led him to the Saint at this time, and thus in the same year that foundations were made in Floreffe (Belgium), and the church and the monastery built in Prémontré (France), in that very same year Norbert was also enabled through the liberality of this Count to make a new foundation on German soil. To do justice

---

[2] Cfr. Madelaine, o. c., 231. Also Tenkoff, p. 7.

[3] Acta SS. *Vita B.* Godefridi, l. c.

to the noble character of the Count, we must not overlook the numerous obstacles he had to overcome before offering himself and all he had to Almighty God.

There was first and foremost his young and beautiful wife, truly devoted to him, and not at all inclined to be separated from a noble and loving husband. To leave her without her consent would be to break his solemn oath taken before God's altar—"till death doth us part." With God's help, however, he succeeded in winning her over to his views, and she also decided to leave the world and give herself to God. One day she will be abbess of the convent of Herfort, where Godfrey's sister Beatrix, also is to take the veil. Still greater difficulty had he in persuading his brother, Otto, who at first refused outright to credit his sincerity. Here again, by the grace of God, he succeeded in obtaining a consent. But we can readily understand that the consent of neither Jutta nor Otto was obtained in a day, but only after a long and painful struggle, and not without help from above; for we must not forget that we are here dealing with great and wealthy nobles. To sacrifice everything and become beggars for the sake of Christ, however great and heroic from a supernatural standpoint, is something from which human nature at all times recoils.

Meanwhile Norbert had come into Westphalia, where, without his knowledge, all these preparations had been made. This was in the month of May, 1122. As soon as Godfrey heard of his arrival he at once hastened to him, and to Norbert's great surprise he offered him the castle of Cappenberg with all its dependencies, its gardens and pastures, its woods and mills. The castle itself was to be turned at once into a monastery for the Saint's disciples. Norbert accepted his generous offer. When, on the 31st of May, the transfer had been made with due solemnity, and Godfrey had given up all he had, he then offered himself, and begged of the Saint to receive him as one of his disciples. To this also Norbert consented, but refused to clothe him as yet with the religious habit, for he foresaw the numerous difficulties which would arise from the Count's generosity.[4]

Meanwhile the necessary alterations were being made in the castle to fit the place for the life of religious, and on the 15th day of August the Bishop of Münster, Thierry de Winzenburch, came to solemnly dedicate the new monastery and provisionary chapel.[5] Norbert installed some of the brethren of Prémontré, and this foundation of Cappenberg made such rapid progress, that in a few years it became the splendor of the Order, ranking as high as Prémontré itself. Norbert himself, as long as he lived, bore the title of Provost of the House of Cappenberg, although during his lifetime, first Cuno, and later Otto, were its actual superiors. But all official documents of that time are addressed to Norbert, Provost of Cappenberg, and the list of Provosts is headed by the name of Norbert. His love for this house was exceedingly great and he often spoke of Cappenberg as the "Holy Mountain."

While a new church was being built, plans were made by the advice of Norbert, for the erection of a "Xenodochium," *i. e.*, a great hospital for the sick of the neighborhood and for travelers, and at the same time an almshouse where large numbers were to be daily fed. "It was Norbert's constant desire," observes Madelaine, "to have the roof of charity in the shadow of the house of prayer."

As soon as these buildings were completed, Jutta expressed her desire of taking the veil in religion, and forthwith a large convent was built at the foot of the mountain for Norbertine Sisters. It was known by the name of "Nieder-Clooster," and was later transferred to Wesel.[6]

Godfrey's brother Otto, greatly influenced, no doubt, by the noble example of his brother and sister, also determined to become a religious, and in his turn offered to Norbert his immense

---

[4] Cfr. Madelaine, o. c., p. 233.

[5] Acta SS. T. II, p. 122-123. Also G. Vanden Elsen, o. c., p. 106, where he observes that on this same day the cornerstone was laid for a new church.

[6] Cfr. Madelaine, p. 234, who quotes Hugo Ann. Praem., T. II, col. 1067.

patrimony, the castles of Varlar and Ilmstadt. Varlar was also in the diocese of Münster near Coesfeld. A colony of disciples came from Prémontré, and Varlar was soon transformed into another Premonstratensian abbey, dedicated to the Mother of God. Four years later when Pope Honorius confirmed the Order, Varlar is spoken of as a very flourishing community. As to Ilmstadt or Ilbenstadt, which had belonged to both Godfrey and Otto, it was also converted into an abbey. It was situated on the other side of the Rhine, about five miles from Frankfurt, in the diocese of Mainz. The Charter of Adalbert, Archbishop of Mainz, is of the year 1123, and gives the religious "living under the Rule of St. Augustine, and the institutions of our venerable brother Norbert," all powers and faculties for the exercise of the sacred ministry. Some years later Pope Innocent II, upon the request of the Archbishop, confided to the Premonstratensians the the care of the souls of that whole province.[7]

While these new foundations were being established, God manifestly aided Norbert in the great work. Funds seem to have been forthcoming whenever needed, and the number of disciples continued to increase every day. Prémontré had in reality become a training station, whither new recruits came to be drilled in monastic discipline and from which they were sent out to the new foundations as soon as they were imbued with the spirit of Norbert. In a word, things were going entirely in accordance with the fondest hopes of our Saint. No wonder, therefore, that we find Satan making violent efforts to obstruct the noble work. He soon found a powerful auxiliary in the Count of Arensberg, the father-in-law of Godfrey, who, when he heard of what he was pleased to call "the most foolish act of his son-in-law," became furious, and accused Godfrey of flagrant injustice to Jutta; for, he claimed that part of the estate of Cappenberg was her dowry and that she had been misled.

[7] Ibidem, Hugo Annales Ord. Praem. Varlaria, col. 1047-1048 (T. II), and also T. I. Ilbenstadium superiis, p. 866.

Godfrey immediately went to him to adjust matters and explain everything, but the Count refused even to listen to him and decided to take by force what he claimed, though unjustly, to be his. In effect he came with a number of armed men to Cappenberg to frighten his son-in-law, but Godfrey faced him fearlessly, for he was convinced that what he had done, he had done solely for the love of God and the welfare of his soul, without violating the rights of anyone. He said to one of his former servants (thus we read in the Acta SS.): "Perhaps his plan is to imprison me, but you can tell our father Norbert, that in case I am imprisoned, I pray him not to take any steps to procure my deliverance. Oh! if I could only be found worthy to die in prison for the love of God."[8]

But now many of his former servants, those who once loved him were turned against him, said openly that the Count had lost his head, and accused Norbert of being an impostor. These men had changed towards the young Count because, although they still had a sufficient income, they had largely been replaced by lay-brothers, and from a worldly point of view the change had not been to the advantage of even those that remained. Even the Bishop of Münster himself, though he was a great friend of the Count and a warm admirer of Norbert, advised Godfrey on the day he dedicated the new monastery, to change his plans for the sake of preserving peace. But Godfrey answered the Bishop as well as his servants by saying: "What we have done, we have done acting on the inspiration of God, and as long as I live, not the world, but God will be served in this place. If you really loved me you would all be happy to see me following God's Holy Will and escaping from the dangers of the world."

The Count of Arensberg refused to be reconciled, and said to all who cared to listen to him, that he was going to kill Norbert and hang his body from the wall of the castle. By the help of a certain Franco, he next decided to take his daughter, Jutta, by force from

[8] Acta SS. Tom II. 13 Jan., p. 130.

her cell; this he did, and led her away from Cappenberg. He had hidden her, but Godfrey sought for her night and day. The rumor was then spread that Godfrey had changed his mind; that he had driven away the canons and was now trying to find his wife and resume his worldly life. When, however, Godfrey showed the people how false was this rumor, and spoke to them of the injustice of this cruel act of the Count of Arensberg, they began to hate and despise the latter, and even dared speak of his cruelty to his own daughter.

At this time it happened that for some unknown reason Norbert was obliged to leave Cappenberg.[9] As soon as the Saint had left, Frederick began to change tactics in regard to his son-in-law, and tried to gain in a friendly way what he was unable to procure by force. He invited Godfrey to visit him in his castle, but notwithstanding his eloquent plea, Godfrey soon convinced him that it was all in vain.[10] This second failure infuriated him; he threatened Godfrey's life and finally decided to bring the whole matter before the Court of the Emperor. To this Godfrey gladly consented.

Be it observed that the Emperor Henry was now just at the most critical period of his life and overwhelmed with cares. Maurice Bourdin, the antipope and a creature of Henry, had been obliged to take refuge in the monastery of Cava. The Saxons were in revolt. The nobility was weary of his fruitless struggles with Rome, which had already lasted over fifty years. The absurdity of Investiture, the impropriety of a prelate receiving the ring and crozier from the hands of a layman had become apparent to everybody, and from all sides came petitions for peace.

It was at this moment that Norbert, who had returned to

---

[9] VandenElsen, p. 108, says that Norbert probably had gone to Prémontré to assist at the solemn dedication.

[10] According to Madelaine this meeting took place on the feast of the Assumption, 1123, but it must have been the year before.

Westphalia, in company with Count Godfrey, went in person to the Emperor, who was holding his Court at Lobwissen. We must not forget that the Counts of Cappenberg had more than once taken sides against the Emperor, and were known to oppose his claims as to Investiture. Through the influence of Norbert, Henry, as he himself distinctly stated,[11] not only favored Godfrey against his father-in-law, but shortly after pardoned the recusancy of both Godfrey and Otto, and restored them to his favor. All this is stated in a public document.

Now, this favorable decision of an excommunicated Emperor, and his subsequent action in regard to the foundations of Godfrey and Otto, which he took under his imperial protection, are most remarkable and show unmistakably Norbert's influence over Henry at this critical period. Can anyone doubt that Henry and Norbert, his former chaplain, held serious converse on the state of the Empire, and that Norbert induced him to sign that long-looked-for declaration made at the Concordat of Worms in the month of September of this same year?

> For the love of God, thus reads the document, of the Holy Roman Church and of Pope Calixtus, as well as for the good of my soul, I renounce all claims to the right of Investiture by ring and crozier. I grant to all the churches within my Empire the freedom of canonical elections and consecrations. I promise peace with Pope Calixtus and the Holy Roman Church, and to give him aid whenever he may claim it.[12]

The end of the war of Investiture was hailed with great joy by all Christendom. True, history has not linked the name of our humble Saint with that most important event, for no one can know

[11] Hugo Ann. Praem. I. Prob. 372, supradicto sacerdote pro eis intercedente. . . . Cfr. also Binterim and Von Steinen.

[12] Cfr. Darras. Gen. History of the Church, Vol. III, p. 200.

exactly what passed between him and the emperor. But when we reflect that Norbert's whole life since the day of his conversion had been devoted to peace-making, that his influence over the hearts of the nobles and the great of his day was truly miraculous—moreover, that circumstances brought him at this time into the very presence of the Emperor, and that to his influence Henry is known to have yielded in regard to Godfrey and Otto—who could doubt that Norbert was a most powerful instrument in the hands of Almighty God to bring about this most momentous event?

Meanwhile, Frederic, Count of Arensberg, had died quite suddenly while assisting at a great banquet, and his death brought peace to the Abbey of Cappenberg. Godfrey soon received the white habit from the hands of Norbert, and became one of his most zealous disciples. His great humility especially was truly edifying. He ever refused to be reminded of his former greatness, and never allowed anyone to render him particular honor. "You make me feel sad," he often said, when reminded of what he had done for the Order, "I am the servant of all." It was his great delight to perform the most menial duties in the house. Many a time he went to the "Xenodochium" he himself had built, and there washed the feet of the poor sick people. Further, in the observance of the prescribed fast and in other mortifications, he was truly admirable and a continual source of edification.

Norbert's desire was to have him in the Abbey of Prémontré. The Saint's desire meant a command for this son of obedience, and both he and his brother went to the mother abbey. Here, in the year 1125, Godfrey received minor orders. Norbert entertained the highest hopes for the future of this saintly disciple. Alas! these hopes were never to be realized, for Divine Providence had disposed otherwise. He who seemed most worthy to become a priest of the Most High, would never with his pure hands touch the Divine Victim. However, he had offered himself "a living host, holy and acceptable to the Lord."

He had been but one year in the Abbey of Prémontré, when

Norbert, now Archbishop of Magdeburg, called his dear son to him. Godfrey hastened to obey, but felt out of place in the midst of the world. He soon begged Norbert to send him back again to the solitude of the cloister, "his paradise on earth," as he called it. Having received the Saint's blessing, he retired to the abbey of Ilbenstadt, and there became the victim of a mortal malady. His brother, Otto, as also the other religions, were all deeply grieved when from day to day his condition grew worse. He, on the contrary, seemed radiant with joy, and often said to the brethren: "But why, after all, did we take the habit of penance? Why did we mortify ourselves, if not to be sooner with our Savior?"

On the 13th day of January, 1127, when all the brethren stood weeping at his bedside, he said to his brother Otto: "I hear a voice repeating, 'Go before him' ..." A moment later he exclaimed: "Welcome, messengers of my Creator!" These were his last words. Angels came to bear his soul to eternal bliss. He was then only thirty years of age.[13]

His first foundation, Cappenberg, was soon considered the mother house of the German province, and in a few years comprised, besides the houses at Ilbenstadt and Varlar, Herfort, where Jutta became Abbess, Clarholz, Scheida, Wesel, Weddinghausen, Wirburg, Quellenburg and Bonlant. Otto became, in 1155, Provost of Cappenberg, and died there in the odor of sanctity, on the 27th of January, 1172.

[13] The feast of Blessed Godfrey is kept in the Order on Jan. 17th.

CHAPTER VII
THE THIRD ORDER OF ST. NORBERT

Certatim populi accurrunt facunda videre
Ora Viri, cunctosque eloquio suo trahit.

Forth thou went a conquering hero;
Passions wild and social bondage
Bent their crippled forms and vanished
'Neath thy rule...

HE fame of the wonderful deeds of the Counts of Cappenberg had spread rapidly throughout Westphalia, and thence into France, where at this time Norbert was well and favorably known. His Order was steadily growing in importance, to the great delight of all good people, but to the extreme annoyance of Norbert's enemies. They began to recognize the powerful influence of Norbert's Institute, and consequently they put forth every endeavor to injure the reputation of Norbert and his disciples.

At Prémontré, Satan was continually trying to cause disturbances among the brethren, and outside of the abbey Satan's followers criticized their work severely. In the case of Cappenberg, they found reason to accuse the Saint of having exercised undue influence over Godfrey, his wife and his brother, with the intention of enriching his Institute. But Norbert remained undisturbed; it was by no means the first time that they had condemned his actions. Besides, his measures at Westphalia caused great admiration; the noble example of Count Godfrey and his brother appealed to the hearts of many, and thus Norbert's reputation, far from being lessened, was considerably exalted. Several of the nobility came at this time to Norbert to offer all they had, and even themselves, with the firm determination to follow Godfrey's example.

Among these one especially must be noticed, since he was to be, in the designs of Providence the cornerstone of a great and new structure to be raised by the Saint. He was a very illustrious person, the most powerful prince in the kingdom of France, and even the first in rank after the king. Theobald IV, surnamed the Great, was the son of Stephen, Count of Champagne and Blois, and of Alice, daughter of William the Conqueror, King of England. In the year 1102 he had succeeded to his father's estates, and, observes Guibert of Nogent, "owned as many castles as there are days in the year."[1] Since the year 1120, when on the 25th of November a terrible accident had befallen his family, Theobald had been deeply religious. He was on his way to England to visit the king, when on that day one of the ships suffered shipwreck off the English coast, and no trace was left of "La Blanche Nef," which had his sister aboard, his brother-in-law and four children of the king.[2] Since that terrible catastrophe the abundance of his wealth and the great honor in which he was held by all, only contributed to render him more humble and charitable. He became the ideal Christian prince, whose only object in life was to secure the happiness of his people, and to encourage them in the practice of virtue. St. Bernard testifies to his integrity when he says in one of his letters:[3]

> When we receive, perhaps, from other princes words true and untrustworthy, it is neither new nor wonderful to us. But in the case of Count Theobald, it is a matter of great surprise that his Yes and No should be without weight, since a word from him is for us equivalent to an oath, and a slight untruth is regarded by him as a grave perjury; since of all the virtues which dignify his

[1] Hugo "La Vie de Saint Norbert," p. 124.

[2] G. VandenElsen, "Het leven van den H. Norbertus," p. 117.

[3] Letter XXXVIII, published by S. J. Eales.

high rank and render his name celebrated throughout the whole world, the chief and most extolled is his steadfast truthfulness.

Such was the illustrous person who came out to meet Norbert returning from Westphalia; he was fully determined to follow the example of Count Godfrey and join the Order. A most flattering proposition, no doubt, to the Founder of a new institute greatly in need of helpers and protectors, and we should expect the Saint to act with him as he did with Count Godfrey and accept his offer without delay! But no; the Saint did not proceed hastily in this matter; and, without either accepting or rejecting the offer, he asked the Count for a few days' time, in order to consult our Lord in prayer, and confide to Him this new project. Could it really be the will of God, the Saint asked himself, that the immense estates and castles of Count Theobald should come to the Order? He knew that in case the numerous castles should really be converted into monasteries, it would cause great disturbance in the feudal hierarchy of the Count's vassals, and perhaps prove even a menace to the peace of the kingdom. On the other hand, he was convinced of the present generosity of the Count in building churches and monasteries, and he knew him to be a father to the orphans, a protector to widows, and a most liberal friend of the poor and the Church. Would it not be contrary to the workings of Divine Providence to change the life of this noble prince, whom God seemed to have predestined to be a great benefactor of whole provinces?[4]

Norbert therefore increased his prayers and mortifications to prepare his heart for guidance from on high. The more he prayed the more he realized that God did not call Theobald to serve Him in the monastery. A sublime thought now entered into the mind of the Saint, no doubt, in response to his fervent prayer. Was there no possibility of opening the doors of his Institute to persons living in the world? Was it not possible to establish some organization which

---

[4] *Vita B*, Ch. XXXIII.

would be halfway, so to say, between the world and the monastery? An organization, which though existing in the very bosom of human society, would have a truly religious soul? This idea gradually ripened in the mind of Norbert, and eventually led to the establishment of the Third Order, known as such the world over.

Theobald was awaiting Norbert's answer with the greatest anxiety. Heaven suggested to the Saint the following reply: "You will not be a religious, you will continue to bear the yoke of the Lord as you have done, and you will add to it that of wedlock."[5] "See," exclaims here the oldest historian of the Saint, "how great was his discernment of spirits! Two princes, Godfrey and Theobald, come to him; one he makes give up all; the other he bids keep all, and possess all as if he possessed nothing."[6]

Theobald, though he seemed greatly disappointed, answered the Saint manfully: "If such is the will of God, it is not for me to gainsay it, but rest assured, venerable Father, that I will not wed anyone but the woman you choose for me."[7] The Count, anxious to be in some way united with Norbert and his great work, asked the Saint before leaving, for a Rule of Life. Norbert was happy to grant this request and drew up a Rule that could without great difficulty be observed in the world, but at the same time sufficiently austere to become for souls of good will, a safe road to eternity and a bulwark against the evils of the age. In addition to this, Norbert gave the Count an outward token or sign of his aggregation to the Order, in the form of a white woolen scapular with which he solemnly invested him.[8] Thus the generous offer of the Count and Norbert's subsequent rejection of it were in the eternal decrees, instrumental in bringing about the foundation of an entirely new institution, "The Third

---

[5] *Vita B*, Ch. XXXIII.

[6] Ibidem.

[7] Ibidem.

[8] Biblioth. Praem. Ord. Lib. I, p. 311 .. . breve scapulare laneum candidum sub laicalibus vestimentis praescripsit. ...

Order." Henceforth in the midst of his glittering court, Count Theobald was always in simple and modest attire, and observed a rule of life far superior to that of the most pious layman of the district.

It is quite certain that before St. Norbert's time no one had ever succeeded in establishing in the Church a state of life midway between the cloister and the world; or, to put it in different words, a religious order which should penetrate into Christian homes in the midst of the world. Therefore, as Father Duhayon observes:

"To St. Norbert is due the honor of having been chosen by God to become an instrument in founding this salutary institution."[9] Also Cardinal Gasquet says: "It is worth remarking that apparently the Canons of Prémontré were the first to conceive the idea, afterwards so largely developed by the mendicants of the thirteenth century, of uniting laymen and women to them by a formal aggregation in what was known as a 'Third Order' with a share in all the prayers and privileges of the brethren.[10]

To our Saint therefore belongs the glory of having pointed out the way to other Founders—a glory and honor which may well be appreciated by the sons of the holy Patriarch and the friends of the Order. The Norbertine Tertiaries were originally called "Fratres et Sorores ad succurrendum," from the assistance given to and received from the Order. This name is also given in the Brief of Pope Benedict XIV, concerning them. It is probable that this brotherhood did not take the name of "Third Order" until the later foundation of similar institutions.

The solemn aggregation of Count Theobald to the Order of Prémontré, could not fail to act as a powerful stimulus to his religious fervor, and as an edifying example to his courtiers and people. Within the very confines of his castle he founded, a few years later, the Abbey of Chateau-Thierry, in order to be able to

---

[9] Manual Historique des Ordres Religieux," pp. 98-136.

[10] "Collectanea Anglo-Praemonstratensia," Vol. I, p. VI.

have at all times the disciples of St. Norbert about him. At the request of the abbot, Godfrey by name, who once belonged to the court of Theobald, and who considered the castle too worldly for a monastery, the abbey was transferred to Valsecret, in the diocese of Soissons, in the year 1140. Although Valsecret was but a short distance from the castle, Theobald insisted on always having two Premonstratensian Canons about him. To these he confided the direction of his conscience, the distribution of his alms, and the spiritual care of the inhabitants of his domains. Fath. Valbonne in his "Vie de St. Bernard," observes: "Two Premonstratensians accompanied the devout prince Theobald on all his journeys. Wherever he held his court, they distributed his alms and secretly carried them to the homes of timid poor. They also gave hospitality to clerics and monks who came to treat with the Count."[11]

When Theobald died, on Jan. 10th, 1151, Norbert indeed was not there to bless and strengthen him, but by his bedside were disciples of the Saint to comfort him in his last hour. His name was inscribed by loving hands in the Necrology of Prémontré and Yalsecret, and the Ephemerides Hagiologicae of the Order give on Sept. 26th, a sketch of his life.[12]

Many followed the good example of Count Theobald and joined the Third Order of Prémontré. The Counts of Brienne, who founded the Abbey of Basse-Fontaine, in the diocese of Troyes, became especially remarkable among the many disciples whom the spirit of the Holy Patriarch had attracted. "And," observes an old writer, "so exact was their fidelity to the Rule drawn up for them by Blessed Norbert, that all could see, that these princes did not wear the white scapular in vain. The integrity of their lives and the purity of their

---

[11] See Illana, o. c., p. 146.

[12] The particulars of the life of Count Theobald have been chiefly taken from "Het Leven van den H. Norbertus," by G. VandenElsen, who relied on "L'Histoire des dues et des comtes de Champagne," by H. D'Arbois de Jubainville. Tom. II.

morals never belied the color of their habit."[13] Soon every district in France and many other parts of Europe gave a number of Tertiaries to the family of Norbert. Here we cannot but sincerely regret the brevity of Norbert's historians. The very names of these first Tertiaries would not have been without value to us, and details of the lives of many more would prove most edifying.[14] Each Premonstratensian abbey had from the earliest times its register covered with names of brothers and sisters "ad succurrendum," but even these registers seem to be lost. Still a long list of names can yet be found in the Necrologies of different abbeys. Some of these have only recently been published, as for instance, the Necrology of the old Abbey of Floreffe, and the Obituary of the Abbey of Silly in the diocese of Séez, France. We shall return to this subject in the second volume.

As to Norbert, one may well be surprised at the marvelous growth of the Saint's work in those days. Thus far we have enumerated the new abbeys at Floreffe, Cappenberg, Varlar and Ilbenstadt. As early as 1121 a foundation had also been made at Viviers, whither a colony of disciples had been called by Hugh le Blanc, Lord of Ferte-Milon. Henry, one of the early disciples, became its first abbot, and is known especially for his great charity. A legend tells us that at the time of a famine, when he was distributing wheat to the poor, the wheat was miraculously multiplied; and, on another occasion, he by his prayer hastened the ripening of the harvest.[15]

In the same year was founded the Abbey of Saint-Josse-au-Bois or Dommartin. There is a description of the origin of this abbey, written in the beginning of the seventeenth century by one of the

---

[13] Acta SS. XX, p. 922.

[14] Cfr. Manual of the Third Order of St. Norbert, translated from the French by Abbot Geudens and published in London, 1889.

[15] Ann. Praem. Ord. T. II, col. 645. Vallis Serena.

religious,[16] in which we read that when Dagobert was King of France, St. Josse (Judocus) having been chaplain to the Duke of Ponthieu for seven years, retired from the world and became a solitary. He built a little chapel in the desert, which ever after his death was used by hermits. Then a certain Milo came to serve God there. The number of hermits having increased, they did not think it right to live without a superior. Milo went to Prémontré, and with the help of Norbert, a monastery was built, but not until all had placed themselves for some time under Norbert's direction. Ten years later Milo, who had been appointed Superior by Norbert, became Bishop of Thérouanne and was succeeded by a religious named Adam, who removed the canons from St. Josse-au-bois to Dommartin, in 1161.

Other monasteries sprang from this abbey governed by Milo. There was first the abbey of Ardenne near Caen. A certain Gilbert, who was from Caen, had, with the other hermits of St. Josse, attached himself to St. Norbert. Having gone to his native town, he was received by a wealthy lord, Aiulphe du Four. He and his wife spoke to Gilbert of a vision they had, in which the Blessed Virgin asked them to build a chapel in her honor on their property, called Ardenne. Thus originated this foundation. At the same time that Ardenne was being built, another branch detached itself from St. Josse to build, in the diocese of Rouen, the abbey of St. Nicholas-de-Thelle, later called Marcheroux. Ulric, the first abbot, had forty canons regular under him. He also founded at a short distance from this abbey, a house for Sisters, the convent of Beaumont-les-Nonnains.[17]

More celebrated than any of these was the abbey of Cuissy. Since 1114 there dwelt here in a deserted place, a Canon of the

---

[16] This description is found in the Arch. Publ. de Caen. Fonds d'Ardenne. Further Cfr. Hugo Annal. T. I, col. 621. Also Calonne "Hist, des Abbayes de Dommartin et St. André-aux-bois." 1875, p. 7.

[17] Ann. T. II, Marchasium Radulphi, col. 127.

cathedral of Laon, Luc by name. Disciples had joined him, and, acting upon the advice of the Bishop of Laon, they all placed themselves under the direction of Norbert. This was in 1122. Two years later Bishop Bartholomew consecrated Luc as Praemonstratensian Abbot of Cuissy. His great sanctity was known to all. St. Bernard corresponded with him about the year 1130, in regard to a convent for nuns, built by Luc near the abbey of Cuissy. (Cfr. Letter LXXIX.) The abbey of Cuissy and the neighboring abbey of Vauclair became renowned for their exquisite calligraphy and miniature-painting, which may still be seen in different manuscripts.[18]

[18] Cfr. De Florival. Barthélemy de Vir, p. 173 et seq. Also General Cat. of the Publ. Library of Laon. I, p. 96, et seq.

CHAPTER VIII
THE APOSTLE OF ANTWERP

Jam Tanchelini per te Norberte nefandam
Conversa ejurat Belgica terra luem.

Vainly Tanchelm strove to sow
Seeds of heresy and woe
In the peaceful land of Flanders...

F anyone thinks that in Christian Europe during the twelfth century people were but blind followers of a fanatic faith, he must indeed be glaringly ignorant of that period of history.

"The disorder and moral relaxation," thus writes the historian Darras,[1] "naturally developed by the War of Investitures, favored the rise, in the Western Churches, of numerous sects more or less closely allied to Manicheism, and tending to raise vice to the dignity of a system. These errors were thus a continuation of the series which had agitated Orleans, Arras and Toulouse, remains of the Eastern Paulicians, and forerunners of all modern systems which, under various names, aim at the overthrow of all authority, of hierarchical subordination, of the family and society. Their doctrinal errors, though agreeing in some points—such as the uselessness of the sacraments, of the invocation and veneration of the saints, and of prayers for the dead—are at variance in others, according to the views of their leaders. But their view of moral obligation is one: denial of all authority and rule—license and scandal. The first of these names which we meet in the twelfth century is that of Peter

[1] Cfr. Darras. "General History of the Church," Vol. III, p. 201.

> Bruys, whose followers styled themselves Petrobusians. He traversed Dauphiny, Provence and Languedoc, destroying and burning crosses, rebaptizing children, teaching that churches are useless, as God wishes no other temple than the universe. He was followed by excited crowds who butchered the priests, plundered and burned the churches and gave themselves up to the most shameful excesses ... Antwerp had been thrown into a state of similar disorder by a fanatic named Tankelin or Tanchelm . . . who revived the traditions of the Adamites and pretended to restore the world to its state of primitive nakedness by recalling its lost innocence."

Tanchelm, a talented but haughty layman, had preached his doctrines in the early years of the twelfth century, in the neighborhood of Antwerp. Thence he went to the diocese of Utrecht. He had also propagated his pernicious doctrines along the banks of the Rhine. Elated by his success, for his followers were many, he put on a monastic habit and went to Rome; there he sought by various means to have the Pope attach the seal of Rome to his nefarious work. Needless to say, he was unsuccessful, and returned by way of Cologne. This was in the year 1112.[2] While in Cologne he was seized by German soldiers and handed over to the Archbishop as a dangerous individual and an impostor, for we must not forget that society was no less interested than religion in the suppression of these sectaries. He was put in prison but escaped, and we read that the following year he was driven out of Bruges by clergy and laity. In 1115 he was driven from Louvain by Godfrey, Duke of Lorraine, and that same year he died a miserable death.[3]

Tanchelm's followers affected a life of poverty and austerity, opposed the power of the Pope and of all ecclesiastical authorities. They called themselves the poor of Christ, the imitators of the Apostles, and accordingly assumed the title of "Apostolicals." They

---

[2] Pertz, Script. XVI. Annales Veterocelles, 1112.

[3] Acc. to Madelaine, p. 271, who quotes Pertz, his skull was crushed by an indiscreetly zealous priest.

not only admired their shockingly immoral leader, "but," observes Abelard, quoted by the Bollandists,[4] "they actually adored him as the son of God." In a letter addressed by the clergy of Utrecht to the Archbishop of Cologne, we find in a few words the synopsis of Tanchelm's errors. "The Pope is nobody; archbishops and bishops are nobody; priests and clerics are nobody; the Church is I and my followers." If we may speak of any heretic excelling in the pernicious doctrines and practices of the Neo-Manicheism of those days, Tanchelm certainly merits that distinction. We read in that same letter, that one day he performed a mock-marriage with a statue of the Blessed Virgin, in a public square, and the people, blinded, came to offer him wedding presents.[5] He and his followers regarded the Blessed Eucharist especially with peculiar horror, which they constantly manifested by the most shocking profanations. Without staining our pages with repulsive details, let it be sufficient to state that contemporary writers declare that the deeds perpetrated by Tanchelm and his followers are too loathsome and horrible for description.[6]

And the poor deluded people! How lamentable to see a country, Christian for generations past, going back not only to pagan immorality, but casting off all moral restraint, and encouraging a purely animal life! We here ask ourselves, how was it possible that a sect, whose doctrines tended to the utter destruction even of all social order, could successfully establish itself in a Christian country? As an iconoclast, Tanchelm held out to the rulers the treasurers of the churches, and as a reformer he pleased the ignorant by removing all moral restraint. Here then is the cause of the rapid spread of this as of almost every heresy.

---

[4] Cfr. Acta SS. T. XX, p. 832.

[5] Ibidem. Epistola Trajectensis Ecclesiae ad Freder. Epis- cop. de Tanchelmo seductore.

[6] *Vita B.* Ch. XXXVI.... Balneum ejus bibebant ... in tantum ut se infelicem diceret quae huic conjunctioni nefariae misceri non meruisset...

Eight years had now passed since the principal author of these monstrous disorders died, and the moral state of the people in Antwerp was most pitiable. Antwerp then belonged to the diocese of Cambray, but at present it is in the archdiocese of Malines. In the year 1119 good Bishop Burchard sent thither twelve of his canons to extirpate the heresy and try to restore order. They were attached to the church of St. Michael, which had been built by Godfrey of Bouillon before he set out for the Holy Land. All were zealous priests who worked hard to restore not only the faith but also virtue to the poor deluded people. Alas! these canons thought the evils too great and too deeply rooted to be eradicated by them. In their distress they returned to Cambray and conferred with Bishop Burchard. The result of this conference was that both the canons and the bishop thought Norbert the very man capable of restoring Christian life in Antwerp.

Norbert was at this time busily engaged in his solitude at Prémontré, confirming his brave but inexperienced sons in their fervor and spiritual life. By word and example he was their leader in the strictest observance of the rules, and by his wise counsels he encouraged them in their daily struggles. No one would have thought him at this time a Saint, the reputation of whose sanctity was attracting the eyes of Europe. He was humble and pious—a true *servus servorum.* But Bishop Burchard, who had known him for years and was well acquainted also with his great success as missionary and convert-maker, valued him at his true worth.

A deputation from the bishop came to Prémontré to explain to Norbert the pitiable state of Antwerp. The man of God, whose zeal for the salvation of souls consumed him, was at once ready to comply with the bishop's request. Was not this, thus he reasoned, a great opportunity to do missionary work? To bring back to God not ordinary sinners only, but heretics—people who had given up their faith—what could be more noble, what work more apostolic? Guided by the Holy Spirit, the Saint not for a moment hesitated, but set out at once for his new scene of labor, accompanied by

Evermode, Waltman, and other disciples, wholly imbued with his apostolic spirit. They were twelve in all, and once arrived at their destination, those fervent apostles lost no time in opening what we would to-day call a great "Mission."

To the credit of the twelve canons who had left, be it remarked here, that their work had not been entirely unsuccessful, for as a result of their efforts a reaction had already set in, and the good and pious people of Antwerp, however small their number, hailed the coming of Norbert as that of their savior. The historian H. Q. Janssen informs us[7] that the Saint upon his arrival found the church crowded with people curious to know what the Saint had to say. The same historian describes Norbert ascending the pulpit—his emaciated features, his white habit, his expressive and charming voice, his gestures. But it was not these that gave him that supernatural power of awakening emotion and stirring his hearers to conviction, it was his own personal holiness. In the "Life" of Bl. Hugh we find only a few words of the first sermon delivered by Norbert on this occasion, but they are of great significance.

> "Brethren," he began, "I am aware that the ignorance of truth, rather than the love of error, is the principal cause of your forsaking the true religion. If truth had been announced to you, I know you would have followed it with as great eagerness as you have followed error. You suffered yourselves to be misled too easily, and now I hope that you will suffer yourselves to be saved easily by us..."[8]

In his first address to the people, instead of censure or reproach, Norbert combined the gentleness of persuasion with the force of conclusive argument. No invectives, no personalities, but in everything charity according to the rule of the Apostle. It was this sentiment which our late Holy Father, Pope Pius X, so beautifully expressed when he said: "Non possumus aedificare Ecclesiam super

---

[7] See VandenElsen, p. 130.

[8] Cfr. *Vita B.* Ch. XXXVI. Also Taiée, Prémontré, I, p. 26.

ruinam charitatis." (We can never build up the Church on the ruins of charity.)

Norbert's disciples followed bis example, and their sermons produced deep and lasting impressions. The most ignorant could not fail to see the immense difference between the preaching of Norbert and of Tanchelm and his disciples. While the latter appealed to violence and vice in a most ostentatious manner, the Saint quietly made an urgent appeal to all that was most noble in man. Moreover, Norbert had come not in the name of Satan but of the Most High, and his conduct and irreproachable life fully justified his mission. Consequently, it was not difficult even for the most illiterate to see on which side was truth.

Antwerp soon bent its head in shame. Striking their breasts with the deepest sorrow, the people came and knelt at the feet of the missionaries to receive pardon from Almighty God. "Men and women," observes Bl. Hugh in his Life, "came to them after having purified their consciences by a sincere confession, and in large numbers brought back to the missionaries the Sacred Hosts, which from ten to fifteen years and more, they had kept in their house's and most sacrilegiously dishonored."[9] Within a very short time, in fact a few weeks, the whole city seemed entirely transformed, and never before did the faithful assist at the celebration of the Holy Sacrifice of the Mass with more genuine piety. The poor people now felt as if they had been living in a dream, and had at last awakened to the reality of their former Christian and Catholic life. The name of Norbert was on the lips of all, and they were unable to sufficiently express their lively gratitude to our dear Saint. Good Bishop Burchard and his Canons also greatly rejoiced on hearing of the happy result. In fact a most sincere enthusiasm was shared by every one, and from that day forward Norbert was called by the "Vox Populi" the Apostle of Antwerp and of the Blessed Sacrament.

The people, as well as the bishop, entreated Norbert to accept

[9] In the museum of Antwerp (No. 107) we find a painting, from the hand of C. De Vos, representing St. Norbert collecting the Sacred Hosts.

the church at Antwerp, and establish there a house of the Order; and the Canons who had been attached to St. Michael's freely offered to move to another part of the city, which eventually they did, and thus originated the famous cathedral of St. Mary at Antwerp.[10] Norbert accepted the liberal offer of the bishop and founded at that place the celebrated abbey of St. Michael, which until the time of the French Revolution, had continued the great work inaugurated by the Saint. He installed Bl. Waltman as its first abbot. Burning with apostolic zeal and faithful to the Counsels of his spiritual father, Waltman sent out disciples to preach the Gospel in the neighboring towns and villages, and so thoroughly extirpated whatever remained of Tanchelm's heresy in this province. Thus the abbey of Antwerp became a great center of civilization, and within ten years established three other abbeys which have since preserved the faith in these provinces.[11]

Once order was restored in Antwerp, Norbert made every endeavor to help the people to persevere in their good resolutions. But among all the aids to perseverance, there was one of which he spoke continually, the one on which, in the Saint's opinion, the future religious life of the people depended, and that was a sincere devotion to the Holy Sacrament of the Altar. Since Tanchelm had tried hard to eradicate all respect for the Holy Eucharist, Norbert resolved to revive it and be its apostle. He ordered special services to be held with the greatest solemnity to make reparation to Our Dear Lord for the outrages He had endured, and for the many

[10] Cfr. Cath. Encyclop. Vol. I, p. 589: "The Cathedral of Antwerp was originally a small Premonstratensian shrine known familiary as "Our Lady of the Stump."

[11] These were: the abbey of Middelburg in Zeeland, and the two abbeys—Tongerloo and Averbode—which exist to this day, both in the province of Antwerp. St. Michael's abbey also founded two convents for Norbertine Nuns, one at Zoetendaal and one at Vroenhout. The latter is at present at Oosterhout in Holland, and has a foundation at Neerpelt in Belgium.

sacrileges that had been committed. Large crowds assisted at these solemnities, and before long a genuine devotion, more fervent perhaps than ever before, possessed the hearts of the faithful.

Norbert found another means of perseverance in a sincere devotion to our Heavenly Queen, and in the establishment of his Third Order. He placed the new abbey church under the patronage of the Bl. Virgin, and at that time implanted in the hearts of the people that filial love for God's Holy Mother, which in due time would manifest itself in the building of a magnificent cathedral in her honor—a church famous for its splendor and exquisite beauty the whole world over. Further, in regard to his Third Order, we find the Bollandists specifying some of its results, so visible at Antwerp about the middle of the twelfth century. There exists a contract of Brotherhood, made in the year 1135, between the Canons of Notre Dame at Antwerp and the Premonstratensian Canons of St. Michael's Abbey, in which it is stated, that those parishioners of Notre Dame who desire aggregation to the Premonstratensians, "can, on taking the Rule and White Habit of the Order, receive the sacraments from them, and be buried by them and in their cemeteries."[12] That in this contract there is evidently question of the Third Order, is further made plain in the Acta SS.[13]

When Norbert finally left the city of Antwerp to return to Prémontré, his departure was deeply regretted by all. The people realized that a saint, to whom they now owed their faith and virtue, was leaving them. They proclaimed him as the Apostle of their city and of the Blessed Sacrament, and, observes a writer of Antwerp in the seventeenth century, in order to proclaim Norbert's great deeds to posterity, the people from that time gave the name, Norbert, to their children. Further, out of gratitude to the Saint, they placed several beautiful windows in the church of Notre Dame at Antwerp, representing the triumphant procession of the people, after their

---

[12] Hugo Annales T. II, col. CCI.

[13] T. XX, p. 922.

conversion by Norbert. They also inscribed under a tableau in one of the chapels of this basilica in which Norbert is represented, these beautiful words:

> Quod Amandus inchoarat,
> Quod Eligius plantarat,
> Willibrordus irrigarat,
> Tanchelinus devastarat,
> Norbertus restituit."[14]

Thus did Norbert become an apostle of the Bl. Sacrament, and because of this victory at Antwerp, the Saint is usually represented holding in his hand a Monstrance, while the heretic Tanchelm lies prostrate at his feet. The Monstrance is the emblem of his devotion to the Holy Eucharist, and the prostrate heretic symbolizes Norbert's triumph over the Sacramentarian Heresy of this fanatic. Two paintings from the hand of Rubens, representing the Triumph of St. Norbert at Antwerp, were preserved in the abbey of St. Michael until the time of the French Revolution. One of these is to be found today in the Kensington Museum in London. A famous painting of this same scene is preserved at Cologne, and one at Magdeburg, besides a large number in the different abbeys of the Order. Bayerlinck, speaking of the Chronicles of Miraeus in regard to Norbert's Triumph at Antwerp, says:

> "The Order of White Canons was instituted by St. Norbert in the most difficult times of the Church, when the Sacramentarian and the Adamite Heresies were raging. The Father of mercies had selected and prepared St. Norbert, like another Alcides, to overthrow this heresy."

Andi Guerinus writes in his commentary on the Canticle of Canticles:

---

[14] "St. Amandus prepared the soil for the reception of the faith which St. Eligius planted, St. Willibrord irrigated, Tanchelm devastated, but St. Norbert restored."

> "St. Norbert with his Holy Order was, raised up by Divine Providence to render conspicuous in his days two great mysteries, viz: The Sacrament of the Holy Eucharist, and the Immaculate Conception of our Lady."

Norbert bequeathed his special devotion to the Blessed Sacrament as a legacy to his spiritual sons. His statues and pictures seem to say to them: "Love the Holy Eucharist; defend and promote devotion to the Blessed Sacrament." To further commemorate the Saint's Triumph at Antwerp, the Order has kept a special feast, which is yearly celebrated with great solemnity in the different abbeys. The diocese of Malines also celebrates this feast, and in all the churches of Antwerp there is held every year a solemn novena in preparation for the Feast of Norbert's Triumph over Tanchelm. On May 17, 1884, a plenary indulgence was attached to its celebration by Pope Leo XIII.

Of the old St. Michael's Abbey nothing now remains. The place where this great abbey once stood, is to-day indicated only by a street named Convent Street. (Klooster Straat). A description of this abbey may be found in the "Acta Sanctorum," as an appendix to the Life of St. Norbert.

CHAPTER IX
THE APPROBATION OF THE ORDER

Approbat Calixtus multisque favoribus ornat
Praemonstratensis germina prima domus.

Pope Calixtus approves the Order of Prémontré
and grants it many favors.

UMORS of Norbert's signal victory over Tanchelm's heresy at Antwerp, soon spread throughout Belgium and France, and the Saint's apostolic labors became the topic of conversation. Good Bishop Bartholomew especially, was full of praise and admiration for Norbert and his disciples, and thanked God for having given so holy and zealous a priest to his diocese. He now urged his former request of having some of Norbert's disciples in his episcopal city.

As the reader no doubt remembers, there was in Laon the abbey of St. Martin, which Norbert had tried in vain to reform, five years before. Since then, things had gone from bad to worse, and conditions were now truly deplorable. There was no longer any discipline and the life led by the canons prevented many from following their vocation to the priesthood. Bishop Bartholomew, deeply moved by the sad state of this abbey, and at the same time anxious to put a stop to its many abuses, begged the Saint for some of his disciples to replace the canons of St. Martin's. At first, Norbert hesitated, because he was still averse to the establishment of abbeys in large cities. However, St. Michael's Abbey in Antwerp was an argument in the bishop's favor, and the Saint was finally forced to yield. As soon as he had given his word, Bishop Bartholomew at once changed the Charter of the Foundation of the Abbey of St. Martin. He made it read as follows:

> In the name of the holy and indivisible Trinity. Bartholomew, by the grace of God, unworthy servant of the church at Laon... Moved by the state of decadence of this monastery, we have determined to confide it to the care and government of Brother Norbert, who, in the forest of Voas at Prémontré, has established the eremitical life under the canonical profession, with a great number of servants of God. When he yielded to our request, it was understood that the church should remain under our jurisdiction, and the jurisdiction of our successors. The brethren, who, attracted by piety, will unite in this place for the welfare of their souls, shall live here canonically under the authority of an abbot, whom they shall have elected according to the Rule of St. Augustine and the Constitutions of the monastery of Prémontré. In case the abbot of St. Martin should fail in the fulfillment of his duties, and, after having been cited by the bishop of Laon and the abbot of Prémontré in the presence of the church of Laon, he should remain obstinate, the abbots of said Institute shall be called together in a General Chapter at Prémontré to discuss his conduct and judge accordingly. If he prove incorrigible, he shall be deposed in conformity with the prescribed rules of religion; and they shall elect another abbot who shall be consecrated and installed by the bishop of Laon.[1]

At the head of the twelve religious who were sent to Laon, Norbert placed Gautier of St. Maurice, one of the seven young students who had first come with Norbert to Prémontré. No better choice could have been made, since Gautier during his four years at Prémontré had distinguished himself by his love for study and prayer. He was a second Norbert, and therefore could conquer the almost insurmountable obstacles to this new foundation.

Upon their arrival, the brethren found themselves destitute of

[1] Among the different seals attached to this document we find the seal of St. Bernard, the illustrious Abbot of Clairvaux. Cfr. Le Paige Biblioth. Ord. Praem., p. 446. Also letter 253 of St. Bernard.

even the necessities of life, except, as the Bollandists observe, for a donkey by the name of Burdin.[2] On the first morning some of the brethren went with this donkey into the forest of Voas to gather wood. On the back of Burdin they brought back a load which they then sold. In this way they were enabled, in the beginning, to buy bread; and many a day did they have to wait till the afternoon before the wood was sold. The monk Hermannus of Laon testifies to the fact that in the midst of this poverty, all the brethren were truly happy and contented. They cultivated the surrounding land and thus soon provided for their material welfare. They then laid the foundation of the abbey church, which exists to this day, and is most remarkable for its architecture. In a word, under the able management of Gautier, who in the year 1150 became Bishop of Laon, St. Martin's was, in a few years, one of the most celebrated abbeys of the Order. Within the short period of twelve years, this foundation counted no less than five hundred religious; and, in wealth, it surpassed all other monasteries of the diocese.[3]

No sooner was a certain regularity established in the abbey, than Abbot Gautier, after the example of Norbert, went out preaching. He went to Germany, the Low Countries, France and also to Switzerland; thus, in a very few years, the abbey of St. Martin had become, in the true sense of the word, another Prémontré.

After Norbert's success in Antwerp, the rapid growth of the Order seems nothing short of miraculous. Every day brought new postulants to Prémontré, and numerous bishops entreated Norbert to send them some of his disciples. When the Saint was at Liege, where Bishop Albéron was holding his synod at the time, he first received a document by which the abbey of Floreffe was confirmed. To show how highly Bishop Albéron esteemed the Order, we here

[2] Acta SS. T. I. Analecta Norbertina, p. 852. Ut praeter unum asinum, Burdinum nomine, nihil pene aliud haberent...

[3] Ibid. Infra duodecim annos plusquam quingentorum fratrum numerus Inveniretur... Adeo ut jum inter praecipua et excellentia Franciae monasteria computetur. Cfr. also Leqeux. Antiq. relig. T. II, p. 81 et seq.

mention the fact that he offered Norbert at the same time the abbey of Mount Cornillon, which, being situated in the diocese of Liege, enabled the bishop to have the religious near him. The bishop then relieved the members of Mount Cornillon from their allegiance to the Victorians at Paris.[4] and placed the abbey at the disposal of Norbert. The Saint sent for religious from the new abbey of Floreffe, and appointed Blessed Luke as the first abbot.

An ancient secular chapter, situated at Wenau, near Cologne, had been placed at the disposal of the abbot of Floreffe, who changed it into a convent for Norbertine Sisters.[5] In the same year a monastery was built on a mountain, named Justemont, in Lorraine, where an early disciple, Zachary by name, became the first abbot. This foundation was made through the generosity of Euphemia, a lady of Vatronville, who acted in this matter upon the advice of her brother Ursion, Bishop of Verdun. Foundations were also laid for the Abbey of Riéval, in the diocese of Toul, through the generosity of the Counts of Barr. The first abbot was Herbert, one of the early disciples from Laon. Nor must we forget to mention that also in this same year, Norbert founded a convent for Sisters in Bedburg, in the diocese of Cologne, near his native town, Xanten. Hugo even adds that at this time a foundation was also made in Poland, where Count Alexander founded and richly endowed a Premonstratensian abbey at Strzelno.[6] But what seems even more wonderful than the founding of all these houses in so short a time, is the fact that never were religious wanting to populate them. Truly, we again exclaim, the blessing of Divine Providence rested visibly on the work of St. Norbert.

---

[4] See G. VandenElsen, o. c., p. 138.

[5] Cfr. Madelaine, who quotes Annal. Ord. Praem. T. II, col. 1159. Further Barbier. Hist. de l'Abbaye de Floreffe, p. 14. Le Paige Biblioth, p. 307.

[6] Cfr. Charles Hugo "Annales Ordin. Praem." T. II, col. 933, et. seq. "Strzelno." Madelaine who, on page 265, quotes Dr. Winter, says that according to the latter this foundation was made only after Norbert became Archbishop.

Although the Order had existed now for three years, thus far it had received only episcopal approbation. True, the Holy Father while at Laon, had encouraged Norbert in his plans, and thus approved of his work, but a papal document confirming the Order had not as yet been issued. It happened that at this time there were two legates of Pope Calixtus II, with the Bishop of Noyon in Picardy. They were Cardinals Peter di Leone and Gregory de Angelis, who had come to publish the resolutions of the Lateran Council. The Saint, now well known for his preaching and miracles, went to them, and, humbly prostrate at their feet, implored as a great favor to receive the confirmation of his Order from them, in the Pope's name. The Legates fully informed of the great good which Norbert and his disciples had effected everywhere, acquiesced willingly. The tenor of the Bull explaining first the spirit of the Order, and further giving to it papal confirmation, is as follows:

> Peter di Leone, priest, and Gregory de Angelis, deacon, Cardinals and Legates of the Holy See—to our venerable brother Norbert and to all his brethren who profess under him the canonical life, health and benediction.
>
> We give thanks to Almighty God, because He has inspired you to renew the praiseworthy lives of the holy Fathers and to raise up an Institute founded on the teachings of the Apostles, which flourished in the early Church, but in our times has become nearly extinguished. For there were in the beginning of the Church two kinds of life practiced by her children; the one by the weak, the other by the strong; the one remaining in small 'Segor' the other ascending the summit of high mountains; the one redeeming sin by penance and alms, the other working to acquire eternal merits by the continual practice of virtue; the one engaged in worldly affairs, the other, raised on high, despising and forsaking worldly goods.
>
> But the kind of life which, by its fervor, is disengaged from worldly things, is again divided into two classes having nearly the same spirit; the first is that of canons, the other of monks. The latter has by God's mercy not ceased to shine in the Church; but the for-

mer, which by relaxation was almost extinguished, has in our days by the mercy of God begun to acquire new life and vigor. The holy Pope and Martyr, Urban, instituted it; St. Augustine gave it his rules; St. Jerome reformed it by his letters. We should therefore deem it not a less meritorious work to re-establish under God's inspiration and with His help the apostolic or canonical life, so well known in the primitive Church, than to preserve the monastic life sustained in its splendor by the Holy Spirit.

"We, therefore, by the authority of the Holy See whose Legates we are, approve your state of life, and in the name of God we exhort and beseech you to persevere in it. We also grant to all those who profess the canonical life in your monasteries and with the help of God remain faithful, the blessing of the Holy Apostles St. Peter and Paul, and the pardon of their sins. We forbid that anyone dare undertake to change the state of your Order, the benefits of which have been shared by so many countries, that many more may obtain the blessing of your administrations. We also decree that no member of your Order, from levity or even under pretext of leading a more austere life, be allowed to change from your Order into another, with- out the consent of the Abbot and of the whole community, and we forbid any Abbot or Bishop to receive such without the necessary testimonials as to this unanimous consent.

You, therefore, dearest brethren in Christ, endeavor with renewed zeal to fulfill most faithfully what you have promised to the Lord. Let your light shine before men that they may see your good works and glorify your Father Who is in Heaven. It is in the name of the Father, and of His Son and of the Holy Ghost, that we confirm your Institute, that it may stand forever. Should anyone offend against these decrees, and after two or three warnings not give satisfaction, let him be punished according to the canonical penalties.

Peter di Leone, priest and legate of the Holy See.
Gregory de Angelis, cardinal-deacon and legate of the Holy See.

Written at Noyon, 4 Kal. Julii (June 28th) of the year of Our Lord, 1124, the sixth of the Pontificate of Pope Calixtus II

Thus at last was Norbert's Order approved and confirmed by the highest authority on earth, and from that day forward it took its place among the Orders of Canons Regular. Great must have been the joy of Norbert and the brethren when the seal of Rome had been set upon their noble work, and this papal approbation, added to the good will of bishops and priests, gave a distinctive character to the work of the Saint, to the great consternation of his opponents. Not all bishops and priests looked upon the work of Norbert with the same admiration. Once it became known that the new Order had been approved by the papal legates, several critics openly disapproved of many things the Saint had introduced, and which they were pleased to call useless innovations. Among these critics were Rupert, Hugh Metel, Hugh Farsit, Gautier, Bishop of Maguellone, and others. Rupert reproached Norbert for having added to the Rule of St. Augustine observances of too great severity; he accused him of lack of charity, since Norbert had never a good word for the monks of Cluny; he complained that the superiors of the Premonstratensians were called abbots and bore the crozier, and further, he thought it unworthy of priests and especially of an abbot, to work in the field, look after cattle, and clean the stables.[7]

Hugh Metel even went to the above named Cardinals and reproached them for having given their approbation to the Order of Norbert, first, because unlike canons, they wore woolen habits instead of linen; and secondly, unlike monks, they went out preaching. These were his reasons for calling this new canonical life scandalous.[8]

Hugh Farsit made use of the very same arguments in his opposition, but his mode of expressing them was more offensive.[9]

---

[7] Cfr. Migne Patrol, lat. T. 170. 535-536. Also Dom Martene. Amplissima Collect. T. IX. Liber de diversis Ordinibus et Professionibus quae sunt in Ecclesia. 1053.

[8] Hugo. Sacrae Antiq. Mon. T. II, p. 386. Epist. XLI.

[9] Cfr. Histoire Litt. de la France T. XII, p. 294. Fr. Hugonis Suessoin. de Epistola ad Patres Confluentiae congregatos.

Bishop Gautier, in his turn, attacked Norbert, but on an entirely new point. He reproached him for having changed the Roman Breviary, but the good bishop was evidently misinformed, as we know from the writings of Cardinal Jacques de Vitry[10] and also from the celebrated treatise on the Liturgy by Cardinal Bona.[11] Besides, the Annalist Hugo observes that in the Bull of Pope Honorius II, it is clearly stated that the Premonstratensians in regard to psalmody and other ecclesiastical offices, are to conform themselves to other Canons Regular.[12] It is quite evident, says Madelaine, that Nor- bert never tried to make innovations in liturgical matters. If to-day the Norbertine liturgy is in some respects different from the Roman, it is because, in the course of time, the Roman liturgy has undergone changes.

The new Order was thus attacked on account of the habit the religious wore, the work they did, the ritual they used; nay, even their name had become a subject for dispute. The following dialogue was held between a religious of Cluny and a monk of Citeaux:

The Clunyite: "St. Augustine has written his rule not for monks but for canons regular. These men pay no attention when one calls them monks."

The Cistercian: "Whether they wish to be or not, they are monks, or they don't belong to any Order."

The Clunyite: "Pray, brother, why would you make yourself odious to canons regular wearing a cassock or wearing a surplice, Norbertines or other?"

The Cistercian: "If I refuse to a Norbertine the name of Canon to give him the name of monk, have I taken from him an honorable name to give him one that is less glorious? Like all those who live in community, the Norbertines are monks. Moreover, I find in the history of the Church a number of Saints who were monks, but I

---

[10] Cfr. Hugo "Dissert. sur la Canonicité de l'Ordre de Prémontré" Luxemburg, 1700, pp. 313-316.

[11] Cfr. Bona "De variis Ritibus divinae Psalmodiae," Ch. XVIII, par. 6.

[12] MSS. of Hugo, p. 28.

never met a single Saint who had been a canon."

The Clunyite: "St. Augustine was a canon; is he not a Saint?"

The Cistercian: "He called himself monk in many of his sermons, in particular in the sermon where he speaks of himself and the clerics. The Norbertines show bad taste in refusing through self-love the title of monk in order to be called preachers and pastors."

The Clunyite: "Be careful. You are doing them a double injury. You call them monks, and moreover you call them Norbertines, and they do not wish either name."

The Cistercian: "Do you know why?"

The Clunyite: "That is their business. I think, judging from their long cassocks, that they desire to be preachers and pastors of parishes, which is not allowed to monks. Perhaps they do not wish to be called Norbertines, because, as some say, their founder, master Norbert, has apostatised. You can see him, after having made profession to walk barefooted, riding a splendid horse, attending banquets, and living at the Court of Emperor Lothaire."[13]

It is quite evident from this dialogue, and also from the above quotations, that neither the person of Norbert nor his work was spared. These criticisms moreover were freely discussed by clergy and laity. Nor should we think lightly of these seemingly unimportant subjects under discussion, for they were far-reaching in their consequences. The simple change, for instance, of the material of the habit signified, as we know, the union which Norbert had tried to bring about between the monastic and the canonical life. However, general opposition is often but a proof of the great influence of an Order.

To return to our Saint. After Norbert had received the approbation of the Order from the papal legates, he at once left Noyon and went to visit the late foundations at Laon, Cuissy and Viviers. On the day he arrived at Viviers, they brought before him a farmer possessed by the evil one. After invoking the aid of the

---

[13] Cfr. Dom Martene. "Thesaurus Anecd." T. V. col. 1614. The dialogue was held between 1153-1171. Madelaine, p. 302.

heavenly Queen, Norbert cast out the devil by a single sign of the Cross.[14] It was on this journey also that Norbert went to pay his respects to the bishop of Soissons, and to ask him to confirm the rich donations of Yvo of Cathena and his wife Helwidis. Five years previous, this noble woman had asked Norbert's prayer that God might deign to bless her marriage. The Saint had prophesied at the time that one day she herself with more than one child, would join a religious order. She had come now to Norbert to offer herself with her husband and little children, and all the wealth they possessed to help the Saint in his noble work.[15]

Notwithstanding the criticisms of his enemies, Norbert remained undisturbed, and continued his good work most zealously. One of his critics, however, or rather enemies, he seems to have noticed more than the others, and that was Abelard, of whom we spoke above. Ever since his condemnation at the Synod of Soissons, where Norbert had exposed him as a heretic, Abelard had been persecuting Norbert and his disciples by biting sarcasm and ridicule. At this time Abelard was teaching a large body of students at the "Paraclete." This "Paraclete" was situated in the duchy of Champagne, whose duke, Theobald, was Norbert's most ardent admirer, and even a member of the Order. Wo do not know whether or not it was through Norbert's influence with Count Theobald that Abelard was forced to close his school, but the latter complained bitterly of the Saint's opposition to him at this time. Says Jos. McCabe, in his "Peter Abelard" (p. 226 et seq.):

> We may take Abelard's statement literally. Bernard and Norbert were doing the work of his rivals and were doing it effectively. They who had supported him at Soissons or afterwards, were being poisoned against him. Count Theobald and Geoffrey of Chartres are two whom he probably had in mind. He feels that the net is being drawn close about him... From that time he became morbidly sensitive and timorous... He must fly from France... etc.

[14] Cfr. G. VandenElsen, o. c., p. 143.

[15] Ibidem, p. 144.

Though Norbert's enemies and critics were quite numerous, yet his sincere friends and admirers surpassed them by far. Their testimonies force upon us the conclusion that Norbert, during this period of error and confusion, had rendered splendid services to religion and to society. Guibert, Abbot of Nogent, who knew the Saint most intimately, describes him as the greatest man then living in France, because of his penetrating intellect, his knowledge of the interior life, of the sacred mysteries of our holy religion and of the treasures of Holy Scripture.[16] Anselm, Bishop of Havelberg, speaks in glowing terms of his zeal, his virtues and of the universal admiration in which he was held. Hermann adds that since the time of the Apostles, no man had rendered such great services to the Church. And even Gautier, Bishop of Maguelonne, though one of Norbert's critics, refers to him as an incomparable preacher, well versed in the Holy Scriptures and remarkable for the holiness of his life.

These and a number of similar testimonies of contemporary writers, give us a high idea of Norbert's piety, his wisdom and zeal, and at the same time show us clearly why some feared him and tried to depreciate him. However, among all the friends and admirers of St. Norbert, the great St. Bernard, who in one of his letters (LVI) refers to him as the chosen organ of the Holy Ghost, the channel by which God manifests His will to man, stands out quite prominently. Since his friendship will necessarily increase our love for Norbert, the following chapter will deal with the mutual relations between these two eminent men of the twelfth century.

---

[16] For references see the Preface of "Vie de saint Norbert," by Charles Louis Hugo.

St. Norbert and St. Bernard before the Emperor Lothair

CHAPTER X
ST. BERNARD AND ST. NORBERT

Lotharium eloquii mira dulcedine tractum,
Mellifluumque sibi jungit amore Patrem.

By the sweetness of his eloquence
Norbert drew to himself the Emperor,
And by his love won the Mellifluous Doctor.

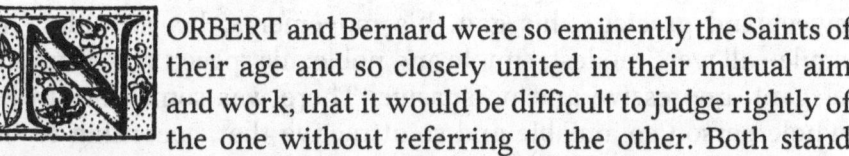

NORBERT and Bernard were so eminently the Saints of their age and so closely united in their mutual aim and work, that it would be difficult to judge rightly of the one without referring to the other. Both stand forth as the great pastors, preachers and reformers of the twelfth century; both appeared in the Councils of the Church as well as of the State, and without ever ceasing to be holy and mortified religious, both were the ruling will of the times.

Permit me first to call attention to the close similarity of their life-story. Bernard, the future Saint and celebrated Abbot, was born in the castle of Fontaines near Dijon in Burgundy, when Norbert was in his eleventh year. Each had a very pious mother, and the birth of each was preceded by most remarkable circumstances. While Hadwigis heard a heavenly voice telling her of the future greatness of the child about to be born, the mother of St. Bernard had a terrible dream of a white dog barking incessantly, which dream was thus explained by a man of great sanctity: "Fear not; you shall be the mother of a child who, like a faithful dog, shall one day guard the House of the Lord, and bark loud against the enemies of the Faith."[1]

His biographer informs us that, "when Bernard was nineteen years old, sparkling with all the brightness of youth and genius, he no longer felt within him the transport of his former fervor; his piety, devoid of all consolation, weaned, so to speak, from all its sweetness, it seemed no longer to have either light or heat; the springtime, with him, was past; the shadows of night were around his soul, and the voice of the turtle was no longer heard therein".

Like Norbert, Bernard is said to have possessed remarkable personal beauty. "His figure was perfectly proportioned, his manners elegant and dignified, his eye full of fire, his countenance sweet and gracious; his gait, his movements, his attitudes, his smile—all were modest, simple and noble; his speech was naturally elegant, impressive and persuasive. There was something in his whole person so amiable and so attractive that, according to the expression of one of his biographers, he was more dangerous to the world than the world to him." (p. 33.)

One day, on his way to visit his brothers, who were with the Duke of Burgundy, as he rode along, silently and in deep thought, the world with its perturbation and perpetual vicissitudes seemed to pass before him as a vain show, and suddenly a voice sounded in the depths of his heart—"Come to Me all you that labor and are heavy laden, and I will refresh you; take my yoke upon you and you shall find rest to your souls." At these words a heavenly longing took possession of Bernard's heart, and thrilled him to the very marrow of his bones. He stopped at the church door, entered, and, prostrate before the altar, poured forth his soul to God. This event, with all its circumstances, Bernard often recalled, and used to relate it to the monks of Clairvaux. "I am not ashamed to confess," said he, "that frequently, and especially at the beginning of my conversion ... etc." (p. 36.)

In the year 1113, Bernard, now twenty-three years of age,

---

[1] Cfr. "Life and Times of St. Bernard," by M. L'Abbé Ratisbonne, translated from the French, p. 18.

entered with thirty companions, the monastery of Citeaux, where a few years later he became abbot. From that time on the Order of Citeaux began to flourish and numerous other houses came into existence. One of these, the monastery of Foigny, in the diocese of Laon, was apparently the place where the two Saints first met. When this monastery was dedicated, Norbert was present, and, shortly after the dedication, we find Bernard in the company of Norbert at Laon, on the occasion of the transfer of St. Martin's Abbey to the Premonstratensians. St. Bernard with Drogo, Simon and other friends of Norbert, signed the solemn charter.[2] This meeting took place in the latter part of the year 1124, and was the beginning of a life-long friendship.[3]

Though their respective Orders were entirely distinct and separate, the Saints were ever closely united, for the life-aim of both was "Reform." They deplored the morals of their age, everywhere corrupted, and particularly those of the ministers of the Church, many of whom they led to a better life. Both were the antagonists of the able and brilliant Peter Abelard, and while Bernard was engaged in preaching missions to the simple people of Languedoc, Norbert was found in Belgium and the Low Countries engaged in the very same work.

Again, the schism caused by the antipope, Anacletus, found in Bernard as well as in Norbert, its most strenuous opponent, and as Norbert had been closely criticized, St. Bernard was also menaced by a storm of violence, and the most unjust reproaches pursued him even in his monastic cell. Bishops, alarmed at the power of a simple monk, denounced him at Rome, where the whole college of Cardinals even found fault with Bernard. The Pope himself alarmed at these complaints, ordered the celebrated Cardinal Haimeric, the

[2] Madelaine, o. c., p. 157, observes, that it seems beyond doubt that both Bernard and Norbert assisted at the Council of Soissons in 1121, and that consequently their friendship dates from that time. He relies on the Acta Sanctorum.

[3] Cfr. Histoire de l'abbaye de Foigny, p. 11.

Chancellor of the Roman Church, to remonstrate with St. Bernard.[4]

The mutual esteem and admiration of the two Saints is clearly evidenced in many of St. Bernard's well-known letters, from which we also incidentally learn how nobly Bernard assisted Norbert in the propagation of the new Order of Prémontré. Thus we read in a letter addressed to Geoffrey, Bishop of Chartres:[5]

> I am quite ignorant respecting the matter of which you inquire of me; namely, whether the Lord Norbert is about to go to Jerusalem. For when I saw him last, a few days ago, he said nothing of it to me, though I was honored in being permitted to drink in words from his mouth, as it were from a sweet-toned flute.

"High praise for Norbert," says Mabillon, "from such a man, especially since Bernard did not easily yield to any kind of imaginativeness!" It is certain that Bernard had at once recognized the Saint in Norbert, and took counsel of him on many occasions. Thus we read in the same letter: "But when I asked him what he thought concerning the Antichrist, he declared himself quite convinced that Antichrist was to be revealed during this generation, that is now . . ."[6]

Norbert, on his part, also found in Bernard a safe counsellor and guide, and it was through this mutual friendship that many customs of the Cistercians were introduced into the Premonstratensian Order. Thus the well-known "Charter of Charity," which in thirty articles, fixed the usages of the Cistercian Monks, was adopted by Norbert in its entirety. In fact, every observance of monks which

---

[4] Cfr. "Life and Times of St. Bernard," edited by Samuel J. Eales. Vol. I, p. 147.

[5] Ibidem. Letter 56. See also foot-note on this page wherein appear the above quoted words of Mabillon.

[6] We remarked above that many were persuaded Antichrist was on the point of appearing. They were led to believe this by the iniquity of the times and the appearance of many of the signs foretold by Christ. VandenElsen ob serves, however, that Norbert referred to the coming of the antipope, Anacletus, as the advent of the Antichrist

Norbert found to be compatible with the life of priests, he adopted and introduced into his houses. No wonder, therefore, that the friendship between the two Saints was very intimate, and that we see them side by side, continually fighting the great evils of the times. Neither can it cause much surprise that friends as well as enemies of these Saints named them in one breath.

We observed above how Abelard referred to both as the two apostles who were doing the work of his rivals, and doing it effectively. Rupert, a monk of Cluny, said sarcastically that all existing religious Orders had to make room for the rising Cistercian and Premonstratensian Orders.[7] Again, when the antipope, Anacletus, manifested a desire to enter into negotiations with the German Emperor, Lothaire, the latter sent, in concert with the Pope, St. Bernard and St. Norbert (then Archbishop of Magdeburg) to Anacletus. "But," observes the biographer of St. Bernard, "the two servants of God found the antipope so hardened in his pride that they soon gave up all effort of reconciliation."[8]

Special mention must be made of their friendly relations with Count Theobald, of whom we spoke above as the first member of Norbert's Third Order. Of the many letters written by St. Bernard, we find several addressed to Count Theobald. Thus one time he wrote to him about an unfortunate man, named Humbert, who had been vanquished in a duel, in consequence of which he was deprived of his eyesight and property by the order of Count Theobald. Be it observed that just at this time the Count was doing all in his power to repress entirely the fighting of duels, which was everywhere else tolerated by other princes. However, in this particular case the Count apparently misjudged, for it was said that Humbert was innocent. So the latter had made an appeal to St. Bernard, who in consequence wrote the Count several letters, and at the same time implored the assistance of all those whom he knew

[7] Rupertus Lib. IV, in Regulam S. Ben.

[8] St. Bernard by M. L'Abbé Ratisbonne, p. 197.

to have influence with the Count, in the poor man's behalf. How greatly he relied on Norbert's power, is shown in the following words: "I entreat you, then, by the mercy of God, that you pursue your good purpose, and not permit the wicked to boast that the poor man is ruined; rather take means for the fulfillment of the promise you have made to Dom Norbert and to me, that you would restore the patrimony of Humbert to his wife and children."[9]

How highly Bernard thought of Norbert's sanctity, appears from a letter written to Bruno, Archbishop-elect of Cologne: "And you have also the Lord Norbert, whom you may conveniently consult in person on all such subjects. For that good man is more fitted than I to explain the mysterious workings of Providence, as he is nearer to God by his holiness."[10]

"Norbert," observes Dr. Winter,[11] "was very closely united to St. Bernard. The letters of the latter give ample testimony of the esteem he had for Norbert. And undoubtedly we should be able to show Norbert's high appreciation of St. Bernard, were it not for the fact that his writings have been lost."

In the "Life and Times of St. Bernard," the following reference is made to St. Norbert, by the author, M. L'Abbé Ratisbonne (p. 221):

> "In this same year, and almost at the same time, the 6th of June, 1134, another friend of St. Bernard expired, in the full vigor of his age—his faithful fellow-laborer in Italy—the venerable Norbert, founder of the Premonstratensian Order. His various and intimate relations with the Abbot of Clairvaux, the great congregation of which he laid the first stone, and lastly, the edification which he afforded to his age, by his sanctity, his learning, and his labors, oblige us to enter into some details in this place concerning this great man..."

Then follows the life-story of our Saint, after which the author

[9] Cfr. Letters 33-35-38.

[10] Ibidem. Letter VIII.

[11] Cfr. "Die Praemonstratenser," p. 288.

continues, speaking of Norbert's Order:

> "This useful institution, closely allied to that of Citeaux, arose with almost equal rapidity. Bernard and Norbert, attentive to the needs of their time, mutually supported each other in their common efforts to supply them. Both, united in the pure desire of good, labored in the various Councils at which they assisted for the reestablishment of religion. They had recently united to extinguish the schism in Italy, and they had both resisted the pretensions of the antipope. . . . The death of Norbert, whose labors in Germany and Italy had so perfectly seconded the mission of the Abbot of Clairvaux . . . grievously affected the heart of St. Bernard . . . etc."

After our Saint's death, however, St. Bernard continued to evince affection for Norbert's Institute in various ways, and was ever solicitous about the welfare of the Premonstratensian Canons. He often sent letters to the different abbots giving them advice and assistance in maintaining religious discipline, and even in finding new recruits for the Order. He kept constantly in touch with them, and eagerly watched the development of Norbert's great undertaking. An illustration of this we find especially in one of Bernard's letters addressed to Norbert's first disciple, Blessed Hugh, then Abbot of Prémontré. Apparently there had been some misunderstanding between them, and the gentle answer of Bernard amply shows his interest in the Order.

"I have read," writes Bernard,

> "what you have heard of me, and I fear, for you write bitter things against me, but I hope with more severity than truth. What wrong have I done. Is it that I have ever loved your person, been kindly disposed to your Order, and helped whenever I could? If you believe not my words, let my deeds be my witness. Indeed, my conscience tells me that I ought to have been commended by you. But since you have seen fit to speak and write against me, I will lend power to my words from the testimony of my actions... It goes, indeed, against the grain. I may seem to be boasting of my good deeds, and this is not seemly; but you compel me to act as a fool. Whenever have you

or yours wanted my help and failed to receive it? In the very first place, the land of Prémontré, in which you are living, was formerly mine, and you had it as a gift from me.[12] For our brother Wido[13] (so the first inhabitants of the place called him) had given it to me through the bishop. Next, it was principally through my efforts, that the monks of Beaulieu[14] affiliated themselves with you. When king Baldwin was alive he gave me the place of the Holy Samuel at Jerusalem, and at the same time a thousand crowns with which to build; I gave you both the site and the money. Many know how hard I labored that you might have the church of St. Paul at Verdun; and you enjoy the fruit of my labor. If you do not admit this fact against you, my letters to Pope Innocent, of blessed memory, are in existence, as true judges and living witnesses to the truth of what I say. Your brothers of Sept-Fontaines hold from me the place which they occupy,[15] which the first inhabitants called Francs-Vals.

For which of these facts do you wish to leave your friends? Are you not returning evil for good? For you threaten to break your compact,[16] to sever the peace that there is between us, to give up

---

[12] Cfr. above p. 64.

[13] This Wido is referred to on p. 64 as Guy. We read of Wido, says S. Eales, in a foot-note to this letter, in the history of the monastery of Vicoigne, near Valenciennes (Spicil. Vol. XII, p. 534), where Wido or Guy, "a Breton by birth, a priest by office," is said to have lied at Prémontré at the time that Norbert went there, and to have given place to a greater than he, by retiring to Vicoigne, where he laid the foundations of a monastery which he put under the care of Walter of St. Martin of Laon, as Abbot.

[14] Beaulieu was a house of Canons Regular in the diocese of Troyes and was ceded to the Premonstratensians in the year 1140. Bernard's letter (407) was written to Odo, Abbot of Beaulieu.

[15] Sept-Fontaines was in the diocese of Langres.

[16] Manrique describes this agreement, which was entered into, in A. D. 1142, between the Cistercians and Premonstratensians for the sake of peace, as fixing two leagues between their monasteries and one between their granges or farms. Hence Bernard says, a little further in the letter, that the house of Basse-Font was outside the limits agreed on.

fellowship, to break our unity..."[17]

Although the above quotation, and in fact the whole long letter is a gentle rebuke to Abbot Hugh, it explains at the same time most fully how great Bernard's interest was in the welfare of the Premonstratensians. We shall now quote from another letter of St. Bernard, in which he highly appreciates the Premonstratensians. This letter was written, in 1142, to Milisendis, Queen of Jerusalem, daughter of king Baldwin, and wife of Fulk.[18]

> You see how greatly I presume on your goodness, since I venture to recommend others also to you. However, it would be as unnecessary as presumptuous, perhaps, for me to say much in commendation of these brethren of Prémontré, for they so commend themselves by their own merit that they have no need to be commended by another. They will be found, if I mistake not, to be men of wisdom, fervent in spirit, patient in tribulation, powerful in word and work. They have put on the whole armor of God and have girded themselves with the sword of the Spirit, which is the Word of God, not against flesh and blood, but against spiritual wickedness in high places. Receive them as warlike and yet peaceful; gentle towards men, warlike towards evil spirits. Rather, I should say, receive them as Christ Himself, who is the cause of their pilgrimage.

So closely united did these two great Orders of the twelfth century work side by side, that Lawrence of Liège in his "Lives of the Bishops of Verdun" likens the Orders of Citeaux and of Prémontré, to the two Cherubim which shadowed the Mercy Seat. He calls them the two famous Orders which by their zeal for souls have protected the Church in those evil days, and whose great influence can never be overestimated.[19]

---

17 This letter was written in the year 1150 and is in the collection of S. Eales No. CCLIII (253). The quotations as well as the foot-notes are taken from this collection. P. 735, et seq.

18 Letter CCCLV. (355) op. cit.

19 Spicii. V. XII, p. 325.

CHAPTER XI
THE WONDER-WORKER

De grege dum Saevus tenerum Lupus abstulit agnum,
Raptor cum praeda, Te revocante, redit.

Deseases fled thy touch; the famished came
And all were soothed by thee in Jesus' name.
More wondrous still, a wolf thou didst compel
To guard the trembling sheep. . . .

HAVING completed the great work of establishing the new foundations, Norbert again returned to Prémontré. It now pleased Divine Providence to confirm the work of the Saint by many miracles. Miracles indicate man's restoration to his primitive state and remind us of the power which he received in the very beginning over nature, which he was called upon to command, in the name of the Creator. On the testimony of the Apostle, this power may undoubtedly be regained by man: "For every nature of beasts, and of birds, and of serpents, and of the rest, is tamed, and has been tamed by the nature of man." (St. James' Epist. III.-7.) When divine love is reborn in man's soul, he finds in that love all knowledge, all virtue, all power. The kingly scepter is, as it were, restored to him. Such was St. Norbert; the world obeyed him, and the spirits of this world trembled at his voice; the fallen angels themselves bore witness to his sanctity and greatly feared him. Contemporary writers relate numerous incidents which attest this supreme authority. We cannot here relate them all, but will limit ourselves to a few. While they may, perhaps, provoke a smile from the incredulous, they will at the same time manifest to many others

Norbert's nearness to God.

We have seen how Satan endeavored from the very beginning to destroy the work which Norbert had so happily begun, and now he continued his attacks upon Prémontré, striving to frighten and discourage the religious. Thus we read that their sleep was almost nightly disturbed by violent shaking of the walls of the monastery or by forms of the most hideous creatures.

One night Norbert was absorbed in prayer in the little chapel of St. John, which chapel the reader no doubt remembers. A new temple had long since been erected, but the Saint experienced greater devotion in the poor little chapel, on account of the great things which had taken place within its walls. The night was far advanced when Norbert arose from prayer in order to give a short rest to his fatigued body. Suddenly he saw before him an ugly bear, his claws outstretched and his mouth wide open as if on the point of devouring him. For a moment the Saint seemed overcome by fright. He recalled the fact that he had locked the door of the chapel and had not heard the least noise. Realizing that it must be Satan, he offered a short but fervent prayer and made the sign of the Cross, saying: "What do you want, you cruel beast? Depart from here, I command you, in the name of Jesus Christ. You know that you can do no harm without the permission of God, and then to those only who, by their sins, are in your power." At these words of faith and authority the devil at once disappeared.[1]

Immanem Daemon fingit dum Callidus ursum.
Cogitur imbellem mox celerare fugam.

Norbert had power also over dumb animals, a phenomenon which we observe in the lives of so many saints. It is related that a young shepherd who used to watch the flock of the monastery, asked one day what he should do in case a wolf came to attack his sheep, since he had no dog. He was told simply to defend the sheep

[1] *Vita B*, Ch. XLI.

in the name of Norbert. The boy remembered this advice, and when some time later a wolf came and carried off one of the sheep, the boy shouted after him: "Thief! this is the flock of Master Norbert. I command you in his name to give up your prey." And in effect the wolf let loose the captive sheep. (*Vita B.* Ch. XXXIX.)

The valley of Prémontré resembled in very truth the earthly Paradise, wherein these fervent religious led innocent lives, and apparently they also had regained command even over dumb animals. Thus one day a young Brother was sent out to find the cattle that belonged to the monastery. As he was leaving the house, behold! a wolf appeared, and stepping to his side, not only accompanied the Brother, but was even of service to him in bringing the cattle together. Having returned to the monastery, and the cattle being safe in the stable, the Brother locked the doors and went away. The wolf did not seem greatly pleased with these proceedings. When the Brother left, the wolf began making a great noise, scratching all the while the stable-door. St. Norbert heard the noise and said to one of the Brothers: "Why do you not open the door for this traveler who asks our hospitality?" The Brother answered: "Father Norbert, this is no traveler but a wolf who wants to go into the stable." The Saint replied: "There must be some reason for this; tell me what happened to-day with the cattle." The young religious who had brought the cattle in was called to appear before Norbert and made to tell his experience. When he had told all, the Saint said: "See, that I am right. This wolf wants his wages. Give him something to eat." And, adds the early biographer, after this event, the same wolf was often seen accompanying the young Brother.[2]

Until the time of the seventeenth century, there was a tree kept in great veneration by the people, and called "The Tree of St. Norbert." According to popular tradition, the Saint himself had planted this tree. During five hundred years its foliage was always

---

[2] *Vita B*, Ch. XXXIX. Cfr., also P. Alph. de Liguori. Pp. 185-191.

green summer and winter.[3]

There is also found along the road between Anisy and Prémontré a spring of clear water, called until this day "The Well of St. Norbert." A supernatural power is still attributed to the water of this well, by the inhabitants of the surrounding country.[4]

However strange and miraculous the above occurrences seem to be, they are not more marvelous than the wonderful growth of the Order at this time. Prémontré, at the time of its foundation, may truly be compared to the grain, spoken of in the Gospel. Nothing, in fact, could have been weaker, humbler, more abject than this heavenly seed when it was first put into the field of the Church, but the principle of life was within it. Norbert's preaching and the exemplary lives of himself and his followers exercised an irresistible influence. Priests as well as illustrious laymen attached themselves to Norbert and flocked to his foundations. And well may we apply to Norbert's Order the words written by a biographer of St. Bernard: "How many learned men, how many orators, how many nobles and great ones of the earth, how many philosophers have passed from the schools or the academies of the world to the valley of Prémontré, to give themselves up to the meditation of heavenly things and the practice of a divine morality."

Prémontré had become at this time. a "training station," we might say, where hundreds came to enlist in God's army. Here they were practiced in religious discipline, and from here they were also sent out to different posts, the new foundations. Of the numerous foundations made at this time we shall speak presently, but first we shall accompany Norbert on a journey to Ratisbon.

The Saint's stay at Prémontré was not to be of long duration, for he soon found himself obliged to leave his dear valley in order to fulfill his promise to Theobald, Count of Champagne. The Count, as

---

[3] Cfr. Madelaine, o. c., p. 283, who further quotes Vander-Sterre "Vita," p. 408. DeWhagenaere, p. 33. De arbore a S. P. Norberto plantata.

[4] Cfr. VanderSterre, l, c. Notes of de Hertoghe, p. 405.

the reader remembers, never did anything of importance without the advice and direction of Norbert, and was now reminding him of his promise to find him a worthy spouse. When Theobald had offered himself to the Order, and Norbert had refused to accept him, for he knew that it was not the will of God that the Count should be received into the Order, he said that he would never marry anyone except the person designated by Norbert. (See above, p. 140.) Thus the object of Norbert's present journey was to negotiate for a marriage between Theobald and Mathilda, daughter of the Marquess of Crayburg and niece to the Bishop of Ratisbon.[5]

Norbert left Prémontré towards the end of the year 1125 in the company of one of his disciples with whom he usually traveled, Blessed Evermode. He was accompanied also by two deputies of Count Theobald. "Nevertheless," says Hugo,

> "his equipage had nothing of the worldly magnificence of an ambassador, for his humility caused him to observe the strictest rules of holy poverty. Clothed in an old white cassock, over which was thrown a large cloak, and riding on a donkey, he went through Champagne, Lorraine, Alsace and Wurtemberg in such a state of spiritual recollection that nothing distracted him. He spent his time in prayer, meditation and pious conversation with his companions."[6]

Arrived in Ratisbon, he at once went to the Bishop's palace. The Bishop at that time was Hartwic, whom Norbert had learned to know at the court of Henry V. It happened that on the day of Norbert's arrival at the Bishop's house, there was with the Bishop his brother, the powerful Count Engelbert, who had several grownup unmarried daughters. One of these was Mathilda, whom the Saint had selected for the Count of Champagne. When the Saint

---

[5] According to d'Arblois II, p. 263, Theobald was married in the year 1123, because his wife's name is mentioned in a charter of that year. However, there are good reasons to consider this date incorrect as the Charter is but a third copy and d'Arblois observes: "On est souvent en droit de se méfier de la date des diplomes dont on n'a pas vu les originaux."

[6] Cfr. Hugo, "La Vie de saint Norbert" Liv. III, p. 181.

had explained the object of his journey, both the Bishop and his brother most willingly gave their approval to the projected union, which would be as glorious to Mathilda as it was agreeable to Theobald. So Norbert dismissed the two deputies who had accompanied him and sent them back to Champagne to inform the Count of the result of his mission.[7]

He himself remained at Ratisbon, and for some time was the guest of the Bishop. Naturally, a soul so inflamed with zeal for missionary work as was the soul of Norbert, could not remain idle in a diocese where the spiritual wants were so great as were those of Ratisbon. Consequently, full of the spirit of God and of love for his neighbor, Norbert gladly acceded to the wishes of the Bishop, and began preaching in the neighboring towns and villages. The good results of his missionary work were at once apparent. He succeeded in bringing back a large number of sinners to the performance of their Christian duties, restored, as was his wont, peace between enemies, and in a very short time caused a genuine revival of the Catholic faith and its practices in that neighborhood. A great lord by the name of Albert, Count of Pogen, was so deeply touched by Norbert's preaching, and especially by his edifying life, that he not only resolved to change his course of life but even changed his castle of Vindeburg into an abbey of Norbert 's Order, which abbey existed until the middle of the fifteenth century.[8]

Prom the diocese of Ratisbon Norbert went over to the diocese of Augsburg, where among a large number of conversions, the most notable one was that of Verner, Count of Swabeck. To show his great esteem for the man of God, this count founded the abbey of

---

[7] Cfr. Rosenmund. "Les plus anciennes biographies de saint Norbert." Also "L'Histoire des Comtes de Champagne," par M. Arbois de Jubainville loc. cit.

[8] According to Madelaine, o. c., p. 306, this abbey at one time possessed no less than three hundred manuscripts of great value, but at present these are nowhere to be found.

Ursperg in Suabia. This abbey became well known, especially on account of its ninth abbot, Conrad of Liechtenau, who wrote the "Lives of the Saints," in twelve volumes, and also the "Chronicles of Ursperg."[9] It was also at this time,[10] that two noblemen from Spain, who had heard of the Saint and met him, now came to Prémontré and joined the Order. When these two disciples returned to Spain, fully imbued with the spirit of Norbert and his Institute, they there began propagating the Premonstratensian Order. Seventy years later, St. Dominic, the Founder of the Friar Preachers, will live in one of these foundations and freely borrow from the Premonstratensians whatever he finds suitable for his own Order, i. e., Rule, Habit, and to a great extent also the spirit of Norbert's followers. We therefore read in the Life of St. Dominic: "If we compare the plan of St. Dominic with that of St. Norbert, who had preceded the former by nearly a century, we shall find a very striking similarity between them."[11] Norbert finally left Ratisbon about the middle of January, 1126, without having fully attained his object, that of seeing Count Theobald married. Circumstances prevented the immediate celebration, as we shall see in the following chapter. The Saint meanwhile will make a journey to the Holy City. However, before accompanying Norbert on this journey to Rome, we must here especially notice his great love for the poor, which at this time he so constantly manifested.

A long drought, followed by a terrible winter, (1125-26) was causing untold suffering among the poorer classes, throughout the provinces, and St. Bernard as well as St. Norbert, at this particular time especially, did all in their power to relieve the sufferers. Both considered the wealth of the churches to be truly the patrimony of

---

[9] Ibidem. The "Lives of the Saints," written by Conrad, were consumed by fire, and his Chronicles were altered during the Protestant Reformation. Cfr. Hugo Ann. T. II. Ursperga.

[10] VandenElsen, o. c., p. 173.

[11] Cfr. "History of St. Dominic," by Aug. Drane, p. 163.

the poor, and so they helped them with a lavish hand in their hour of need. We read of St. Bernard that he had adopted as many as two thousand poor men, whom he marked with a particular sign, (*accepit sub signaculo*) pledging himself to suppprt them as long as the famine lasted.[12] Of Hugh of Grenoble we read that he sold the precious vases of his church in order to relieve the suffering. Neither did the rising Premonstratensian Order fail in its mission in these dreadful days. Norbert himself gave the example by begging bread for his beloved poor, and in his sermons he urged the great precept of charity, while his disciples in the different abbeys, imbued with Norbert's spirit, gave away whatever they had. We read, for instance, that the brethren at Cappenberg were actually suffering want in consequence of their liberality towards the poor. At Prémontré the same condition prevailed, and the Saint rejoiced exceedingly on finding this true spirit of self-denial among his brethren.

"Such was the noble use," observes the biographer of St. Bernard,

> "made of those riches which the frugality of the religious and the piety of the faithful caused to abound in monasteries. Religion, which makes itself all things to all men, administered the public funds during the minority of nations; she gave back as interest what she secured as capital; she received the superfluity of the rich to satisfy the wants of the poor; and, thanks to the monastic institutions, the evil of mendicity was never, in the Middle Ages, what it has become in our times."[13]

The famine passed, charity for the poor of the different abbeys continued to such an extent, that Norbert, charitable as he was, found himself obliged to regulate the zeal of the brethren. For this reason he prescribed the following rules, which were binding at all times on all the brethren of each and every abbey. A copy of them

[12] Neander "Histoire de saint Bernard," p. 14.

[13] Abbé Ratisbonne, o. c.. p. 111.

is still to be seen in the Public Library at Laon:

> In the name of the blessed and undivided Trinity. Amen. Of all that the brethren possess or acquire, one-tenth part is to be given to the poor; it is God's tenth. If the income of the house amounts to ten silver solidi, eighteen poor people are to be clothed of the one-tenth: eight during the winter, ten during the summer, one on each great feast day. Thus during the winter, one shall be clothed on the feast of All Saints; one on Christmas; one on the day of the Circumcision; one on Epiphany; one on the feast of the Purification of the Blessed Virgin; one on the day of the Annunciation; one on Holy Saturday and one on Easter. They shall receive new pieces of clothing, namely, a shirt, breeches, stockings, socks, shoes, a tunic, and a cloak with a cape, or with furs. The other ten poor shall be clothed in summer; one on the day of the Ascension; seven during the seven days of the week after Pentecost; one on the feast of the Apostles St. Peter and St. Paul, and the tenth on the day of the Assumption of the Blessed Virgin. As clothing they shall receive a cape, a shirt, breeches, socks and shoes. From the day that he receives his clothing, the poor man must, if he does desire, be kept in the 'Xenodochium' for eight days and be given his meals. If after this distribution has been made, something remains of the 'Tenth' of God, this money will be used for strangers and guests. On Holy Thursday every priest and deacon, after washing the feet of the poor, will give them for the sake of charity and with the consent of the superior, one piece of his own clothing, as his cape, or his fur, or his tunic. After this charity and the meal which will follow, the poor will not remain for seven days, but shall leave our monastery in peace.[14]

As is quite clear from the above remarkable ordinance, St. Norbert considered the poor as much his children as his disciples, and as far as possible, wanted them to be on a footing of equality. Norbert's love for the poor is further proved by the fact that many a time, before he was able to build a suitable place for the brethren

[14] MSS. in the Library of Laon. "Res Praemonstratenses." T. I. Matricula Ord., p. 182. Eleemosynae Norbertinae, ex vetustissimo Eccl. Praem. cartulario., p. III. No. 108. In nomine Sanctae, etc. Cfr. Le Paige, p. 394.

in a new foundation, he insisted on having a "Xenodochium," where his poor and sick could be properly cared for. Listen to the following maxims which Norbert never tired repeating to his disciples:

"To harbor poor people, and to share what we possess with them, is the source of abundant plenty.

"He who of his own free will has become poor for God's sake, ought never to complain when he is treated and clad like the poor.

"Having dwelt at Court and in the midst of wealth, I have learned by experience that there the heart is never satisfied, but that when far away from these, the heart is always at rest.

"Riches pass away, but holy poverty is a lasting good and a token of a happy eternity."

It was in this manner that Norbert by word and example enkindled in the hearts of his disciples so great a love for the poor that their generosity, many a time, exceeded their means. We read of the abbey of Cappenberg, that one day the brethren had absolutely no food in the house when the hour came for dinner. The Saint, who was there at the time, was notified of the fact, but undisturbed, he went to the refectory with the brethren and said the prayers as usual. When the brethren were seated, neighbors came, seemingly by chance, but rather led by Divine Providence, and brought food in abundance. "And," adds the biographer, "from that day forward the abbey was never in want, neither for the brethren nor for the poor."[15]

Truly, it is only the living faith of the saints and their childlike confidence in God's Providence that could inspire them with this noble spirit of self-denial. To share with the poor, not of one's abundance, but of one's necessities, and to do so constantly for higher motives—here is the real virtue of charity. And according to the words of the Savior: "Whatsoever you have done to the least of My brethren, you have done to Me," great will be the reward of those who practice it.

[15] Vita B, Appendix Cappenb. c. II.

CHAPTER XII
HIS SECOND JOURNEY TO ROME

Herbipoli gemino Matronae lumine cassae,
Afflatis tenebras jussit abire genis.

On Easter Sunday, at Wurzburg,
Norbert gave sight to a blind woman
by breathing on her eyes.
(Antiphon of the Office)

IT was about the middle of January, in the year 1126, when Norbert, in the company of three of his brethren, set out from Ratisbon for the Eternal City. The object of his journey was to obtain the Pope's approval of his Order, for although it had received the papal approbation through the Legates at Noyon, there was still persistent opposition to him and his Institute. The more the Order grew the more marked became the opposition, and now learned and powerful men had actually gone to Rome to influence the Pontiff against the Order.[1] The Saint, therefore, had determined to see and speak with the Holy Father personally, and to obtain His approbation, also his encouragement, such as he had received from his two illustrious predecessors, Calixtus and Gelasius. The present occupant of the St. Peter's Chair was Honorius II, who had been elected on Dec. 21, 1124.

According to VandenElsen, St. Norbert was also accompanied on this journey by the celebrated Augustinian Abbot, Gerhoch of

[1] Cfr. VandenElsen, o. c., p. 180.

Reichersberg, who occupied an important position in the German Church of the twelfth century.[2]

Winter was nearing its close when the Saint and his companions at last stood beneath the walls of the Eternal City. What were the feelings which must have animated Norbert's soul, when, on approaching Rome, his thoughts reverted to his former visit, fifteen years before! Then he was the vain young man, the proud courtier, and belonged to the household of one who had made the Pope a prisoner; now he is the penitent—the missionary—the spiritual father of a household of hundreds and hundreds of children entirely devoted to the cause of God's Representative.

Pope Honorius was a great patron of learning and virtue. He had listened to the critics of Norbert, but he had heard such praise of him and his Order, that he received the Saint with all possible marks of respect and veneration. In fact the two earliest biographers of the Saint point with legitimate pride to the great honor and marks of esteem which the Holy Father bestowed upon the man "who had already done so much for the welfare of the Church, and to whom the future would point as a savior."[3] The Holy Father at once recognized Norbert's sincere humility, admired his wisdom and sanctity of life, and saw in him the true reformer. In consequence he most willingly gave Norbert his blessing and encouragement, and the fullest confirmation of his Order.

Honorius gave the Saint three different "Bulls." The first, dated February 16, 1126, confirms the foundation of different abbeys. Another received by Norbert on the next day, refers to the Motherhouse of Prémontré alone. Both these "Bulls" were delivered

---

[2] Ibidem, p. 182. A description of the character and work of this celebrated Abbot may be found in the Appendix to the Letters of St. Bernard, edited by S. Bales, Vol. III, p. 194. In the same place is also found the letter he wrote to St. Bernard, and his Treatise respecting Simoniacs. VandenElsen further says that Gerhoch had been cited to Rome on account of indiscreet zeal.

[3] Cfr. Madelaine, o. c., p. 310.

to Norbert by Cardinal Haimeric, the great friend of St. Bernard. The third is dated February 27, 1126, and was also given at the Lateran. This third concerns the house of Cappenberg in particular, which it places under the special protection of the Holy See. The most important of the three is the first, by which the different foundations are confirmed in general. It reads as follows:

> Honorius, bishop, servant of servants of God. To our beloved sons, Norbert, our brother in Christ, and the canons of the church of St. Mary of Prémontré, and to their successors having made profession of the religious life, forever. Those who follow in the footsteps of the Apostles, renounce the pomp of the world and their possessions, and apply themselves with all their might to the service of God, if they will have persevered in the good work they have begun, they will receive, on the day of Judgment, the robe of immortality and eternal glory.
>
> Therefore, since you by the inspiration of divine grace have determined to live religiously and to lead a canonical life according to the Rule of St. Augustine, We confirm your Institute by the authority of the Apostolic See, and We exhort you to be firm and to persevere with a view of the remission of your sins.
>
> We decree that it is forbidden to any one to change the order established according to the Rule of St. Augustine in your churches, where the brethren live who have made profession of the canonical life; that no bishop dare, in the future, drive away the brethren of this religious order from your churches; that no brother having promised to lead the canonical life dare leave your churches or monasteries without the consent of the community. If he does leave, no bishop nor abbot nor monk may receive him unless he presents letters from the community.
>
> We further hereby also confirm the goods and possessions which you hold justly and legitimately, among which we have thought well to mention the following by name: The church of St. Martin at Laon, in the diocese of Laon; the church of St. Mary at Floreffe, in the diocese of Liège; the church of St. Mary and the Holy Apostles Peter and Paul at Cappenberg, in the diocese of Münster; the church of St.

Mary at Varlar, in the same diocese; the church of St. Annal, in the diocese of Metz;[4] the church of St. Michael at Antwerp, in the diocese of Cambray; the valley of Premontre from the place called Halierpré to the valley of Rohard, with the three adjacent valleys, and from the river going to Vois, according to the location of the valleys; the two parts of the tenth which you hold of the farm of Crespy from the bishop of Laon, and all that has been given to you in this same place by our beloved son Louis, King of France; the freehold of Clairefontaine, the freehold of Ramignies with the mill, three farms at Bolmont, a farm at Anisy with the mill, a farm at Fraisnes; at Souppy three and a half farms and the freehold called Bonnuel; at Soissons a house with vineyard and land; vineyards in Laonnais, Broiencourt, Wissignicourt and Montarcenne; and besides, all that you in the future through the concessions of pontiffs or the liberality of kings and princes, or through other honest means, may be able to acquire canonically, We desire that you and your successors who will remain firm in the profession you have embraced, possess in an unviolable manner.

We forbid any person to dare trouble your churches, to take your property, keep it, diminish it or trouble you by bold vexations. We ordain that your goods be kept entire to serve for the sustenance of the brethren and the poor, having regard, nevertheless, for the rights which belong to the diocesan bishops. If then in the future any person, be he an ecclesiastic or a secular, knowing this, Our regulation, will have acted in opposition to it, and if after two or three admonitions he refuses to give satisfaction, he shall be deprived of his authority and dignity; and he should know that he will have to appear one day before the Divine Tribunal to render an account of his iniquity. For the present he shall be excluded from all participation in the Body and Blood of our God and Redeemer, our Savior Jesus Christ, and on the final judgment day he shall be submitted to rigorous vengeance.

In regard to those, on the contrary, who will respect the right of

[4] In regard to the church of St. Annal, in the diocese of Metz, Madelaine observes that this church is not mentioned in any catalogue, and we read in MSS. of Hugo, T. I., p. 77: "Fatemur ignorare ubi steterit..." VandenElsen is of the opinion that the cathedral of Metz is meant, whose patron was St. Annal. Cfr. Madelaine, o. c., p. 3101, and VandenElsen, p. 185.

your churches, may the peace of Our Lord Jesus Christ be with them; may they receive in this life the fruits of their good works, and in the life to come, may they find the reward of an eternal peace. Amen.

> I, Honorius, bishop of the Catholic Church.
> Given from the palace of the Lateran by the hand of Haimeric, Cardinal-Deacon of the Holy Roman Church and Chancellor, XIV Kal. Mart. (February 16th). The year of the Incarnation of Our Lord, 1126, the second year of the Pontificate of Lord Honorius, Pope.[5]

Thus at last Norbert's wish was gratified in every respect. Christ's Representative had fully approved of and confirmed the work of the Saint, and thus silenced his enemies. One finds in the church of Mortain in the diocese of Constanz, a valuable painting representing this memorable scene, Norbert kneeling before Pope Honorius, who hands him the Bulls of approval and confirmation of the Premonstratensian Order."[6]

While at Rome, Norbert, in company with his three disciples, daily visited the tombs of the Apostles and the many places

---

[5] Le Paige, Biblioth. Ord. Praem., p. 392. It is to be noticed that not all Premonstratensian Foundations are named in this Bull. Madelaine observes (p. 310) that the only reason for this was a lack of definitive organization in the places omitted. However, VandenElsen says that the Saint did not possess the houses of Cuissy, Steinfeld nor Mont-Cornillon, but that these had taken upon themselves to follow the rules of the Premonstratensians without abdicating the right to their properties. He further continues that in virtue of the Bull of 1124, given by the Legates, the sons of Norbert were canonically ranged among the canons regular, living under the Rule of St. Augustine. The Bulls of 1126 confirm the former and recognize their houses and lawful possessions. He further adds that only since 1131 the Premonstratensian Order has been recognized by another Papal Bull as an Order separate and distinct from all other Orders of canons regular.
In regard to the third Bull (see above p. 191), this same author, quoting "Analectes pour l'histoire eccl. de Belgique," XII, p. 35, says that the Bull approving and confirming the abbey of Floreffe, was received by Norbert on March 4th.

[6] Madelaine, o. c., p. 307.

consecrated by the blood of the martyrs, as St. Lawrence, St. Agnes, St. Cecilia. The thought of what these holy apostles and martyrs had suffered and done for the glory of God and of the Church, filled him with a burning desire to work and suffer like them. Almighty God will soon grant him this desire, but in a manner wholly unexpected by the Saint.

It happened that one day, when Norbert and his companions were in prayer and meditation, all distinctly heard a voice intimating that Norbert was soon to be bishop of Parthenopolis (Magdeburg). When they arose from prayer not one dared to speak of the incident, for although all had heard the same prophetic words, they were afraid to think of any separation, and therefore kept the secret, each in his own heart. It was sad news for all, but Norbert especially was overpowered by grief at the thought: first, of the dignity and responsibility; and, secondly, of the consequent separation from his brethren, for never for a moment did the Saint doubt the reality of this prophecy.[7]

Having received for the last time the apostolic blessing from Pope Honorius for himself and his brethren, Norbert left Rome, eager to return to his brethren and communicate to them the great favors he had obtained from the Sovereign Pontiff. One of his companions he sent by way of France to inform Count Theobald of his return. The Count had been anxiously awaiting him in order to be able to complete the arrangements for his marriage with Mathilda.

Norbert himself made the journey once more by way of Germany, preaching in the towns through which he was obliged to pass. Everywhere Almighty God blessed the word of His apostle, and not only did he succeed in making numerous conversions, but he also was enabled to make different new foundations, and thus perpetuate his noble work. He founded not far from Nemmingen, the monastery of Roth in the diocese of Constanz, through the

[7] *Vita* Pertz, Ch. XV. Manifeste auditum est quod Pathenopolis futurus esset antistes. . . . Vita B, Ch. XXXIV.

generosity of Henna, baroness of Wildenberg. Burchard became its first superior, and few monasteries in Germany have exercised greater influence than this foundation. It became the mother of other houses, one of which, the abbey of Witten near Innsbruck, is in a flourishing condition to-day.[8]

The abbey of Roggenburg in the diocese of Augsburg, situated two miles from Ulm, was also founded at this time. The monastery of Ursperg, only recently founded, sent there the first religious. In the seventeenth century this abbey of Roggenburg was especially known for its rich and excellent library. Like most of Norbert's foundations, it also had a convent for nuns nearby, which convent existed over two hundred years.[9]

Although wherever Norbert went the people were always greatly edified at what they saw and heard, no town felt the effect of Norbert's zeal and charity more than Wurzburg. At the time of the Saint's arrival the place was in mourning for the death of its bishop, Rudger. Although the good bishop had died the year before, the people now more than ever felt their great loss, for a young cleric, Gebhard of Henneburg, unworthy as he was, tried to raise himself to this episcopal see. However, as we learn from a letter written by the Pope, on March 4th, Gebhard's candidacy had been rejected. We have reason to suppose that Norbert came to Wurzburg with a particular mission from the Holy Father regarding this matter, since his coming was known in the place. Upon his arrival clergy as well as laity went out in large numbers to meet him, and urgently requested him to celebrate the sacred functions

---

[8] Cfr. Cath. Encyclop., Vol. XV. "Weissenau," another daughterhouse of the Abbey of Roth.

[9] Cfr. Suevia Ecclesiastica, p. 722. Also Annal. Ord. Praem., T. II, col. 697, et seq. "Rothum" and "Roggenburgum."

during Holy Week and Easter.[10]

When on Easter Sunday the Saint was celebrating High Mass in the cathedral of Wurzburg before a large assembly of people, a miraculous cure at once convinced all the people of his sanctity. They had already, no doubt, a great opinion of his holiness, for, says the biographer, during this Solemn Function a blind woman was carried before the altar. She was known to all, and great was the people's expectation when after the Communion of the Mass, she loudly begged the Saint to restore her sight. Norbert, touched with compassion and seeing her great faith, went to her immediately, as if driven by a divine impulse. After a fervent prayer he breathed on her eyes, and who can describe the enthusiasm of the people when, to the great astonishment of all, the woman instantly recovered her sight.[11]

This great miracle witnessed by the whole city, deeply touched the hearts of all, and greatly increased their veneration for Norbert, who used this popularity to make his preaching more effective. His holiness was proclaimed everywhere, and people said of him that by the breath of his mouth he made the blind to see, and by the unction of his words he opened the eyes and touched the hearts of the most obdurate sinners. Two of the most prominent men of the town, Canon John and his brother Henry, were so deeply impressed by Norbert's sermons and so much edified by his simple manner of life, that both renounced the world, joined the Saint in his apostolic work, and with their property founded the abbey of Oberzel, situated one mile outside the city of Wurzburg. This foundation, though at first nothing but a small oratory in honor of St. Michael, prospered greatly under the management of John, who in due time

---

[10] VandenElsen, o. c.,_ p. 189, who further quotes W. Bernhardi, p. 108, and Hefele, V. 442.

[11] Cfr. *Vita B*, Ch. XXXIV. *Vita*, Pertz, Ch. XV. Pertz VI. Sigeb. contin. Praem., p. 449—the Office of St. Norbert and further every biographer of the Saint.

became its first superior. The monastery was built later, a little further away, and was then called Unterzell. Pope Innocent II solemnly confirmed this foundation, on the 20th of February, 1133.

Soon the Saint no longer felt at ease in the city of Wurzburg. The great miracle was on the lips of all, and the people were so enthusiastic and so full of admiration for Norbert, that they proclaimed him their new bishop, adding that such was plainly the will of God.

Therefore Norbert and his companions, fearing lest the prophetic words heard at Rome, might already be verified, secretly fled from the city, and resumed their journey homeward.

Leaving Germany the Saint had to pass through Lorraine. The Duchy of Lorraine was then governed by Simon, son of Thierry-le-Vaillant. The duke went out to meet the Saint and begged the illustrious traveler to make a stay at his castle of Prény, where in consequence Norbert and his companions were received with the greatest ceremony.[12] Thanks to the generosity of this Count there was founded here the abbey of Sainte Marie-au-Bois, which abbey Norbert placed under the direction of Richard, one of the early disciples of Laon, who wisely governed the house for nearly thirty years. During the seventeenth century this abbey was the place where a reform of the Order to its original strictness, was inaugurated by Abbot Servace de Lairvelz.[13]

The month of May was nearly over when Norbert arrived again at his dear Prémontré. We can better imagine than describe his joy on entering the house of his choice, after this long absence. And when he beheld once more his beloved disciples, and related to them the great success he had met with everywhere on his

---

[12] The ancient registers of the castle describe the order of ceremonies and also contain a list of the expenses made by Simon, Duke of Lorraine, for this festive reception of Norbert. Cfr. Hugo "Vie de Saint Norbert," p. 191.

[13] According to Hugo, o. c., p. 194, this abbey, which in the seventeenth century was transferred to Pont-á-Mousson, is being used today as a small seminary.

journey—when he told them of his reception at Rome where he received the Pope's confirmation of the Order, and when he further imparted to them the apostolic blessing of the Pontiff . . . how fervently all must have thanked and praised God for His great goodness towards them!

On the other hand, the soul of Norbert was deeply moved at the dire distress in which the brethren were on account of their great charity for the poor during the famine. True, they had been able to supply daily 500 poor people with the necessities of life, but only by observing the strictest fast themselves. Norbert found them all emaciated and pale, and truly deserving of compassion. He consoled them, therefore, with those sweet and tender words which so spontaneously flowed from his heart.

Once back in the quiet of the monastery, Norbert was perfectly happy and busied himself with the affairs of the house, and especially with the instruction of the brethren morning and evening. In explaining to them the spirit of the Order, which was union of the active and contemplative life, Norbert insisted on the practice of monastic virtues no less than on the study of the Scriptures, which, as future missionaries, they could never know too well. An extract of one of these allocutions of Norbert to his disciples has come down to us and is as follows:[14]

> My dear children, never be tired of studying these writings, in which you find a short exhortation to remain faithful in the service of God. For the Word of God is fiery, as the prophet says: it is inflamed with the fire of the Holy Ghost; it consumes vices and promotes virtue; it bestows wisdom on well disposed men, and provides for them heavenly food. Therefore Our Savior has said: Blessed are they who hear the Word of God and keep it. In this manner also Mary Magdalen, by listening attentively and devoutly to the Word of God, is said to have chosen the best part, which Martha, so solicitous in her

[14] Sermo Sancti Norberti, taken from the "*Vita*" by Abbot Van der Sterre (1630).

outward administrations, was not able to obtain. Listen, therefore, cheerfully to the Word of God, keep it judiciously and observe it faithfully, in order that at the end of time you may rejoice to hear these consoling words of Christ: Come ye blessed of My Father, possess you the kingdom prepared for you from the foundation of the world. (Matt. XXV. 34.)

St. Norbert is Consecrated a Bishop

CHAPTER XIII
FAREWELL TO PRÉMONTRÉ

Tempora Norberti nunc Magdeburgica cingit
Inter Teutonicas Infula prima Mitras.

Norbert, Champion of the Lord,
Vowed to lead with fearless word
His warriors on, Magdeburg is seeking thee—

WHILE busily engaged in the training of young religious at Prémontré, Norbert was not less watchful in regard to the other houses. Up to this time all the foundations were governed by simple superiors, without either the title or dignity of abbot. Now, however, his first care was to make preparations for the solemn benediction of two abbots: Gautier for the monastery of St. Martin at Laon, and Henry for the house at Viviers. Bishop Bartholomew conferred the abbatial dignity upon Gautier, and Lisiard, Bishop of Soissons, upon Henry.[1] Thus were Gautier and Henry the first disciples of Norbert to receive the dignity which the saint himself refused. They were abbots, however, without either ring or mitre, they bore only the crozier as the symbol of the authority they had over their subjects.[2] In 1225, the Provost of St. Mary's at Magdeburg received from Pope Gregory IX authorization to wear the mitre and other episcopal insignia. Other abbots also have asked for this privilege, and the

[1] Cfr. *Vita B*, Ch. XXXV. Also Pertz VI. Sigeb. Contin. Praem., p. 449.

[2] Cfr. Hugo "Annales Ord. Praem." T. I. Praefatio IX.

custom has become general.[3]

At the urgent request of many bishops new colonies were constantly sent out from Prémontré at this time, and numerous foundations made. The practice of the Saint, previously referred to, namely, of incorporating into the Order existing houses of secular canons, greatly increased the number of Norbert's disciples. In this manner the houses of Viviers, Cuissy and Braine had already become Premonstratensian abbeys, and it was at this time that the abbey of Steinfeld adopted Norbert's rules and constitutions. This abbey, situated but a few miles from the city of Cologne in the valley of "Eifel," had for some years been inhabited by canons regular of Springirsbach, who now, upon the advice of Frederic, Archbishop of Cologne, sought from Norbert the favor of affiliating themselves to this Order. The superior of the canons was appointed Provost of the community by Norbert, and he obtained in 1126 from Pope Honorius II confirmation of the church and monastery of St. Mary of Steinfeld, it being now a Premonstratensian foundation.[4] This superior's name was Evervinus of Helfenstein. We read of him in the works of St. Bernard. He wrote a letter to St. Bernard about the heretics infesting the diocese of Cologne, and this letter became the occasion of two of St. Bernard's sermons.[5]

---

[3] Be it observed here that there always has been some difference between the houses in Germany and those in other countries in regard to the title of the superior. The German superiors were never called abbots, but provosts. As early as 1146, all superiors of the Order were permitted by a Bull of Pope Eugenius III, to receive the abbatial benediction but did not make use of the privilege until 1225. Cfr. Madelaine, o. c., p. 317.

[4] Cfr. Hugo Annals, T. II. Steinfeldia, col. 851, et seq. Miraeus, Chron. Ord. Praem., p. 45, ad annum 1126.

[5] Sermons LXV and LXVI (of St. Bernard) thus says S. J. Bales, which begin from the exposition of that verse, "Take us the little foxes" (ii, 15), the Saint composed against the heretics of Cologne, having been induced to do this by a letter written to him by Everwin, provost of Steinfeld, which letter he seems on that account to have placed at the head of those two sermons. "Works of St. Bernard," Vol. IV, p. 4. The letter is also found in

The abbey of Steinfeld is, moreover, well known on account of Blessed Herman Joseph, the popular Saint for youth. When only twelve years old, Bl. Herman Joseph became a postulant in this monastery. This was in the year 1162. He died 79 years later, having been throughout his life an example of piety and obedience, and above all a child of Mary, favored by her in a most wonderful manner.[6]

In the preceding chapter we observed that Norbert, when leaving the city of Rome, had sent one of his companions to Count Theobald to advise him of Norbert's return. So about this time a messenger from the Count came to Prémontré requesting the Saint to accompany Theobald to Ratisbon, to conclude negotiations for the intended marriage. This messenger seems to have been the Bishop of Chartres himself, who was a friend of both Theobald and Norbert. We infer this from the fact that, at this time the Saint informed Bishop Geoffrey of his vision in regard to his future bishopric. Although Norbert knew not how nor where, he was convinced that it was to come that year, and since the see of Magdeburg was vacant at the time, he told the bishop in confidence why he feared to undertake this journey.[7] On the other hand, however, Norbert knew how much he owed to the generous Count Theobald, and that moreover he himself had been instrumental in bringing about the coming marriage. Thus when the Count himself

---

the same volume, p. 388, and shows plainly that Everwin was the apostle of Cologne as Norbert was the apostle of Antwerp. In the first vol., p. 66, Eales observes: "I have not the least doubt that these heretics of Cologne were produced in the workshop of Tanchelm."

[6] Cfr. Life of Bl. Hermann Joseph by Wilfrid Gallway, where it is also stated (p. 18) that the once famous monastery of Steinfeld is no more, but that a reform school has been erected on the place where the old abbey stood.

[7] This fact is stated in the Acta SS. (T. XX, p. 853) as follows: "Colloquens familiari suo Domino Godefrido Canotensis urbis episcopo, dixit ei se per visum cognovisse quod ipso anno futurus esset episcopus.. . ." Cfr. also Hugo "La Vie de saint Norbert," p. 202.

came to Prémontré and insisted, the Saint no longer refused, although filled with strange forebodings.

Norbert seemed to know that he was to leave Prémontré for good, and was sad at heart. Having received Norbert's promise, Count Theobald left Prémontré, and no sooner was he gone than the Saint called the religious together and addressed them in the most tender words, as a father speaking to his children for the last time. This allocution, by some called the Sermon of St. Norbert, by others his "Farewell Address," has happily been preserved.[8] It forms Norbert's spiritual testament to his beloved children, whose sadness and bewilderment on this occasion, can better be imagined than expressed. As tears and sighs expressed the grief of the inhabitants of Miletus on the departure of St. Paul, the Apostle, so now at Prémontré did sorrow find expression in tears and sighs. Although the exhortation might seem rather lengthy to insert here, still it is so clear a reflection of Norbert's soul, that we can not refrain from giving a translation:

> We exhort you, dearest brethren, to be most diligent in the service of God, to Whom you have consecrated yourselves by the solemn profession of your vows. For, having of your own free will and for the love of God renounced your earthly possessions, and also your entire selves, you are obliged daily to carry the Cross of Christ: that is, you are obliged continually to mortify your passions and spend your days in works of penance, suffering patiently the trials which will not fail to come to you from all sides.
>
> This indeed, is the narrow road to heaven, our true country. This is the road which Jesus Christ has pointed out to us by His life and

[8] Cfr. Hugo, o. c., p. 202-206 who speaks of this address as a letter which Norbert sent to the canons later. The early biographer says plainly "Valefaciens autem fratribus suis." *Vita A*, Ch. XVI. Cfr. also VanderSterre "*Vita S. Norberti*," pp. 261-270. Sermo . . . Fath. Jerome Hirhaim, Abbot of Strahov, Prague, has paraphrased this address in his instructions to the religious. "Sermo S. Norberti enucleatus" in fol. 1676. Cfr. Madelaine, o. c., pp. 322-326.

His death, His words and His deeds, and which infallibly leads to their heavenly country all who persevere to the end in that path. You cannot go to Christ unless you enter upon this narrow road with courage and confidence, and do your best to follow it. An Apostle has said: "For he also that striveth for the mastery, is not crowned except he strive lawfully;" (II. Tim. II. 5.) and another: "He that saith he abideth in Him, ought himself also to walk, even as He walked." (I St. John II. 6.) Walk therefore cautiously in the way which God has shown you, lest you be overtaken by death. Let your obedience be prompt, your poverty voluntary, and your chastity above suspicion. Without these three virtues, that which constitutes our Order is wholly destroyed.

You have promised stability or perseverance in this holy place; remain, therefore, faithful in the service of God, and never grow weary of your duties in the monastery. Never leave except when you are obliged to do so on account of temporal affairs, and in case of necessity, lest these useless excursions rob you of the sweetness of a virtuous life and of the consolation which you find in meditating on the divine mysteries; and lest also these excursions lead you astray and cause you to love the wicked world wherein there is no place free from corruption. For, as a fish out of the water is entirely deprived of its natural and necessary element, and hence soon dies, so a vagrant religious frequently found in the midst of a wicked world, deprived as he is of the protection of the cloister, far away from the example and salutary lessons of his brethren, soon falls into sin and gets entangled in the snares of everlasting death. Flee, therefore, my dearest brethren, the company of worldly persons as a fish avoids a dry place, but love the cloister which protects you and keeps the mind pure. For you make an unworthy use of the glorious name of your religious vocation, if by your earthly desires you show that you are more attached to the world than to God.

Remain, therefore, constantly in the monastery, and remain there united by the bonds of charity. Keep a particular watch over your tongue in order that by avoiding murmuring, detraction and envy, you may all have, in the words of our Rule, one heart and one soul in the house of the Lord. For a slanderous and deceitful tongue is a restless evil and full of deadly poison. It never ceases to do harm and to destroy the sweet peace of the monastery, and unnerve the piety of the community. It is therefore commonly said of those: "A quarrelsome and grumbling monk is never a true monk."

Therefore I repeat, put a restraint upon your tongue. Raise up your hearts to the kingdom of heaven where true joys are to be found. Animated by holy desires take your flight with the saints in the regions above in the contemplation of the divine mysteries. Bear with grief the burden of your bodies, so that you may say with the Apostle: "I desire to be dissolved and to be with Christ," (Phil. I. 3) and with the Psalmist: "Bring our souls, O Lord, out of the prison of our bodies." (Ps. CXLI. 8.) And thus you will reign eternally with Christ, Who reads our innermost thoughts.

Though outwardly fairly clad with the white habit—a symbol of simplicity and innocence—but inwardly miserable, deprived of the spirit of religious perfection, should any one of you not observe the discipline of the Order, but despise the wholesome lessons of his superior and even perhaps the superior himself, let him remember that the thoughts of our hearts are known to God, and that, unless he repent in time, he will not escape the eternal torments of hell wherein there is no order, but where an everlasting confusion dwelleth.

Endeavor, therefore, to avoid the terrible judgments of God by constantly doing His will in fear and righteousness, in order that God may keep you in holy religion, and that in His mercies He may preserve you from everlasting punishment in hell. God will abundantly reward those who are faithful in His service, for God gives a great reward for a small service, as He Himself promised His disciples, who having abandoned all they had, asked what should be their reward: "You shall receive a hundredfold and possess life everlasting." (Mat. XIX. 29.) May Jesus Christ lead you there. Amen.

After this exhortation, having impressed once more on the minds of the brethren the necessity of practicing charity towards the poor and the sick, Norbert gave over to Hugh the government of his dear monastery. He then mounted his donkey and took the road to the castle "Chateau Thierry" where Count Theobald impatiently awaited his coming. That God might bless the object of their journey, Norbert induced the Count to receive the Sacraments of Penance and the Holy Eucharist.[9] Finally, towards the end of the month of June, all started on their way to Ratisbon.

The Count was escorted by his court and, surrounded by several members of the nobility, was advancing with great pomp and splendor. Norbert was riding on his donkey, accompanied by two of his brethren with whom he spent the time in prayer and pious conversation. According to a plan prearranged by the Bishop of Ratisbon and Norbert, the bridal parties were to meet on the border of Germany.[10] Think of the great disappointment of all, when on reaching the place, they were met, not by the Marquess of Crayburg and his daughter Mathilda, but by deputies who were sent to inform them of the serious illness of the bride. This sad intelligence was a terrible trial for the Count and his friends; the more so because some of his party expressed their doubts about the illness of the princess, and saw in it an excuse for breaking the engagement.

After holding counsel among themselves, it was decided that Norbert was the only man able to assist the count in the unpleasant situation, and he was to do this by going himself to Ratisbon, to ascertain what were the real conditions. Norbert, seeing the reasonableness of the request, for the Saint himself was greatly perplexed, consented to the proposal, and the Count gave him eight silver marks to defray the expenses of this journey. The money, however, Norbert at once dispatched to Prémontré, where he knew it was greatly needed for the poor.[11] He thus undertook the journey as he always did, without money, but with a great confidence in Divine Providence.

Be it observed here in a few words that Norbert never really

---

[9] Cfr. Madelaine, o. c., p. 330. Hugo, o. c., p. 210.

[10] VandenElsen says that the meeting was arranged for the city of Metz; he bases his opinion on Hermann and on Hugo, who on p. 191 speak even of the great banquet prepared here for this occasion. VandenElsen, o. c., p. 194.

[11] Cfr. Hugo, "La Vie de saint Norbert," p. 213.

fulfilled this mission, for the princess had truly been indisposed on her way to Metz. After she recovered, all took place as prearranged. The Count and Mathilda were happily joined in the bonds of matrimony, probably by Norbert himself.[12]

On his way to Ratisbon Norbert was obliged to pass through the city of Spires, where at that time a solemn Diet of Bishops and German princes was being held under Lothaire III. The news of Norbert's arrival soon spread through Spires, and Lothaire, having heard so much of his numerous miracles and heroic virtues, expressed a wish to see him and consult him in regard to some important affairs which were being treated at the Diet. How accidental it all seemed, and yet we shall soon see clearly that it was the work of Divine Providence.

There were present at the Diet, first of all, two Legates of Pope Honorius, Cardinal Gerard, who afterwards occupied St. Peter's Throne under the name of Lucius II, and Cardinal Peter of the title of St. Marcellus. Besides, there was Adalbert, Archbishop of Mainz; Albero of Metz, afterwards Bishop of Treves, and a number of bishops, abbots and nobles. Then there was, and this is most important to know, a large deputation of clergy and laity from Madgeburg, who had come to solicit from the papal Legates and King Lothaire a successor to Archbishop Rudger, who had died, Dec. 20th, 1124. Thus far there had been a disagreement whenever an election had taken place for a successor. In fact, things were in such a state in Magdeburg that King Lothaire had celebrated Easter in that place in order that by his presence and authority he might

[12] Thus VandenElsen, p. 195. We further know that out of this union were born ten children, some of whomare well- known persons in history. Thus the eldest son, Henry, who married the daughter of the King of France, went twice to Jerusalem with the Crusaders, and his son became King of Jerusalem, in 1205. The fourth son became an Archbishop and even Cardinal and Legate of the Roman Church in Gaul. His name was William. It was in order to gratify his wishes that Alexander III conferred on the see of Rheims the right of consecrating the French King. Confer H. d'Arblois de Jubainville. S. Eales, op. cit., p. 769. (Vol. II.)

bring them to an agreement, but without success. Now these deputies had come to Spires in order to try to settle affairs before this solemn assembly.[13] This question was just being treated when the Saint's arrival was announced.

Norbert was well known to all these dignitaries, since his disciples were represented in the dioceses of nearly all the bishops present. Again, the great miracle of Wurzburg, where the Saint had restored the sight to a blind woman, was still fresh in the memory of all, for Wurzburg is in the neighborhood of Spires. No wonder therefore that Norbert's arrival was hailed by every one as the coming of a man sent by God to help them solve their difficulties. He was at once asked to speak, and took for his subject the very difficulty that occupied the minds of all. He spoke of the duties of superiors, the obedience of subjects, and thus came to the government of churches and the election of its pastors.

His persuasive eloquence produced marvelous results, say the biographers, and soon the election for the see of Magdeburg was taken up with great earnestness. By one faction, Conrad of Querfurt had really been elected, but his election had for different reasons not been confirmed. However, he was again a candidate with Albero of Metz. When after the first election the ballots were counted, Norbert, who was unaware of his having been proposed as a candidate, heard to his great consternation, his own name mentioned several times. Trembling with fear he decided to leave at once, and protested with all his might. His departure was prevented, however, and what is more, suddenly Albero of Metz arose in the assembly and declared openly that Norbert was the future bishop by God's choice, and that it was useless to deliberate any longer.[14] At this moment all present arose and proclaimed Norbert as the new

[13] Cfr. Hertel "Leben des H. Norbert." Also Tenckhoff. p. 29. Further Chron. Gratiae Dei—Ann. Saxon. VI, 763 ad annum, 1126.

[14] Cfr. Acta SS. T. XX, p. 854. Also Pertz Gesta Alberonis (VIII). . . . Suis effecit ingeniis Albero quod domnus Norbertus, vir famosae religionis, eamdem ecclesiam regendam suscepit.

Archbishop of Magdeburg. Again Norbert tried to escape from the hall, but the deputies of Magdeburg followed him and carried him in triumph before the papal Legates and King Lothaire, crying: "Him we want for our Bishop and Father."[15]

Norbert, with tears in his eyes, entreated both the Legates and the King not to confirm this election. But it was all in vain; on the contrary, the Legates as well as the King made use of all their authority to oblige Norbert to yield. The Legate, Cardinal Gerard, arose then in the assembly and spoke these solemn words: "And We, in the name of the Father, of the Son, and of the Holy Ghost, We elect and name for your Bishop, Master Norbert, a man of tried virtue, whom God, We are fully convinced, has sent here for this purpose."

Norbert then submitted to what he was now convinced was God's holy Will. And thus was fulfilled the prophecy made to his mother Hadwigis, at the time of his birth, and also the prophetic words heard in Rome.

Wonderful indeed are the ways of Divine Providence! The Saint had been detained on his way to Ratisbon, whither he was going to find a bride for Count Theobald, and God had prepared a spiritual bride for himself in the church of Magdeburg. The chronicler of Brandenburg concludes the description of the above events with these words: "Thus the emperor himself had proclaimed Norbert as Archbishop; the Legates in the name of Pope Honorius confirmed the nomination in the midst of loud acclamations of all the representatives of the church of Magdeburg."[16] "And," says the chronicler Hermann, "A Te Deum was solemnly intoned to thank God for this unforeseen but happy turn of events."

Kneeling before the King, Norbert then received the pectoral

---

[15] *Vita B*, Ch. XLII. "Hunc in Patrem eligimus; hunc pastorem nostrum approbamus." Cfr. Pertz VI. Sigeb. Contin. Praem. ad annum 1127. The indication of the year, observes Madelaine, is without doubt a mistake, since it is certain that this event took place in the month of July, 1126.

[16] *Vita A*, Ch. XVI.

Cross,[17] while Cardinal Gerard addressed him with these words: "By the authority of Almighty God, the Holy Apostles Peter and Paul and of Lord Pope Honorius, I command you no longer to resist this call from God. As a faithful and prudent servant, administer the treasures of the Word of God which are confided to you, that on the great day of the Lord you may hear these consoling words: 'Well done, faithful servant, enter into the joy of the Lord'."

Norbert now took leave of the Legates and the King, and poured forth his heart in prayer to God. Kneeling before His altar, the Saint shed an abundance of tears. The recent events seemed like a dream to him, and the thought of his future dignity and responsibility made him suffer a veritable agony. When he arose from prayer he said: "Not my will, but Thy will be done, O God," and with these words he was consoled and strengthened.

---

[17] Ibidem: Ad imperatoris genua humiliatus, virgam pastoralem, quae quasi in manibus ejus inserebatur, accipere coactus est. . . .

THIRD PERIOD

From the time Norbert becomes Archbishop until his death

1126-1134

FIDE ET PATIENTIA.
FIDES.
PATIENTIA.
SANCTVS NORBERTVS
Candidi Præmonstratensium Canonicorum Ordinis
Antesignanus et Parens, Antuerpiæ Apostolus,
Archiepus Magdeburgensis, totiusq; Germaniæ Primas.

CHAPTER I
THE ARCHBISHOP

Nudipes ignaro fert a Custode repulsam,
Ad Magdeburgensem dum trahitur Cathedram.

Norbert is escorted to the Magdeburg Cathedral, but being clothed in the garment of poverty, and barefooted, he is refused admittance by the doorkeeper.

WHILE the Saint was still at Spires, solemn preparations were made for his departure and subsequent entrance into Magdeburg. The people first of all prevented Norbert from going to Ratisbon in person, and obliged him to delegate one of his disciples to terminate the affair of Count Theobald. They further sent messengers to Prémontré and other abbeys announcing the great news of Norbert's election, and, to show their great respect for the Saint, they made festive preparations for his departure. Thus it happened that on one bright morning in the month of July, a great number of people had assembled in the streets of Spires to receive the Saint's last blessing. Otto, Bishop of Halberstadt, and Ludolph, Bishop of Brandenburg, both suffragan bishops of Magdeburg, were present to accompany their new Metropolitan, and great was the enthusiasm of all when at last the Saint arrived on the scene.[1] Norbert came not only without any retinue or pomp, but barefooted and clothed in the religious habit of his Order. "Never," says the biographer, "did any one see so much greatness and humility combined."

[1] Cfr. Madelaine, o. c., p. 343. Tenckhoff, o. c., pp. 10-30.

Having said farewell to the good people of Spires, the episcopal cortege went northward, and, passing through the different towns, was received everywhere with the greatest honors. People ran out of their houses to proclaim their great admiration for Norbert, and to beg him for his blessing. But the Saint seemed deaf to the acclamations of the people, and began to realize more and more the weight of this great dignity. " Norbert knew," observes Illana, "that he was about to become the victim of his pastoral ministry, but that such was God's holy will."[2]

After several days of journeying, and when at last Magdeburg came in sight, the Saint, at the thought that he was about to enter the city, over which he was to preside, and for which, as its archbishop, he would have to render an account one day to God, suffered his tears to flow freely. In his great humility he further dismounted from his donkey, says the earliest biographer, took the shoes from his feet, and walked barefooted the last miles of his journey.[3]

On the other hand, an immense crowd of people, all in festive attire, had eagerly been awaiting his arrival, and as soon as the party came in sight, they all went forth to meet their new Archbishop. There was a number of nobles from the city and the province, the clergy, the people, in a word, a large and enthusiastic multitude. Great were their expectations when they came to meet their Archbishop Norbert, renowned for his preaching and miracles. Imagine therefore their surprise when they saw the poor beggar walking the streets barefooted on this hot summer day, covered with dust and sighing sadly under the burden of this new dignity. Their emotions and impressions varied, for while some were greatly edified, others at once recognized a singular reformer, and from that moment disliked him. Still this did not diminish the spontaneous

---

[2] Cfr. Illana, p. 140.

[3] *Vita B*, Ch. XLII. Cfr. also Le Paige, p. 395 and Acta. SS. T. I. Julii. *Vita S, Ottonis* cap. II.

enthusiasm of the people at large, and amidst a universal rejoicing did Norbert make his entrance into the city. This was on July 18, 1126.

He was conducted to his Cathedral, where the Saint consecrated himself and his diocese to God, and asked God to bless them. From the Cathedral the procession went through the gardens of the episcopal palace. It was on this occasion that a very remarkable incident occurred, truly evidencing our dear Saint's character.

From the above description we know that Norbert's appearance was poor and beggarly, and thus it happened that the porter at the door of the palace failed to see anything in him but a poor tramp, and rudely shut the door in his face. "Don't you see," he said, "that you will be entirely out of place among all these nobles?" The Saint only smiled, but those around him who saw the porter's mistake, became confused and cried out to him: "But he is our Bishop and your Master!" The poor man, through fear and shame at this blunder, was about to run away and hide himself when Norbert stayed him and smilingly said: "Fear not, my good man, for you know me better than all those who have raised me to this high dignity, and now force me into this palace."[4]

The news of the incident spread rapidly throughout the city, confirmed the impressions of those who had been edified at his appearance, and made the new Archbishop at once the friend of the poor and the humble. These felt that the saintly Archbishop was theirs, and great was their joy and gratitude. When eight days later Norbert received the episcopal consecration, these good people had their houses decorated and the whole city was in festive attire.[5]

---

[4] *Vita B*, Ch. XLIII. Repellitur ab ostiario ... Hic est episcopus noster et dominus tuus ... Subridendo dicente: Ne timeas ...etc.

[5] Some historians, misled by Herman of Laon, have erroneously said that Norbert's consecration took place in Spires immediately after his election. Cfr. Madelaine, p. 341. Others have expressed their surprise that the Saint suffered himself to be invested by the king (see above p. 211) before he was consecrated and thus recognized the investiture by a layman which he always most strenuously had opposed. However, in the Council of the

Numerous bishops, priests and nobles, and thousands of people had come to Magdeburg to witness the grand ceremony of Norbert's consecration, which took place on the feast of St. James, July 25, 1126. The consecrating bishop was Udo, Bishop of Naumburg, who was so impressed by the Saint's humility, that from that day forward he considered him a saint, and regarded him with the greatst admiration.[6] There were present also Bishop Ludolph of Brandenburg, who had accompanied Norbert on his way to Magdeburg; Bishop Godebold of Meissen, and Bishop-elect Meingotus of Merseburg, who is later to be consecrated by our Saint. These were his suffragan-bishops. A number of other bishops were present, among whom is especially mentioned Otto of Halberstadt, a native of Magdeburg and a constant friend and admirer of Norbert. Other particulars about the consecration the chronicler does not mention.[7] However, our imagination can easily supply that which is wanting, and especially picture Norbert, the humble missionary and convert-maker, in the midst of all this splendor, where he himself was the center of attraction. Who can doubt but that in the midst of it all the Saint was in spirit in his dear valley of Prémontré, thinking of his children. As we remember, on the first night in the little chapel of St. John, the Saint radiant with joy, had exclaimed: "This is the place of my rest, and the haven of my salvation," and now guided by God's Providence he finds himself at the head of a great diocese, far away from his beloved brethren. However, let us not forget that one of Norbert's most

---

Lateran, held three years before, special provision had been made for the election of German bishops . . . "who shall receive investiture of their fiefs. . . . If Germans, before—if Italians, after their consecration. . . ." Cfr. Alzog. Manual of Universal Church History, Vol. II, p. 536.

[6] Winter, p. 329. Octava hinc die, hoc est in festo Beati Jacobi, ab Udone Cicense Episcopo, aliis . . . consecratur.

[7] Cfr. Chron. Magdeb. which may be found in volume XX of the Acta Sanctorum, p. 52.

celebrated sayings was: "He who has God on his side, is troubled at nothing." (Qui Deum habet pro se turbatur in nulla re.) Norbert felt that he was where God wanted him to be.

Anyone acquainted with existing conditions in the beginning of the twelfth century, will know that the position of a zealous bishop in those days was by no means an enviable one. Over the nobility of his province, for instance, he exercised a kind of moral suzerainty; to the bishop came the complaining voice of a maltreated wife, a forsaken heir or an exasperated vassal. His name and episcopal seal gave an authentic character to the most important transactions of various natures. Moreover, by his position he was obliged to take counsel with the emperor, and thus mingle in the general affairs of the Church and State. This position therefore was truly a trying one for all bishops, but more so in the case of Norbert. For when we remember that the Pontificate of the great Hildebrand had been a turning-point in history, and that only forty years had elapsed since then; that the Church was still being purified from those most deplorable sins of simony and incontinence; that the common people, those that were not of the nobility, were considered by the nobles little more than slaves, and moreover that the last traces of the struggle of Investiture were far from being entirely effaced—I say, when we remember all this, we can somewhat realize the delicate position of a bishop, who is resolved to enforce the laws of the Church both among clergy and laity, and determined to defend both the rights and property of the Church against princes and nobles, many of whom, entirely disregarding all claims of justice, had so far played the part of thieves and robbers. But as history abundantly proves, Norbert was equal to the times, and yielded neither the rights of the Church nor his own. Humble he was, but in no sense a weakling.

No sooner had the Saint taken possession of his Archbishopric than he commenced putting order in his own house. His first act was to banish all unnecessary luxuries in regard to furniture and equipage. In doing this he not only followed his own ideas of simplicity and economy, and his love of poverty and humility, but he fully understood that the only way to successfully reform others is by giving the example. At once he met with opposition from the members of his household, who ascribed his innovations to avarice. Naturally their opposition did not in the least deter Norbert who in his own quiet way set aside all superfluity, and dismissed unnecessary servants. He succeeded, the biographer says, in establishing a most edifying discipline among those he retained. As regards his person, in his episcopal palace Norbert continued the austerities he practiced in the cloister, and in a short time his palace in all its internal arrangements and gentle discipline, was truly like a monastery—a place of piety and charity, where the priests of the diocese at any time could find a true father, and the poor a consoler and helper.

Realizing that a bishop is not only responsible for the spiritual welfare of his flock, but also for the temporal affairs of his diocese, Norbert's next act was to examine carefully into the title-deeds of all diocesan property. He soon found that a considerable portion of the lands had come, more or less mysteriously, into the hands of a few powerful noblemen. He found that loans had been made at different times which simply had been forgotten, and in a word that his treasury was in a most deporable condition. In fact he hardly had enough, says the early biographer, to defray the living expenses of his household for four months.

The new Archbishop began to collect whatever title-deeds he could find, and also to make out from old records and the testimony of reliable men, the history of doubtful property. This done, he sent his commissioners to the interested parties to explain the result of his inquiry, and to reclaim the patrimony of his church. When this failed to bring the desired results, Norbert fearlessly employed other means, and even publicly denounced the usurpers. No wonder, therefore, that opposition to Norbert was soon no longer confined to a few dissatisfied members of his household, but spread throughout the diocese. Some, it is true, restored at once their ill-gotten goods, but those on the other hand, who were unwilling to do this, became Norbert's most bitter enemies. They publicly called him a miser, a hypocrite, an adventurer who was fond of money. They loaded him with insults, decried him among themselves, and even encouraged one another in their disobedience, and also in contempt for his person. "Why," they said among themselves, should we suffer a stranger, poor and unarmed, who made his entrance amongst us without anything but his donkey, to give us such haughty and peremptory orders! If he really is a saint, as his friends are pleased to tell us, why does he not then live on the revenue that was sufficient for his predecessor?"[8]

Norbert, in no way disturbed by these angry outbursts of passion, remained firm in his demands, determined to recover whatever belonged to the church entrusted to his care. He now threatened the usurpers with excommunication, which in those days had also civil effects. And this had in many cases the desired result, since we read that by the end of the year a great many had restored their ill-gotten goods. That the Archbishop's popularity had greatly suffered because of these men, will not surprise any one. But the Saint was not seeking popular favor, but doing fearlessly what he considered to be his duty. For this reason Norbert was neither moved by their tears nor affected by their threats. No calumny nor violence could ever make him forsake the duties of his sacred ministry.

It is related that the Saint went to Bolanden where a nobleman lived who was known to be a usurper of ecclesiastical property and a robber of the poor. The Archbishop sent for him and asked him: "How dare you do any injury to St. Maurice to whom our cathedral is dedicated, by taking for your own use that which was destined to be used for God's service?" The man replied that what he had he considered to be his own property, and that he had nothing which did not by right belong to him. After arguing for some time with

[8] *Vita B*, Ch. XLIV.

this man, Norbert foretold him that within one year God would take His own by force. The man was killed a short time after.[9]

With even more severity did the new Archbishop act towards those of his priests who had openly broken their vows and were leading licentious lives. This evil, alas! was great, and deeply rooted, as a consequence of the lamentable Investiture, through which so many unworthy men had been raised to the dignity of the priesthood. Thus says W. S. Lilly:

> "The root of clerical incontinence and simony lay in the custom of lay-investiture, a practice which in effect drew the prelates of the Church into the meshes of the feudal system, and which had attained its most disastrous development in Germany. ... It led in the vast majority of cases to the absolute disposal of ecclesiastical offices by the sovereign—entirely in disregard of the rights of election canonically vested in the clergy and the people—the mode of disposal very frequently adopted being that of open sale."[10]

Norbert, who never measured the success of his work by the rules of human wisdom, hoped, with the assistance of God's grace, to eradicate the evil, and entirely blot out this stain upon his clergy. He began by using the greatest kindness, quietly reminding the guilty ones of the laws and different decrees of the Church. He spoke to them of the sublime character of the priesthood, but at the same time of its enormous obligations and responsibilities. By the sweetness of his eloquence and the power of his arguments, he happily touched the hearts of several of his priests, but unfortunately, others became only more obstinate in their rebellion. Them he threatened with the penalties of excommunication, and when some still persevered in their licentious manner of living, he deprived them of their sacred office, enforced the decrees of Pope Gregory, and applied the censures of the Church.

---

[9] Cfr. G. VandenElsen, who on p. 210 quotes *Vita A*, App. VIII. Geudens, p. 115.

[10] Chapters in European History, p. 157.

It does not seem improbable that at this critical time in Norbert's life he corresponded with his great friend St. Bernard. In a former chapter we spoke of their mutual relations, and how the two Saints helped each other in bringing about the much needed reform. There is a letter of St. Bernard, found in Vol. III of the Work edited by S. J. Eales, already quoted, letter 488, addressed to Brother N. ... The learned author observes in a footnote that it does not appear who was this Brother N. However, there are reasons to suppose that this lengthy letter was sent by St. Bernard to none other than Norbert, and moreover sent at this very time.[11]

Norbert's model in everything was the great St. Augustine, whose Rule he had adopted when founding his Order, and whom, as archbishop, he had chosen for his patron. The great Bishop of Hippo had also made his palace like a monastery, where he lived in common with some of his priests, as did the Apostles. From him Norbert learned, moreover, to have perfect confidence in God and His government of the world. In those dark days of continual opposition the Saint must have often thought of the consoling words of St. Augustine, which according to his biographer formed his habitual thought:

"Thou art just, O Lord, and Thy judgment is right."

Still, it would be really an injustice to the character of Norbert to suppose that he was unduly severe. His invariable rule of conduct was first to try kind persuasion, and only when this failed did he

---

[11] In this letter we read: "Although it would be more fitting for me to receive such exhortation from you, than to address it to you. . . ." Further St. Bernard insists greatly on the exercise of charity in dealing with offenders, citing repeatedly the beautiful examples of Our Savior, and goes on in 24 paragraphs, giving advice to a religious, apparently living away from his monastery, and in the midst of worldly occupations. . . . The whole is certainly a most remarkable letter, and was taken by S. J. Eales from Eugenius de Levis, Presbyter, Anecdota sacra, sive collectio omnis generis opusculorum veterum SS. Patrum, etc. Augustae Taurinorum (Migne Tom. I, Col. 653).

fearlessly enforce the law. Neither did he himself ever make any new regulations in these matters, but only sternly applied and enforced those rules that already existed. The following testimony of him, written by his contemporary, we find in the Chronicles of Magdeburg:

> With the greatest care he performed all episcopal functions. He was always ready to break the Bread of Life for the people, and also was ever an edifying example to all, in his preaching, his conversation and general conduct. He observed with the greatest exactness and piety all the rubrics, and especially those of the Holy Sacrifice of the Mass. Before the kings and princes of the world he always appeared with dignity and reverential authority, before his clergy and religious, with love and humility.[12]

When Norbert had at last overcome much of the opposition, and had re-established the high repute of the priesthood in his diocese, he rapidly rose in the estimation of clergy and people. Many even began to speak of him as the savior of the diocese, and loved him dearly. Yet a great number still persevered in their opposition, and from now on used every means to rid themselves of their saintly Archbishop, and even tried to take his life, as we shall see later.

Meanwhile the time had come when Norbert was to receive the fullness of the archiepiscopal power by the reception of the "Pallium."[13] Since his duties did not allow him to go to Rome personally, it was sent to him in the spring of 1127. We know this from the Chronicles where it is said that Meingotus, who had been elected bishop on the same day as Norbert, could not be consecrated

[12] Cfr. VandenElsen, o. c., p. 212.

[13] The modern "Pallium" is a circular band about two inches wide, worn about the neck, breast and shoulders, and having two pendants, one hanging down in front—one behind . . . is made of white wool, part of which is supplied by two lambs presented annually as a tax by the Lateran Canons Regular to the Chapter of St. John on the feast of St. Agnes . . . is worn by the Pope and by Archbishops. ... An Archbishop is forbidden to perform any episcopal function until invested with the pallium. Cfr. Cath. Encyclopedia.

until March 20, being obliged to wait until the new Archbishop had received the pallium. His consecration took place on Passion Sunday, on which occasion Norbert conferred also other ordinations; among the ordained was a certain Vicelinus, who had known the Saint at the university in Laon, and now presented himself to Norbert to work in his diocese as a priest among the heathens, who were quite numerous at that time in the province of the Archbishop.

To gain an adequate idea of conditions in Norbert's archdiocese one must divide it into two parts. First, Magdeburg, situated on the Elbe, was one of the oldest emporia of the German trade for the Wends, who dwelt on the right bank of the Elbe.[14] After the wars of the years 940 and 954, when the Slavs, as far as the Oder, had been brought into subjection to German rule, Otto the Great set to work to establish an archbishopric, which was finally created in 962.[15] The Western part was inhabited by Saxons, but the Eastern part of the diocese by Wends or Slavs, some of whom had been converted to Christianity, but the majority were still worshiping idols. Norbert's territory was half pagan and half Christian. In the dioceses of Havelberg and Brandenburg, suffragan sees of Magdeburg, conditions were such that the bishops were unable to visit their people except under the special protection of the German King. True, the secular rulers of these two provinces, Pribislau and Witikind, had themselves received Baptism, yet they also were fettered by fear, and unable to propagate freely the religion of Christ. Naturally, pagan temples were found throughout the province, and the Lusatians especially were known to be very antagonistic to Christianity. Consequently, Norbert found in his diocese a great field for genuine missionary labor.

---

[14] The name "Wends" is a much older designation in historical authorities than "Slavs." Both names have been used constantly without distinction by German chroniclers, the former almost oftener than the latter. Cfr. Cath. Encyclop. Art. "Slavs."

[15] Ibidem, Art. "Magdeburg."

At the end of 1126, in an interview with King Lothaire, the Saint had already conceived a plan to evangelize the Wends, and in the beginning of 1127 a missionary expedition left the city of Magdeburg, probably under the direction of Norbert himself.[16] On their way north these missionaries passed through Havelberg where Witikind governed an almost entirely pagan tribe. They went as far as Muritz without finding real opposition, and succeeded in inducing many of the Wends to embrace Christianity. A few years after, when Norbert had been enabled to bring his own religious into the diocese of Magdeburg, he sent numerous missionaries among the Wends, where he also established different monasteries.

Still, it must be noticed that the Apostle of the Slavs is considered to have been St. Otho, Bishop of Bamberg, in Pomerania, and legate of Pope Calixtus II. He had worked among them before Norbert ever arrived in Magdeburg. His second expedition, undertaken in 1128, happened during Norbert's time; and thus we read of Otho that he came to Magdeburg before undertaking the expedition.[17] However, the Premonstratensians also have done great work in bringing about the conversion of the Slavs. Says Dr. Winter: "There is no second example in the whole history of the Church during the middle ages, of any religious Order having completed the conversion of a whole country, such as the Premonstratensians did in Wendenland."[18]

---

[16] Thus Madelaine, p. 354. VandenElsen considers it more probable that the expedition was under the leadership of Vicelinus.

[17] Cfr. Acta SS. T. I. Julii, p. 389.

[18] Winter, p. 31.

CHAPTER II
A SUCCESSOR AT PRÉMONTRÉ

Orbatae domui statuit Norbertus Hugonem
Abbatem, Christo hunc suscipiente Patrem.

The choice of Bl. Hugh to succeed Norbert in Prémontré is shown in a vision to be the will of God.

SPEAKING in a preceding chapter of the Diet of Spires where Norbert's election had taken place, we had occasion to refer to Lothaire, the Holy Roman Emperor and the King of the Germans. Since the relations between the archbishop and the king were very cordial, and especially so because Norbert took an active part in the struggle between Lothaire and Conrad, it seems desirable, before proceeding with Norbert's history, to refer here to the history of Lothaire, and to show how our Saint as archbishop was forced to resume his political life.

The year before Norbert had become archbishop, Lothaire had ascended the throne, since by the death of Henry V the House of Franconia had become extinct. In order to provide a successor to Henry, the ecclesiastical and secular lords of the German states had met in the plain between Mainz and Worms, in 1125. Forty electors had been designated and the choice of the majority was Lothaire of Saxony. However, homage to the elect was refused by Frederick of Swabia and by Conrad of Franconia, both of whom were termed "Hohenstaufen," because of the castle in which their line had originated; both of them were also nephews of the deceased Henry

V; their mother, Agnes, being a sister of that monarch.[1]

The election of Lothaire took place on the 30th of August, and on the following 13th day of September he was crowned at Aix-la-Chapelle. Still this did not prevent Conrad from going to Milan and having himself crowned by Adalbert, the Archbishop. Ill-fated Germany was doomed to another deluge of blood, which lasted until 1135, when Conrad made his final submission. In the midst of these troubles Norbert upheld the cause of Lothaire, and, together with the Archbishop of Mainz and Salzburg, excommunicated Conrad on Christmas day, one week after he had proclaimed himself King of the Germans, and by his sedition and rebellion disturbed the peace of the Church and the State. Rome upheld this excommunication and even renewed it on April 22, 1128, when Pope Honorius also excommunicated the Archbishop of Milan for having unjustly crowned Conrad and for having worked for his cause.[2]

Of Lothaire we read that he was a noble and upright character, courageous and energetic, but that he was terrible to all who were enemies of God and the Church.[3] Small wonder, therefore, that the relations between the Archbishop and the King were of an intimate nature. While the King was assisting the Saint in his great work of reform, Norbert, on his part, fought the king's cause against the usurper. Moreover, since Norbert was no stranger at the German Court, he proved an invaluable aid to the king, who often consulted him on matters of State.

But we shall return now to Norbert in Magdeburg where we left

---

[1] Cfr. Parsons "Universal History," Vol. II, p. 508.

[2] Cfr. VandenElsen, p. 231, who quotes Jaffe, 64—Hergenrother III—252 (54)—Bernh. 52 (6). He observes that the Pope confirmed the excommunication by Norbert and the other bishops through the influence of our Saint who had been commissioned at this time to lay the matter before His Holiness. This opinion is based on a letter of Gerochus to Pope Innocent II. (See Migne CXCIV, 1374.)

[3] Cfr. *Vita B.* Ch. LII and further the Chronicle of Ursperg, quoted by Madelaine, o. c., p. 336.

him busily engaged in looking after the material as well as the spiritual welfare of his archdiocese. We should not forget that Norbert, when he became Archbishop, had not ceased to be a religious. Thus he continually wore the white habit of the Order, and as far as he was able, observed the rule of the abbeys. As a Protestant critic, Dr. Winter observes:[4] Norbert was first of all the reformer of religious as well as of priestly life, and represented in his days a kind of religious puritanism. His mission was to bring the people back to the pure Gospel, and his motto therefore was the motto of our late saintly Pontiff, Pius X, "to restore all things in Christ." Since Norbert had resolved to attain this end by forming priests according to his own ideals, or by conferring the priestly dignity on religious, it can cause no surprise that the Saint was the great protector and friend of all religious in his diocese and at the same time was anxious to introduce into his diocese the priests formed under his own supervision.

There was one monastery especially which was greatly favored by the Archbishop, the Benedictine monastery in Bergen, a suburb of Magdeburg. Often, the biographer says, Norbert used to retire to this monastery in order to avoid the noise of the world and to find repose in the calm of prayer and monastic solitude. He later commissioned these Benedictines to reform the monastery of Ammersleden, which, under their management, became a flourishing institution. He further brought needed reform into the houses of Poelde, Alsleben, Nienburg and Petersberg, and founded the new monasteries of "Gottesgnade" and Leitzkau. Rightly therefore does Dr. Winter (*l. c.*) observe that there was not a monastery in the diocese into which Norbert did not bring reform, for religious were at all times his most beloved children.

However, if the Archbishop loved and protected all religious of his diocese, it is but natural that he often thought of his own dear sons in Prémontré. The Saint realized first of all that his numerous

[4] "Die Prämonstratenser. . . ." Ch. I.

episcopal duties did not allow him to look after the interests of his Order. Thus when unfavorable reports reached the ears of Norbert concerning conditions in his beloved valley, the thought came to him to have someone else replace him; one who could have the entire direction of the Order. This, no doubt, would be better for the brethren, and at the same time would relieve Norbert of a great responsibility. It happened at this time that the Saint was obliged to go to Aachen in the interest of King Lothaire, who was still engaged in his struggle against Conrad. Norbert resolved at the time to go to France and visit different foundations, for he wanted to speak to the brethren of his plans in regard to a successor to himself.[5]

Before leaving Aachen the Counts of Grimbergen came to find the Saint and to offer him their castle near Brussels for a Premonstratensian abbey. Norbert accepted the gift and sent there at once Humbert with some of the brethren. Thus arose the Abbey of Grimbergen, which brought forth in the course of time another house near Mondaye, in France, and exists to this day, though the buildings had to be renewed after the French Revolution.

Alas! who can describe the great disappointment of the Saint when, after a tiresome journey, he arrived at his dear Prémontré, and saw that the unfavorable rumors he had heard were based on sad reality. Conditions had greatly changed since he had left two years before; so much so, the early biographer remarks, that the Order was threatened with utter ruin.[6] Although the joy of the brethren was great at Norbert's arrival, still there was a note of sadness in it all, which the Saint did not fail to notice, and which

---

[5] Cfr. VandenElsen, p. 232, who observes that it is evident from the early biographer that Norbert visited Prémontré at this time, since he says in Ch. XLVIII that the brethren had waited for him for two years. However, Madelaine is not only silent upon this journey but makes it positively appear that Norbert did not go. Cfr. Madelaine, o. c., p. 362.

[6] *Vita B*, Ch. XLVIII. Instantem dissolutionem Ordinis in plerisque locis videntes. . . .

made him realize that his Institute was passing through a severe crisis. The cause of all this seems to have been that, although Hugh had governed the abbey with great zeal and discretion, the brethren had still looked up to Norbert as their superior, as in reality, though absent, he still had continued to be. The Saint assembled the brethren, at once opened his mind to them, and spoke of his future plans regarding the management of the Order.

In order to obtain the necessary assistance of the Holy Ghost in the election of a successor to himself, he desired them to unite their prayers, acts of charity and penance for this intention. Many tears were shed at this unexpected announcement. All loved their spiritual father dearly, and were grieved indeed to lose him as their superior. Norbert, on his part, must have felt even more than they, how great a sacrifice it is to tear oneself away from those we love. He must have remembered that first night in the lonely chapel of St. John—his subsequent successes in building the monastery and the church—the constant influx of new brethren. Again there passed before his mind the many happy days he had spent here in prayer and solitude, while now in his diocese but little time was left him for spiritual exercises. However, Norbert was a strong-willed man, and his mind was made up. He explained to the brethren that it had been obviously the work of Divine Providence that he had been raised to the dignity of an archbishop, and that in consequence of this he was no longer able properly to look after the welfare of the Order. He remained in Prémontré as long as duty allowed him, and when leaving called some of his earliest disciples to come to him in Magdeburg in order to deliberate together on the matter of electing a new General.

On this same journey Norbert paid a visit to his beloved Cappenberg, to console the brethren for their loss of Blessed Godfrey, of whom we have spoken above. He also went to his native town, Xanten, where he was received with the greatest enthusiasm.[7] Those especial canons who formerly had been his enemies, now did all in their power to make due reparation. The church which had been destroyed by fire, in 1109, had just been rebuilt, and the Saint was privileged to reconsecrate church and altars with great solemnity, an immense crowd of people being present. This event took place on July 22, 1128.

Norbert then returned to his diocese and resumed his episcopal duties. Soon the disciples, whom he had called from Prémontré and other abbeys, arrived, and among them was Hugh, who during his absence confided the government of Prémontré to Reinerus, later abbot of Auxerre.

St. Norbert's first biographer gives on this occasion the rule of prudence which our Saint always followed in the transaction of important business concerning his Order or his diocese. He observes that when changes had to be made, regulations to be confirmed, or other important affairs to be regulated, Norbert first invariably asked the prayers and then the opinion of all those who were about him. He never decided hastily, but always sought to know the will of God through the opinion of prudent men. He was further persuaded that the light of the Holy Ghost is obtained not only through prayer, but also through deliberating with good men united in the name of God. Thus then the Saint took counsel; he joined his own fervent supplications with those of the brethren, and deliberated with them on the election of his successor. God graciously heard their prayers, and even deigned to reveal to Norbert that He desired that Hugh, his first disciple, should take his place, and that he would moreover possess the spirit of the Founder himself, in his government of the Order. When after some time the brethren were about to return to their abbeys, with the exception of Hugh, whom Norbert retained for some time with him in

---

[7] Cfr. VandenElsen, p. 237, who further quotes Spenrath "Xanten und seine Umgebung," II, 19.

Magdeburg, the Archbishop impressed on their minds to remember in their election Hugh, his first disciple and faithful co-worker in the foundation of Prémontré.[8] We ought to remark here that up to this time Norbert had always made the appointments, and elections had never taken place. In reality this first election established a precedent which to this day is observed in all the abbeys.

"When the time came," says the biographer, "Blessed Hugh was unanimously elected by the brethren."[9] That his election was undoubtedly the work of the Holy Ghost was again confirmed by a revelation from on high, not to Norbert, but to Hugh himself. For on the very day of the election, Hugh, who at the time was still at Magdeburg, had a vision in which he saw St. Norbert recommending him to Our Blessed Lord, Who received him from the hands of Norbert. Hugh was too humble to speak at once of this vision, but Norbert knew of it and perhaps had seen the same vision, for he said to Hugh: "Dear brother, you will, by the election of our brethren, succeed me in the house of our poverty." At these words Hugh fell on his knees before the Saint and said:

> "I see, O Father, that it is the will of God and that I must obey. I will go in the hope that He Who by His mercy has elevated me, by His grace will sustain me. I must sacrifice my will that I may do the will of God and yours. Still, if on account of my numerous sins God should refuse me His help, then may I be permitted to come back to you, whom I have chosen for the father and protector of my soul."

At this Norbert replied: "You will go in the name of the Lord with confidence, and the hand of God will be with you until the end."[10]

Soon news came from Prémontré confirming the vision of both Norbert and Hugh, and the archbishop was greatly pleased. He did all in his power to comfort and strengthen Hugh, who, though

---

[8] Cfr. *Vita A*, Ch. XVIII.

[9] Ibidem ... In quam convenit amabilis Deo fratrum unanimitas.

[10] *Vita B*, Ch. XLVIII.

reluctantly, at last consented to take upon himself the great responsibility. Norbert gave him directions for the management of the material as well as the spiritual affairs of the abbey, and of the whole Order. Comforted and strengthened by Norbert's blessing, Hugh left Magdeburg, and was solemnly installed and consecrated abbot by the Bishop of Laon. On this same occasion Waltman, Provost of Antwerp, also received the abbatial consecration, and also Richard, Abbot of Floreffe, and Odon of Bonne Espérance.

Once firmly established in Prémontré, Hugh's first work was to find means to promote unity and uniformity in the different foundations. So far the authority of Norbert had been a sufficient guarantee to preserve uniformity, but since his departure for Magdeburg relations between the different foundations seemed to have weakened. Having no court of appeal, local superiors had often found themselves obliged to interpret part of the rules, and adapt them to circumstances. Again, as the reader remembers, there were foundations where only two or three of the brethren had received their religious training in Prémontré, and this was more or less the cause of the little uniformity between some foundations and the mother-abbey, Prémontré, though in individual abbeys, the discipline was excellent, for the brethren were all still in their first fervor.

In order, therefore, to establish unity and uniformity in the Order, Hugh, once he had been elected Abbot-General, called together the different superiors and a General Chapter was held at Prémontré.[11] Present were: Gautier, Abbot of St. Martin at Laon; Richard, Abbot of Floreffe; Henry, Abbot of Viviers; Waltman, Abbot of St. Michael at Antwerp; and Odon, Abbot of Bonne Espérance. No reasons are given anywhere why a greater number of superiors were not present at this first General Chapter, but it seems that the situation was such that it was impossible to wait for

[11] Vita B, Ch. XLVIII.

all to assemble.[12] No doubt the absence of Norbert was also partly responsible. Nevertheless, important decrees were enacted which later on were sanctioned by other General Chapters and Sovereign Pontiffs. According to the positive instructions of St. Norbert, the following resolutions were agreed upon:

1. That all Superiors of the Order, the General, the Abbots and Provosts, should be elected by the brethren, and for life.

2. That the General Chapter should be the highest or supreme tribunal in the Order, and that all the Abbots and even the General should owe obedience to it. Further, that it should be convoked every year at Prémontré, for October 9, feast of St. Denis, and that all Abbots and Provosts were obliged to attend.

3. The fast was changed from a perpetual one to one of seven months, but the use of flesh-meat was never allowed. Fasting was to be observed from the feast of the Exaltation of the Cross until Easter.

4. Special rules were made to guide Abbots, Priors and other officials of an abbey in the discharge of their duties; likewise for the Superiors of convents of nuns, for parish priests, confessors and missionaries.

These were the first written statutes of the Order, and became the nucleus of the Constitutions of the Premonstratensian Order. Naturally, in the course of eight hundred years, changes had to be made from time to time. Official new editions appeared in 1290, in 1505 and in 1630, but of these we will speak in the second volume.

It is quite evident that this first conference of the different abbots did untold good in the way of promoting uniformity. Besides, as long as Blessed Hugh lived, the Chapter was held every year, and the attendance gradually increased. In the second year there were nine abbots present; the third, 12; the fourth, 18; and, before Hugh

[12] Madelaine, o. c., p. 365.

died, there were as many as 120 abbots in one General Chapter.

Norbert, who during these three years of his episcopate had already done so much to reform his clergy, often had expressed his ardent desire of seeing some of his brethren of Prémontré permanently established near him in Magdeburg. In this matter, however, the Saint found great opposition. "The Canons," observes Dr. Winter, "were so little pleased with the reforms of their strict Archbishop, that they refused to admit a number of men of the same spirit into the city." But, in the ways of Divine Providence, "all works to the good of those who love Him."

There was near the episcopal palace a collegiate church dedicated to the Mother of God, where some secular canons lived under the authority of a provost. They were leading a life far from edifying, and when Norbert's efforts to bring about a reform had failed, the only course open to him was to introduce priests formed by himself. But in this he was strongly opposed, especially by an archdeacon, by the name of Atticus, to whom we shall be obliged to refer later.

However, Norbert at last succeeded in prevailing upon the Canons of St. Mary's Chapter, and they gave up their church to the Premonstratensians. The reasons for the change, which was confirmed by Pope Honorius as well as by King Lothaire, are given in a Charter of October 29, 1129: the good of the church and the welfare of the diocese:

> In the name of the Holy and Indivisible Trinity. Norbert, by the grace of God, Archbishop of the Church of Magdeburg. We want it to be known to all present and to come, that We, having considered the state of the Church at Magdeburg, have resolved to revive the splendor of religion in her, to re-establish her in her immunities, to reform in her the abuses which have crept in, and to perfect the good which We have found there established. Now we have seen that the church of St. Mary, situated in this city, has so strangely fallen into decay, inside and outside, that even the buildings are nearly in ruins, and that there hardly remains enough for the sustenance of the twelve

Canons, who, according to the foundation, must celebrate the Divine Office. Part of their funds have been distributed among the officers of the prince, part was wasted by the negligence of the clerics, and the rest has been seized by neighbors, and there is no hope of being able to recover it.

We, therefore, having considered their poverty and their frequent complaints, and wishing moreover to see the Church rather increase than diminish, have obtained from the canons by our prayers, our exhortations and counsels, that they give up their church to the religious who lead the common life under the Rule of St. Augustine, and that they place themselves at our disposal without any restraint. But in our anxiety to place them under claustral discipline and under the government of a dean, we have incorporated them into other churches of the city. Some of them we have placed in the church of St. Nicholas. To others we have assigned part of the revenues of St. Mary's. We have also transferred to our brethren the ancient funds and rights of St Mary's; and in order to procure for them peace and a more solid tranquility, we have ordained that in future they will depend only on us and our episcopal successors.

And in order that these regulations may be permanent, we confirm them by the authority of the Holy Apostles Peter and Paul. To those who will observe them we wish peace and the remission of their sins. But if any person of whatever condition he be, dares to destroy the fruit of our labor, and by a bold attempt, to disturb the poor of Christ, let him be anathema until the day of the Lord.

Done in the year of the Incarnation of Our Lord, 1129, on the 29th of October, in the abbey of St. John the Baptist (of Bergen), a suburb of the city of Magdeburg (the signatures of eight canons follow).[13]

As soon as Norbert saw his cherished plan realized, the old Chapter of St. Mary was changed into a mission-house, and Evermode, one of the first disciples and a most faithful companion of Norbert in his apostolic labors, became the first Provost of the young community. The house became the center of missionary activity, for these holy and zealous missionaries revived by their

[13] Cfr. Hugo Annal. Ord. Praem. T. II. Probat., col. CVIII.

exhortations and edifying lives the faith in the archdiocese, and went out from there propagating the Gospel among the Wends, of whom we spoke in the last chapter. Moreover, as there was such a great want of priests and especially of good priests in those days, Norbert soon entrusted several other parishes to the care of his brethren, and with their assistance succeeded to a great extent in reestablishing the full practice of religion in his archdiocese.

CHAPTER III
PERSECUTION

Vix Canonum Sacra jura Foves, Fervensque tueris,
Mox Enses, Hastas effera turba movet.
Stas tamen Impavidus; turbaeque, Hostesque recedunt.
In Sacra jus gladii nilque valere docent.

Great Pastor! Model of thy flock! Thy mind,
Fixed on eternal interests, entwined
Round God's unchanging Church, thy constant care;
They struck thee with the sword. . . .

(Office of St. Norbert)

LTHOUGH Norbert's success in bringing about reforms in his diocese and in recovering the patrimony of the Church won the love and admiration of many, as we observed above, it also was the cause of embittering his opponents. Who has ever ventured to attack inveterate abuses without meeting desperate opposition? Calumny and persecution have invariably been the portion of all those who would follow the Crucified Redeemer. "Blessed are they who suffer persecution for justice's sake."

Since Norbert's brethren from Prémontré had come into the city, and his enemies, to use their own words, had to deal no longer with one reformer but with many, they no longer were satisfied with abusing their Archbishop in words, but, blinded by passion, they actually made an attempt on his life. Satan incited some wicked laymen and dissolute priests to conspire against the energetic Archbishop and kill him. A plot was formed in Magdeburg and the soul of it was the archdeacon, Atticus, also known in history under the name of Hatseco or Jetzo. This cleric, who by his position exercised great influence throughout the diocese, bore Norbert a mortal hatred, and showed himself until the end, Norbert's most bitter enemy.[1]

On this occasion he and some of his colleagues, fearing to act openly, bribed a low individual to murder Norbert. The plan was attempted on April 12, 1129. We read in the original biography of the Saint, that on the 10th of April, the Archbishop was still twenty miles away from Magdeburg, at Goslar, where on that day he, with King Lothaire, signed in the old castle at Kaiserburg, a solemn Charter for the erection of a Sisters' convent at Altena or Elten. Immediately after, he returned home in great haste to be able to celebrate the Divine Services of Holy Week in his Cathedral.[2]

When on Thursday the Saint was hearing confessions, and people came in large numbers imploring God's pardon of their sins, there was seen among the penitents a young man, dressed in a long cloak, who asked to be immediately admitted into the presence of the Archbishop to make his confession. The porter announced the young man, but the Saint answered, not to let him enter. The young man urged once more his request, and the Saint obliged him to wait in the episcopal palace until the crowd had been heard.[3]

Evidently God had revealed to His servant the conspiracy, for when at last the Saint was near the false penitent, he cried from afar: "In the name of God I command you to remain where you are and not approach your Archbishop." The young man appeared greatly astonished, but Norbert without asking any further questions told his attendant to take off the man's cloak. Behold a large knife, which the man was trying to conceal! The Saint asked him why he had come thus armed. Trembling and dazed, the wretch

---

[1] Winter "Die Prämonstratenser", Ch. I.

[2] *Vita B*, Ch. XLVI.

[3] Ibidem. Also Tenckoff, p. 12-32.

fell at once on his knees and began to implore for mercy, candidly confessing that he had been bribed by someone to take Norbert's life, giving the names of the instigators of the whole plot.[4] To the great horror and astonishment of all present, it was then discovered that Atticus, the Archbishop's archdeacon, was the leader of the conspirators. Like another Judas, he had actually sold the life of his master, and an act of religion and piety was to cover his crime. Great was the indignation of all present, and the name of Hazeko was repeated by all as a synonym for Judas. Norbert himself, however, remaining calm and resigned, said to those around him:

> Why are you surprised? Must I be more privileged than Jesus Christ, my Master, Who on this very night was delivered over to His enemies by one of his twelve Apostles? How great would be my happiness if on the day and at the hour He expired for us, I could die for Him by the hands of those whom I counted among my friends! The day on which pardon was offered to sinners, mercy to those without hope, and life to the dead, that day would truly be a great day to die! By preventing my death you have only prolonged my trial; you have increased my work and postponed my rest. Regarding these instigators, they were my friends and will remain my friends. Besides, today is no day for vengeance, but for mercy. It behooves us to imitate our Leader, Jesus Christ, Who has said: "Do good to those who hate you; pray for those who persecute and calumniate you." And further: "Father, forgive them, for they know not what they do."[5]

These words and beautiful sentiments reveal clearly the soul of the hero and the saint, and justly might we think to find Norbert's enemies at his feet imploring his pardon. At least we should expect to see them deeply touched by the Saint's readiness to forgive, but, strange contradiction! Norbert's great kindness produced only the very opposite effect, and actually contributed to harden the hearts

[4] *Vita B*, Ch. XLVI. "Proditionis hujus rei inventi sunt qui . . ."

[5] Ibidem. "Isti erant et sunt amici. ..."

of the conspirators and confirm them in their diabolical design against the life of our Saint.

A very bold plan was now decided on, and one of the clerics of the household of the Archbishop had taken the execution upon himself. It was the Saint's custom, whenever he was able, to go with his Canons to the church at the silent hour of midnight to take part in the singing of the Divine Office. His usual place, on account of his dignity, was to walk last in the procession. The bold assassin knew this; and, having hidden himself in one of the dark passages, had decided to stab the last person. Amidst the tumult and consternation that would follow, and aided by the darkness of the midnight hour, he thought to escape safely.

Now on the very night chosen it happened, for some unexplainable reason, that the Saint instead of walking the last, was in the midst of his Canons, when they were going into the church, and thus the assassin stabbed the chaplain of the Archbishop instead of Norbert. With a loud cry: "I am killed!" the cleric fell at once to the ground, and all the brethren, shocked and amazed, ran to his assistance. By the sound of the voice the assassin perceived his mistake, but ran away. The Canons pursued him, but Norbert, grasping at once the situation, and realizing that his own life had been threatened, recalled them and said: "Let him go in peace and let us not render evil for evil. My hour is not yet come. Let us wait till it please the Lord to take me. Those who have armed this man do not rest, and have sworn my death. However, they will only succeed in showing forth God's all-guiding Providence, Who wants to make use of me to do His work."[6] This was all the vengeance which Norbert's charity, so much stronger than the hatred of his enemies, allowed him to take. None of the biographers mention a single word from which could be inferred that the assassin had even been pursued or punished. On the other hand, we read that Norbert continued his work with the same fearlessness, at all times

[6] *Vita B*, Ch. XLVII.

enforcing the laws of the Church. However great was his charity, his courage in the midst of these trials is no less remarkable. Neither calumny nor violence could make him forsake even for a single day, the duties of his sacred ministry. One of Norbert's sayings, which he never tired of repeating, was: "Calumny is the test of a patient and generous heart, which bears with it rather than give up working for God." Or again: "He who has God on his side is troubled at nothing." And, relying on these principles, Norbert fearlessly continued excommunicating incorrigible clerics and laymen, and insisting on the temporal rights of his Church.

On the 13th of June, 1129, we find the Saint once more at Goslar, present at the Diet where he was occupied with matters of Church and State. Here he remained some time and returned to Magdeburg in time to celebrate the feast of Sts. Peter and Paul. During this absence dark clouds of opposition had thickened and gathered, threatening a severe storm on the least provocation.

As the reader remembers, the introduction of the Premonstratensians into St. Mary's Chapter at Magdeburg was one of the Archbishop's greatest crimes, in the eyes of his enemies. As a matter of fact, the presence of these zealous men had been a continual source of reproach to them, and their constant good example had reminded them of their own duty in a more convincing and powerful manner than even the words of Norbert. Again we may rightly suppose that Norbert naturally favored these brethren since they were truly apostolic men, who worked day and night for the glory of God and the salvation of souls. This had caused feelings of jealousy. Furthermore, the marked preference of Norbert for his confreres had not only irritated the clerics but had given rise to a rumor that the Archbishop was but waiting for an opportunity to introduce his sons into the Cathedral. This suspicion they thought confirmed when Norbert upon his return from Goslar, announced that, since the Cathedral during his absence had been desecrated, it was going to be reconsecrated.

Madelaine observes that neither the two early biographers nor the chroniclers of Magdeburg designate the crime by which it was desecrated. However, the fact of the desecration is beyond the shadow of a doubt, for it is mentioned by all historians. It seems as if, through a feeling of shame, they did not want to specify the nature of the crime by which the house of God had been profaned. At any rate, the Archbishop was bound by the laws of the Church to purify the temple, and so he made his intention known to the assembled Chapter.[7]

At this meeting some of the Canons, instigated by the archdeacon Atticus, objected. They would not hear of having the ceremony performed; unless, first, they knew the names of the guilty parties; and, secondly, the name of him who had made the Archbishop acquainted with the fact. This condition the Saint boldly refused to comply with, adding that he would not celebrate the Holy Sacrifice in the Cathedral as long as it remained in its state of profanation. Meanwhile, Atticus and his friends had spread the rumor among the people that the profanation of the Cathedral could not be proved, and that the Archbishop had some other object in view in this reconsecration. They wanted to submit the case to a synod before which the guilty party was to be cited to prove the crime. This opposition, says Dr. Winter, is unexplainable, if the canons had not thought to see another intention in this reconsecration; that is, a formal transfer of the Cathedral to the Premonstratensians. Atticus further insinuated to the people that Norbert's object was to take away from the Cathedral the precious relics and give them to Premonstratensian churches.[8]

But when there was question of God's honor, Norbert was not the man to fear opposition. From the pulpit of the Cathedral he

---

[7] Cfr. Madelaine, p. 394, who further quotes *Vita B*, Ch. XLIX: "Quoddam infortunium" ... *Vita A*, Ch. XIX, "Contigit in ecclesia majori rerum quippiam." Chron. Magdeb. No. 6. Nefando crimine violata. Cfr., also Acta SS. T. XX. p. 52.

[8] Cfr. VandenElsen, o. c., p. 258.

therefore announced to the people of Magdeburg his firm intention of reconsecrating the Cathedral and explained the reasons that forced him to perform this ceremony commanded by the laws of the Church. But the poor people, deluded by Atticus and his followers, shouted their disapproval. This happened on the feastday of Sts. Peter and Paul. Since the Archbishop had failed to celebrate on this great day solemnly in the Cathedral, as was his wont, the people were angered and excited. Atticus tried by different means to goad the anger of the people, and he fairly shouted out to them that the only cause of this great disturbance were Norbert and his new Canons. The next day was a Sunday. No Mass on that day in the Cathedral might have serious consequences, reasoned the Saint. Consequently, Norbert took counsel with his suffragan bishops, for unless the Church were reconsecrated the archbishop would not allow the Holy Sacrifice to be celebrated. The result was that the Saint resolved to perform the ceremony privately, and purify the Cathedral during the stillness of the night.

Anselm, Bishop of Havelberg; Godebold, Bishop of Meissen; Provost Frederic, some of the good canons of the Cathedral and a few of Norbert's brethren entered the church during the night of the 29-30th of June, to assist their Archbishop in the sacred function.[9] Attired in their pontifical vestments, these holy prelates were performing the sacred ceremonies in the stillness of the night, when all of a sudden wild cries rend the air, the doors are being battered down, and all the people are gathered around the church, shouting for the life of Norbert. The reader, no doubt, fully understands what has happened.

As soon as the Saint and his assistants had begun the ceremony, Atticus and his satellites had roused the inhabitants and spread the rumor that Norbert and his Frenchmen had taken possession of the Cathedral. They further added that now they were breaking down the altars, ransacking the shrines, and that they intended to remove

---

[9] Chron. Magd. (Acta SS. T. XX.)

all the treasures they could lay hands on, especially the relics. They of course knew that at this time nothing would irritate the poor deluded people more than the danger of losing their precious relics.[10] Neither were they in this mistaken. The rage of the people knew no bounds. Besides, to add to the great excitement and the general commotion, Atticus ordered someone to ring the big bell of the Cathedral, and in a moment's time a most excited and turbulent mob surrounded the church, shouting: "Our relics are being stolen!" Though these wild cries frightened those who were assisting the Archbishop, Norbert remained calm and without any sign of fear. He advanced towards the door and would have gone out to the crowd in order to pacify the excited people if he had not been prevented by the assisting bishops and priests. The latter forced the Saint to go with them and seek a place of safety in the old tower built, in the time of Otto I, like a great fortress.[11]

Here the bishops and the canons, all still wearing their sacred vestments, sang at this midnight hour the Matins of St. Paul, whose feast was being celebrated on that day. Thus the Saint in company with his friends passed that memorable night, a prisoner in his own cathedral. How appropriate under these circumstances must have been the Office of the Apostle of the Gentiles! The biographer says that the Saint and his companions found abundant strength in the recital of this particular Office, since by it they were most vividly reminded of the many times that St. Paul himself had been made a prisoner for having upheld the cause of his Divine Master.

Truly a most admirable contrast which has not escaped the different biographers: In the street, wild shouts and cries are rending the air—a maddened mob is clamoring for the life of their

---

[10] Madelaine, on p. 395, enumerates different contemporary writers who all agree in stating that the people were actually misled by this ridiculous calumny. He moreover quotes *Vita B*, Ch. XLIX, where it says, Quod fregisset episcopus altaria .. cum omni etiam thesauro ecclesiae fugere disposuisset.

[11] *Vita A*, Ch. XIX, also Chron. Magdeb. No. 6.

archbishop; high in the tower, solemn and grave voices are chanting the praises of the Lord, and celebrating the heroic virtues of the great Apostle! Strengthening and consoling one another, these saintly men thus awaited the end of the tumult. Yet a few of them murmured and lost courage, saying: "Why did we follow this man? We are going to perish with him." But like the great Apostle, Norbert also tried to console them and spoke to them words of courage and Christian resignation. "My dearest brethren," he said, fear not; it is for God's cause that we suffer. That which is happening now is permitted by His Providence. When a good work is opposed by an enemy, it is God Who permits him to oppose it. Take courage and trust in God." Norbert continued thus to exhort them the more touchingly, and prayed the more fervently as some showed signs of failing. As the Saint himself afterwards remarked, he was less afraid of death for himself, than he was troubled at the thought that some might lose heart and fail.

The captivity lasted from midnight until late in the day, while the hostile crowd was swelling continually and shouting wildly. When some, says the biographer, heard the Saint's voice chanting the Divine praises louder than the others, it seems as if Satan actually took possession of the mob. Cries were heard for the Archbishop's life. "Kill him," they shouted; "die he must!" Truly a vivid picture of the manner in which the Savior Himself had been condemned; and the poor people, like the Jews of old, were made the tools of unscrupulous leaders. At last, when the day was far advanced, some succeeded in scaling the tower, and forced an entrance to where the Saint and his companions were. Like a furious mob, so entirely unlike their real selves, they rushed into the place with drawn swords, shouting for Norbert's blood. However, the Saint had no sooner seen them enter than he advanced to meet them. "You seek but one person," he said; "behold, here I am. Spare those who are with me for they do not deserve death."[12] And,

---

[12] Vita A, Ch. XIX.

marvelous to relate, when Norbert, who still wore his pontifical vestments, pronounced these words with that perfect calm and dignity worthy of an Archbishop, the invaders stood as if nailed to the ground.

The next instant one simple look of their fearless Archbishop threw them down on their knees; overwhelmed with fear and trembling, they begged his pardon. What is more, the sight of their saintly Archbishop had so completely changed them that these very men protected Norbert against the attacks of other assailants, who by this time were entering the place, and so from being his greatest enemies they at once became his actual protectors.

Norberto insidians latro, sed proditus, Ipsum
Patronum causae gaudet habere suae.

While these things were taking place within the tower, a number of those without, thinking that by this time the Archbishop had been killed, now rushed into the room to finish their diabolical plot, and it happened that at this moment one of Norbert's servants was struck; he fell to the ground mortally wounded. The Saint, seeing this, hastened at once to the side of his dying servant, and when some of his friends wanted to restrain him he said: "No; it will never be said that one of mine has fallen while I was still alive." The man who had struck the servant now seeing the Archbishop alive before him, became mad with rage, raised his blooddripping sword and struck Norbert on the shoulder. The sword, however, rebounded and did not inflict a wound. But as the sword was still wet with blood, some fell on Norbert's mitre, and this blood stain remained thereon until his death.

Meanwhile the Archbishop's clerical enemies had come together in the Cathedral and deliberated among themselves as to how to exploit the present riot to their advantage. To take away all suspicion from themselves, they now took the relics, which they found, of course, intact, and went out to show them to the people.

They tried to calm the multitude, saying how shameful it was for the flock to attack their pastor. But they did this not without a reason. For after causing the disturbance, these leaders now came out feigning to be adverse to the use of any violent means, and even showed a false sympathy for their persecuted Archbishop. What, then, was their object?

They spoke to the people of the greatness of their Archbishop, and at the same time tried to make Norbert and his people believe that it was not his person that had caused the riot, but the presence of these Frenchmen in the city. They further urged Norbert in the presence of this large concourse of people to promise on the relics of the Saints that he would at once remove his religious from the Chapter of St. Mary. The Saint, hearing this request, became indignant; and, though he was apparently surrounded by his bitterest enemies, and actually in danger of being killed, he answered frankly that he did not think it just or right to "buy the peace of man by destroying the work of God." His brethren had been placed in charge of St. Mary's for the welfare of religion, with the full consent of both the Pope and the King, and therefore he not only declined to remove them now, but declared that he would never remove them.[13]

In the meantime Henry, the head magistrate of Magdeburg, who had been absent from the city, had returned; and, hearing what had occurred, came hurriedly upon the scene and ordered the crowd to disperse peacefully. He added that whatever grievances they had, they were at liberty to come to make them known to him. The coming of the magistrate at this particular moment may well be regarded as truly providential. Had it not been for his timely arrival, the Saint's positive refusal to dismiss his canons from the city would undoubtedly have caused a new outbreak. However, as it was, calm was restored.[14]

---

[13] *Vita B*, Ch. XLIX. *Vita A*, Ch. XIX.

[14] Acta SS. T. XX. Chronic. Magdeb. No. 6.

Norbert returned with his colleagues to the Cathedral, and, full of joy, celebrated a Mass of Thanksgiving to God for His protection. Before beginning the Holy Sacrifice, he thus addressed from the foot of the altar those present: "Behold what I have been falsely accused of having broken and removed! they are still here whole and entire in the same place where they were before. Judge for yourselves if I am guilty of the sacrilege of which they have accused me."

He then began his Mass, and was obliged to read the Epistle and the Gospel himself, because his ministers—thus we read in the Chronicles—had retired, being fatigued and still very much frightened. When the Mass was over Norbert returned to his palace, rejoicing that he had been found worthy to suffer for the sake of justice, and that God had visibly protected him in his tribulations.[15]

[15] *Vita A*, Ch. XIX.

CHAPTER IV
DRIVEN FROM HIS SEE

Coelitus illaesus, stricto licet ense petitus.
Pectora dat propria, non violanda, Gregi.

They exiled thee; vainly their darts were flung
Around thy tranquil soul....

ONE would be justified in thinking that after the storm described in the last chapter, the sky would have cleared for at least some time. Alas! the biographer informs us that on the very next day new attacks on the life of the Archbishop were planned. Complaining that they had been deluded, and saying that Norbert had escaped them by some secret magical power, his enemies thought of more effective means to rid themselves of the "reformer." Deep down in their hearts they fully realized that the Saint's uprightness and strength of character had caused the ill success of their plan, but this very thought embittered them all the more. As a consequence of all that had occurred, they could not deny that the Archbishop had gained instead of lost in the estimation of the people. However, one of the qualities of hatred is a certain tenacity with which it pursues its evil designs. Regardless of consequences, hatred strives hard in pursuit of its victim.

Norbert's enemies thus met on the very next day in secret. Incredible as it may seem to us, these men determined to do away with Norbert at all costs, resolving on the following plan, truly diabolical in its very conception. The day before the awful murder was to be committed, all bound themselves to take a large quantity of intoxicating drink in order to have the murder attributed to the effects of drunkenness. Furthermore, it was agreed that any one of them who should break this agreement was to have his property confiscated.[1]

Accidentally the plan came to the ears of some of Norbert's friends. These at once went to the Saint to warn him of the new danger that threatened his life, and to urge him to leave the city for some time. But the Saint sternly refused. First of all he could not believe how a man could be capable of doing such a foul act; and, secondly, if things actually proved to be thus, the Saint told them that he joyfully anticipated the hour when he should receive the crown of martyrdom in the episcopal city. He continued to perform undisturbed his daily duties and tried to enforce the laws of reform, seemingly unaware of any plot against his life.

Finally came the day agreed upon by the conspirators. As if acting upon a given signal, an excited crowd rushed into the streets of Magdeburg with wild cries and shouts, more in the manner of savages than Christian people, and made their way towards the Provostry of St. Mary, where they knew they would find Norbert at that hour. The magistrates, however, having undoubtedly been forewarned, were awaiting them, and succeeded in quelling the first riot. The crowd was driven back, but alas! only to return immediately with reenforcements, so that the magistrates were unable to keep the people in check. As on the former occasion, savage cries were heard: "Death to Norbert!"—"Kill him!"

While this wild crowd was trying to gain entrance into the Provostry, the Saint was quietly occupied, and upon hearing the great noise inquired what it meant. He was then told that the worst had come to pass, and that outside the monastery there was a large crowd looking for his life, and fully determined to drive the religious away from the monastery. When this was told to Norbert, the Saint answered smilingly: "They will never succeed, for that

[1] *Vita B*, Ch. L—*Vita A*, Ch. XIX. "De ebrietate Parthenopolitanorum." Both biographies give all the details of this diabolical plan.

which has been planted by the hand of God cannot be destroyed by the hand of man." Full of confidence in God's Providence, he wished quietly to continue the work in which at the moment he was engaged, but the magistrates themselves and all Norbert's friends and children begged him to spare himself for the welfare of his diocese and his Order. At last the Saint consented, and, truly sad at heart, fled from Magdeburg. When he saw the furious mob assembled before the gates of the Provostry, he shed tears of compassion for his poor deluded people, and offered a short but fervent prayer to ask the Holy Spirit to guide him in the direction of these precious but misguided souls.

He first came to the Abbey of St. John the Baptist, the Benedictine abbey at Bergen, where he was most cordially received by his friend, Abbot Arnold. However, he did not remain here very long. After making arrangements in regard to the most pressing matters concerning the administration of his diocese under present conditions, he did not want to expose the religious of Bergen to the attacks of an excited populace, and departed from here for his episcopal castle of Gevekenstein, near Halle. In this place the poor Archbishop had thought to retire and find at least a few days of rest and solitude, in which he could ask God for strength, and find consolation in prayer. However, his enemies had foreseen this plan, so well did they know the Saint, and thus before he arrived the whole place had been surrounded by his enemies. How bitter and hard it must have been for the saintly Archbishop to find himself thus treated by his own children. But Norbert, like the royal Prophet, who while being hunted down by his unnatural son Absalom, suffered the persecution with meekness, went from the castle to the Augustinian monastery of Petersberg, situated on a high mountain.[2] Here the Saint was received with due respect and honor by the Provost, who was most happy to assist his exiled Archbishop.

---

[2] Hugo "Vie de saint Norbert," p. 296. According to Winter, p. 42, and Herstel, p. 81, Norbert went to the monastery of Neuwerk.

The Saint's next act was to take counsel with his friends in regard to the best way of proceeding under the circumstances. Many hours did he spend here before the Blessed Sacrament at the feet of the Master asking for guidance from on high. But his negotiations to restore order by peaceful means to the people of Magdeburg were all in vain. At last then his resolution was taken, and from his place of retreat the Archbishop pronounced the excommunication over all those who should persevere in their opposition to his episcopal authority. Truly may we believe that the Saint had been forced to take this extreme measure, and only adopted it when all other means, inspired by kindness and goodness, had been exhausted. As the biographer observes, Norbert's fatherly admonitions had only added fuel to the burning rage of his enemies, and thus had it become necessary to try to win by severity what could not be won by kindness.

Having pronounced the excommunication, the Saint's heart seemed at rest; and finding another "Prémontré" in the monastery of these Augustinians, considered his exile a real blessing. "Being used to the daily exercises of the monastic life," says Hugo, "he was most happy to be able to join his voice in choir with those of his hospitable friends, and he distinguished himself from the other monks only by the severity of his penance and his piety." How fervently must the Saint have prayed during these days especially, and asked God's pardon for the sins of his people. Like another St. Paul, he offered himself to God for their salvation. And see! the All-Good Father graciously heard his prayer and caused a sincere repentance among the people of Magdeburg.

With Norbert's excommunication it seemed as though a curse had fallen upon the city. Sober reasoning had by this time replaced their wild passion, and the people now felt a great loss in the absence of their Archbishop. They sincerely regretted their hasty actions and, wonderful to relate, this time, even the instigators themselves admitted their guilt and were deeply ashamed of their diabolical deeds. Once the people realized how strangely they had allowed themselves to be misled, they called a public meeting in the center of the city, and here resolved to send some of the most prominent citizens as their deputies to the abbey of Petersberg to entreat the Archbishop to forgive them and to return to his flock.

We can easily imagine how great Norbert's joy must have been at this happy turn of affairs. The good Archbishop received the deputies with the love of a father, who after a long separation, sees his beloved children once more. He most gladly forgave them all. And when they further offered him a sum of money as a compensation for all he had suffered, Norbert sternly refused, saying that his only compensation would be their sincere repentance.[3] However, in regard to his poor servant who had been wounded during the first riot, and whose house had been pillaged and pulled down, for him Norbert insisted on full reparation for all the loss and injuries this poor man had suffered. Norbert then withdrew the excommunication which for six weeks had rested upon the city.[4]

The deputies gladly promised to make the restitution Norbert desired, and hastened back to Magdeburg where their message caused general rejoicing. They at once gave orders to have the house of the wounded servant rebuilt, and further gave him forty silver marks in reparation for what he had suffered.

To try their fidelity and sincerity, Norbert postponed his return for two more weeks. When the people heard this, they at first were disappointed; soon, however, they came together and discussed plans suitable to make due reparation to their good Archbishop for all the injuries he had endured. The whole city now was anxious to make amends, and thus it was decided by all to go to meet Norbert and lead him in triumph back to the city, whence only a few weeks before he had been forced to flee as an exile.

---

[3] *Vita B.* L. Plus animas Deo quaerere venerat quam pecunias. . .

[4] Acta SS. T. XX. Chron. Magdeb. Post sex hebdomadas . . . absolvit. . . .

According to Madelaine,[5] they first escorted him to the episcopal castle at Gevekenstein where Norbert had been refused admittance shortly before, and from thence they brought him to Magdeburg. It was in the latter part of the month of October when Norbert was led in triumph back into the city amidst universal rejoicings. He was surrounded by nobles, and thousands of people proclaimed him as their great and saintly Archbishop.[6] Although but few particulars of this grand reception have come down to us, Norbert's address on this memorable occasion has happily been preserved by history. Upon his arrival the Saint at once entered the Cathedral, which was but a few weeks before the scene of so many indignities; and when Norbert saw himself followed by his people, he mounted the pulpit and spoke:

> My dear brethren, it was with great sadness that I left you, but through the mercy of God it is with exceedingly great joy that I return and appear in the midst of you. The enemy of peace who finds his delight in sowing discord and hatred in the world, has been the cause of this cruel separation. Having laid the foundation of his empire by division, this obstinate hater tries to perpetuate it by discord, in order that by separating the flock from its pastor, the sheep may wander at the voice of a mercenary, and be thrown into the abyss. Such have always been the tactics of this eternal enemy of souls; such also is the source of the misunderstanding now so happily ended. Jealous of the unity between us, Satan has been the cause of this division, by which he has tried to overthrow the good understanding between the pastor and his people, and to destroy that peace which is as necessary for the common happiness of the public as it is for the salvation of the flock and the ministry of the pastor. Almost overcome by the tempest, I could not calm it by my prayers, so I was obliged to turn away from it to go elsewhere. But, thanks be to God! Jesus Christ, Who seemed asleep when the tempest was raging, has now granted our prayers. He has commanded the winds and the sea, and there is again a great

---

[5] Madelaine o. c. p. 402.

[6] *Vita B*, Ch. LI.

calm. The peace which the evil spirit had taken away from us has been restored by the God of peace.

My dear brethren, have an ardent love for this peace; seek it incessantly and guard it diligently. Let our hearts remain united in the bonds of charity. As we read of the first Christians, let there be but one heart and one soul amongst us, and let us work together in the union of this charity. Fear not, my dear children, that what you have done has ill disposed your pastor toward you. It is true, you have wronged not me, but that sublime priestly character with which God has honored me, but I hope from the mercy of Him who knows how to pardon that your tears of sorrow have already effaced the fault you have committed.

Let us therefore now pray to the Father of mercies and the God of all consolation to preserve this peace amongst us, which though we have not merited, we intend to merit from now on. Let us endeavor by our good works to make reparation for our sins. Let us insure our calling in order that God may be glorified by us all forever and ever. Amen.[7]

This forgiving and touching address of the Archbishop on this memorable occasion caused many tears to flow. More than ever did the people realize what a holy and zealous Archbishop they had in Norbert, and from that day they became so firmly attached to him that no calumnies, whatever their source, could separate again the flock from its pastor. Thus was the word of the Apostle verified that "all things work to the good of those who love God." And when the Saint solemnly intoned the "Te Deum," observes Dr. Winter, he not only celebrated his own victory, but also the victory of the brethren of St. Mary's. Since their coming to Magdeburg they had been calumniated and persecuted; they had come with the approbation of the Pope and the King, but until now, their foundation had not been canonically confirmed by the Archbishop. This event,

[7] Hugo, "Vie de Saint Norbert," p. 299. Hugo has taken this discourse from a MSS. containing fragments of the life of St. Norbert.

however, truly crowned Norbert's successful undertakings.[8]

From the very day of Norbert's return to his episcopal city, no people could show themselves more submissive than his. And the early biographer relates that from that day on, Norbert was most successfully engaged in the work of the sacred ministry. He then continues that Norbert was an angel at the altar, a true father in the confessional, another St. John the Baptist in his daily life. A true apostle of peace, his great aim was to establish peace between man and God, as well as between man and his neighbor. He was severe on heretics and schismatics, in fact, on all those who sought to disturb the peace of the Church. He was a father to the orphan, and he comforted the heart of the widow. In a word, Norbert "broke the jaws of the wicked man, (oppressors of orphans and widows) and plucked the spoil out of his teeth."(Job XXIX.) He was always cheerful and most affable to all alike. Assiduous in upholding the doctrines of the Church, he was a no less zealous advocate of her discipline. For this reason he made his regular visitations in his diocese, reforming abuses wherever he found them, without respect for persons. A holy and zealous priest, he was also the pattern of bishops.[9]

During this period of successful administration of the diocese, the Saint by no means neglected to look after the welfare of his Order, and several new foundations were made at this time. There was a monastery at Poelde, in the Duchy of Gruebenhagen, morally and financially in a pitiful condition. Norbert introduced there his own brethren, and their coming was the beginning of fervor and

---

[8] Cfr. Winter, o. c., Ch. I. Madelaine observes, on p. 404, that all the early MSS. agree as to the year in which these events occurred, being the third year of Norbert's episcopate. Only Vander-Sterre says that it occurred in the fifth year; and the Bollandists, following his opinion, describe the above related scene as having taken place after the Council of Rheims (1131). This, for different reasons, seems very improbable.

[9] Cfr. *Vita B*, Ch. LII.

prosperity.[10] About this time was founded the abbey "Gottesgnade" through the generosity of Otto, Count of Reveningen and Crudorp.

The Count himself renounced the world and made his religious profession in the Cathedral of Magdeburg, where Norbert had given him the white habit. In the chronicles of this abbey, published by Dr. Winter, we read that the first provost of this community was Emelrick, whom Norbert had brought with him from France, and who later became a bishop in the East. For the clerics and laymen who formed this community, Norbert prescribed the regular statutes in conformity with the Rule of St. Augustine, "but," continues the author, "he allowed them, as he had also done in Magdeburg, to wear black capes over their surplice, and to cover their habits with mantles; he gave them the Breviary and the Gradual of the Cathedral of Magdeburg and of secular canons, which he himself had learned and followed formerly at Xanten."[11]

Thus did God draw good from evil, both for the Saint's diocese and for his Order, and Norbert was fast approaching the attainment of his ideal, namely, to bring reform in the Church of Christ.

---

[10] Acta SS. T. XX., p. 52. Also Hugo Annal. Ord. Praem. II. col. 575. Poeldia.

[11] Winter "Chronic. Gratiae-Dei," pp. 329-332.

ST. NORBERT AND HIS BRETHREN BEFORE POPE INNOCENT II

CHAPTER V
THE DEFENDER OF THE PAPACY

Norberti studiis Anacleti schismate presso,
Legitimo Capiti Roma quieta subes.

Through Norbert's zeal the schism of the antipope was ended and Rome restored to God's true Representative.

HAT Norbert's zeal for the welfare of religion was not merely confined to his Archdiocese, but extended to the Church Universal, we learn especially from the part he took in the suppression of the schism of Peter di Leone. Before proceeding with the Saint's history, therefore, it appears necessary to give a short account of this nefarious schism, to show the more clearly the importance of Norbert's work.

After the death of Pope Honorius II, which took place about the middle of February, Gregory, Cardinal-Deacon of the title of St. Angelo, had duly been elected to succeed him. He was clothed in the Pontifical robes and enthroned in the Lateran basilica, on the 17th day of February, 1130, taking the name of Innocent II. "On the same day," observes Darras, "Peter di Leone, of a recently converted Jewish family, whose wealth commanded great influence in Rome, was elected by some dissenting Cardinals; he seized St. Peter's Church by armed force, stripped it of all its wealth, and was crowned by his partisans, with the title of Anacletus II."[1] He was, moreover, bold enough to send notice of his election to all Christian

[1] Cfr. History of the Cath. Church, Vol. III, p. 217.

princes and to compel the lawful Pope Innocent to leave the city. To estimate more fully the grave consequences of this act the reader ought not to forget that we are writing, not of the twentieth century, but of the twelfth, when there was neither telegraphic communication nor the press to reach the world with the rapidity of thought, and contradict false announcements. Moreover, Peter di Leone was Cardinal at the time, and thus a great many did not even think of questioning the report. In fact, he it was who, together with Cardinal Gregory, now the lawful Pontiff, had given in 1124 the first papal approval of the Order of Prémontré, by a Bull to which both these Cardinals had affixed their seals. The consequences therefore of Peter's assuming the papal crown in opposition to Gregory were very deplorable, and created lamentable confusion. Ordericus declares that "in most monasteries two abbots arose and in bishoprics, two prelates strove for the chief authority, one of whom adhered to Peter (Anacletus), the other to Gregory (Innocent)." And St. Bernard, speaking of this anti-pope, says in one of his letters:

> "The enemy of the Cross of Christ (I relate it even weeping) carries his audacity so far as to drive from their (Episcopal) sees the holy men who absolutely refuse to bend the knee before the beast of the Apocalypse. ... He endeavors to raise altar against altar ... to intrude abbots into the places of abbots, bishops into the places of bishops, to thrust out Catholics, to advance schismatics. . . ."[2]

And in letter CXXIV St. Bernard says of Peter, that either he is "of Antichrist or the Antichrist himself."

Incidentally, we might call the reader's attention here to a former letter of St. Bernard quoted above. From that letter it appeared that the present schism had been revealed to our Saint two years before it actually occurred. St. Bernard at that time thought Norbert's prediction a mere illusion, but now when he saw Peter di Leone usurping the Chair of St. Peter, and followed by a dissolute

---

[2] Cfr. "Works of St. Bernard," by S. J. Eales. Letter CXXVI. See also General Preface, p. 35.

mob, breaking altars and selling holy vessels to cover the expenses of a cruel war, he remembered the words of Norbert; and thus Bernard himself speaks of Peter as the Antichrist, who now had appeared and was making war against God and His Church.

When the conflicting reports in regard to the new Pontiff reached the ears of the Archbishop of Magdeburg, he at once took steps to find out the true state of affairs in Rome. He wrote to the Archbishop of Ravenna and to the Bishop of Lucques in Tuscany, who were in a position to know the truth about the election. Though the letters of the Saint have been lost, the answers of the two Italian prelates still exist. Archbishop Gautier wrote to Norbert as follows: "Upon receipt of the letter which Your Grace has deigned to send me without knowing me and without ever having seen me, I was greatly rejoiced in the Lord, because, though bodily separated by a long distance, we are united through charity."

He then relates how, after the death of Pope Honorius, Cardinal Gregory had been duly elected, and continues: But after this election, Peter Leonis, who for a long time had aspired to the Papacy, now assisted by the violence of his parents, the spilling of blood and the profanation of holy images, impudently took the red cape, distinctive ornament of the Pope, and feared not to usurp in a simoniacal manner the Holy Roman Church, our Mother. Since these facts are known to all the churches of Italy, we recognize without a shadow of doubt, we salute and venerate as Pope and Lord Apostolic, Innocent II, a man wise, prudent, chaste, humble and full of virtue, who has received the divine consecration from the venerable Cardinals. In regard to Peter Leonis, who is truly a son of a roaring lion, we condemn him and reject him as an intruder, an apostate and a heretic. We beg the prudence of Your Grace not to hesitate...

He further begs Norbert to use his influence with Lothaire, King of the Romans, to induce him to come to Rome at once, and to confirm the bishops of Germany in the union of the Catholic faith. He then concludes, recommending himself to Norbert's pious prayers, and wishing the Saint "long life and health for the welfare of a great number of people and for the glory and honor of the Church."[3]

The answer of Henry, Bishop of Lucquez, was still more explicit on the fact of the election. He relates to Norbert, "his Father and Lord," how, when Pope Honorius was dangerously sick, the Cardinals met in the church of St. Andrew the Apostle, and decided that the election of a new Pontiff should be entrusted to eight persons: two Cardinal-Bishops, the one of Preneste and the one of Sabine; three Cardinal-Priests, Peter of Pisa, Peter Rufus and Peter Leonis; three Cardinal-Deacons, Gregory of St. Angelo, Jonathas and the Chancellor Haimeric, in such a manner that when Pope Honorius, who then was in his last hour, came to die, he who should be elected by these eight men or their majority, would be recognized by all as the new Pope. The Cardinal-Bishop of Preneste decided, moreover, with the consent of all the others, that if anyone should oppose the election thus made, he would be subject to excommunication; and that if anyone should try to elect another, this election would be null, and that he, thus elected, should be incapable of ever obtaining any dignity in the Church. Peter di Leone confirmed this decision with his own mouth, adding that no one need fear any coming schism in the Church. "... But he and Jonathas separated themselves from their colleagues...."[4]

These are the two letters addressed to the Archbishop of Magdeburg in answer to his queries, which letters incidentally have revealed to modern historians the exact circumstances of the election of Innocent, and the intrusion of Anacletus. It is needless to add which side Norbert chose.

Now, as we have said, Anacletus, once master of Rome, had dispatched letters to all Christian sovereigns announcing his

---

[3] Mansi. Concil. XXI, p. 432, et seqq. "Visis Sanctissimae Paternitatis Vestrae litteris ..."

[4] Cfr. Madelaine o. c., p. 412, who moreover quotes the letter in full in the appendix. No. XII.

election to the pontifical throne. The bearer of the letter to the German King Lothaire was Albero, Archbishop of Bremen and Legate of the anti-pope in Germany, who used all his influence to gain the king for the party of his master. This same Albero bore also a letter from the anti-pope to Norbert, because Anacletus knew him to be the king's friend and adviser. In this letter the anti-pope spoke in the most flattering terms of the Archbishop of Magdeburg and the great work the Premonstratensians were doing, at the same time reminding Norbert of the fact that he as the Pope's Legate had at one time done Norbert a great service by approving his Order. He further begged the Saint to follow his party and use his influence with King Lothaire and the German Court.[5]

But Norbert, not satisfied with the accounts he had received from the above mentioned bishops, had also obtained information from Haimeric himself, the Chancellor of the Roman Church,[6] who confirmed Norbert in his belief regarding the nullity of Peter's election. Consequently the Saint treated the letters from Anacletus with contempt, and replied, that far from using his influence in favor of the anti-pope, he would most assuredly direct it against him.

Meanwhile the adherents of Anacletus did all in their power to gain Lothaire over to their party. Pressed for a decision, the king convoked a Diet at Wurzburg (or Wissemburg) in the month of October, 1130. Norbert was the soul of this assembly, and by his powerful eloquence caused the king to declare that he recognized Innocent II as the legitimate Pontiff, and at the same Diet Peter di Leone was excommunicated.[7] Norbert did more. When Pope Innocent had been compelled to leave Rome, he had turned towards

[5] VandenElsen, o. c., p. 281, who further quotes Hugo, according to whom Anacletus made great promises in the letter to Norbert, the nature of which, however, is not revealed.

[6] Anacletus reproached Norbert for having listened to Haimeric. Cfr. Hugo "Vie de saint Norbert," p. 309.

[7] Cfr. Tenckhoff, p. 35—Hefele "Hist. des Conc." T. VII, p. 210.

the shores of France, which had received the august exile with all honor due to his great dignity.

At this time His Holiness was at Chartres, and through the influence of Norbert, a meeting was arranged between the Pope and the King at the Council of Liége,

> where the Emperor Lothaire came to meet him (Pope Innocent) with an enormous attendance of Archbishops, Bishops and Dignitaries of his realm; and in the center of the great square before the cathedral church, the Emperor, as if he had been the Popes equerry, approached the Pontiff respectfully on foot, in the midst of his procession, and with one hand kept off the crowd with a rod, while with the other, like a servant conducting his lord, he led by the bridle the white horse on which the pope was mounted. Then, as the ground was sloping, he supported and almost carried the Pope, and thus greatly increased the dignity of his Paternity (the Pope) in the eyes of all.[8]

Truly a great triumph for Norbert, to see his loyal efforts thus crowned with success; and the consequences of this public acknowledgment on the part of Lothaire at this particular time cannot be overestimated.

Anacletus was duly informed of Norbert's activity, and must have been acutely and incalculably disappointed. But he dissimulated his anger and used the greatest moderation in his dealings with our Saint. It happened that Atticus, the former Archdeacon, whom the reader will not forget as the leader of Norbert's enemies in Magdeburg, had just at this time made an appeal to the court of the anti-pope, against his Archbishop, who was Norbert. It seems beyond doubt that this Atticus, or Hazeko, having been repeatedly found guilty of injustice in the execution of his office, had at last been suspended by the Archbishop, and

---

[8] This quotation is taken from the "General Preface" to the Works of St. Bernard, by S. J. Eales, pp. 39-40. Although Norbert's name is not mentioned just here in connection with this event, further quotations will prove the above statement. Cfr., also Madelaine o. c., p. 415. Hefele loc. cit. Acta Sanctorum T. I. Maii, p. 527.

dismissed from his office. Now against this judgment of Norbert, he had appealed to the anti-pope, and even personally gone to Rome to defend his cause.

Anacletus on his part thought to find in this event a favorable opportunity of coming in contact with Norbert, and in order perchance to gain him eventually to his party, proceeded with the greatest caution. He began by requesting the Archbishop of Magdeburg in the most polite terms to appear before him. In his request, which is dated May 18, 1130, it was stated that it was less to judge him than to have the pleasure of seeing again an old friend. The concluding words are: "We desire to love you with our whole heart, and to honor you with all our power, you and the church confided to you."[9]

When, however, Norbert failed to take any notice of the request, Anacletus cited him to Rome a second time, and commanded him to reestablish Atticus in his former position. But the Saint treated this second letter as the first, and finally the anti-pope Anacletus, excommunicated Norbert, the Archbishop of Magdeburg, in the following words:

> We have ordered you to appear before us during the Octave of St. Martin, but you, unfaithful son, son of Belial, you have not only treated with contempt our paternal commands, but by your sarcastic discourses you have even dared to attack us, and through us the Chair of St. Peter. And to give a semblance of truth to your slander you have said publicly that We have come to the highest Apostolic Office, not by the election of the clergy but by the intrigues of our family, the strong arm of our brother and the spilling of blood. I know from what source you have these calumnious inventions; it is Haimeric, a man dismissed from the College of the Cardinals, who has furnished you with the material.
>
> You further have communicated these lies to His Majesty, King Lothaire, whose confidence you are abusing scandalously. You further pride yourself on having him for friend and protector, as if a crime

[9] Hugo "La Vie de saint Norbert," p. 311.

could be condoned by the dignity of its protectors. We are astonished to see so great a Sovereign the champion of an infamous lie, and more amazed still at finding this pious king allowing you to bark like a dog against the majesty of the papacy. For I know that you are going about to all the bishops and nobles of the realm to make proselytes for a criminal, who is the antichrist, and to take the people away from under our authority. What evil spirit drives you? What has the Catholic Church done to you? That We gave you so many tokens of our affection, that We have given freely (gratis) Our approbation to your Order when We were in France, is all this the reason why you erect an idol in Germany, and raise altar against altar? The unity of the Catholic Church can no longer suffer the excesses of this shameful schism. We therefore feel ourselves obliged to cut with a knife the wound which We were unable to heal with balm of love.

Consequently we condemn you and your followers as we do Jannes and Mambres, Dathan and Abiron. We deprive you of all your ecclesiastical and civil rights, and deliver you to eternal damnation. Given at Rome, from St. Peter's, Jan. 29, 1131.[10]

"I really do not know," says Abbot Illana, "why Anacletus and Hazeko went through all this trouble, the one to write such a letter and the other to deliver it, since both knew the character of Norbert." And in very truth, the injuries enumerated by the anti-pope, irritated at not having been able to gain for his own cause a man like Norbert, seem to us now the most magnificent eulogy of the conduct of our Saint during the schism of 1130. Moreover the excommunication of the Archbishop of Magdeburg did great harm to the cause of Anacletus himself, especially in Germany. The people, who held their Archbishop in the highest veneration, when they saw him thus grossly insulted by one who claimed to be the Vicar of Christ, became more and more convinced of his intrigues and excesses. On the other hand, Pope Innocent greatly encouraged Norbert, and especially after the Council of Rheims showed Norbert how deeply grateful he was for the work the Saint was doing for the

[10] Hugo l. c. This letter was found in the archives of Mont Cassin and sent to Hugo in 1704. Cfr. Madelaine, p. 418.

welfare of the Church.

At the Council of Rheims, Norbert had assisted as ambassador of Lothaire, and his arrival is thus described by the chronicler:[11] "At that time our Bishop Bernard with Norbert, Metropolitan of Magdeburg, who in those days enjoyed great fame and renown in the Church of God, arrived in the city of Rheims." Norbert was commissioned to hand over to the Pope a letter in which King Lothaire again protested his deep respect for Pope Innocent, and announced his readiness to undertake the expedition to Rome against Anacletus. No more welcome news could have been given to Pope Innocent, and he therefore showed his deep appreciation in a letter, addressed to the Saint shortly after, from which the following words are taken:

> It is known to all with how great firmness and perseverance, you, reverend brother Norbert, Archbishop of Magdeburg, have taken upon yourself the defense of the unity of the Catholic Church and how your burning piety and prudent foresight have stood like an unassailable wall around the house of God against the advancing schism of Peter di Leone. You have done all in your power to gain the good will of the King, princes and others, clerics and laymen, to preserve the unity of the Catholic Church and to bring by your eloquent and powerful discourses all under obedience to Us and to St. Peter.[12]

Thus we have the testimony of Pope Innocent as well as the indirect praise of the anti-pope, showing Norbert's great activity in this schism. Among the writings of St. Norbert, which, alas, are lost to us, Le Paige names a "Treatise for the defense of Pope Innocent against the anti-pope Peter Leonis."[13] Considering the great part our

---

[11] Cfr. Pertz Script. XII, p. 642—also Acta SS. T. I. Maii., p. 528.

[12] This remarkable letter, observes VandenElsen, p. 290, is found in Ludwig "Relig. Manusc. XII, dipl. miscell. IV. 388. Also Jaffe R. P. 5441—and Migne CLXXXIX, 167. A similar letter had also been received by St. Bernard on Feb. 17, 1132.

[13] Le Paige "Biblioth ... p. 304. "Scripsit ... praeclarum opus pro defensione Innocentii Papae secundi contra Petrum Leonis filium, pseudo-papam..."

Saint took in this struggle of the whole Church against one man, the loss of this paper is most unfortunate. Cardinal Gerard Caccinianimici, who watched over the interests of Pope Innocent in Germany, confessed loudly that by the efforts of Norbert Germany persevered in her obedience to the legitimate Pontiff. Norbert was thus for Germany what St. Bernard was for France, so that we can truly say that the two great defenders of the Church in these calamitous times, were Bernard and Norbert.

At the close of the Council of Rheims the Pope proceeded to Laon, whither Norbert accompanied him, as he had a great desire to revisit his dear Prémontré. The Saint travelled in the company of Bartholomew, the good Bishop of Laon, who still continued to love and protect the Order Norbert had founded. It is not difficult to divine the topic of conversation as the two bishops travelled once more over the roads in the neighborhood of Laon. How vividly they were reminded of the days when Bishop Bartholomew went forth with Norbert in search of a place suitable for a monastery. How wonderfully this work had developed under Divine guidance!

When at last Norbert arrived in the monastery he was received by the brethren with the greatest enthusiasm. However great was the joy of Norbert's arrival to the brethren, that of his own heart surpassed it, when he saw the fervor of the religious.[14] When once more he walked the old familiar halls, and joined the brethren in the singing of the Divine Office, how deep down in his heart he must have envied them their peaceful religious and regular life. How different it all was from his daily life as head of an archdiocese, especially in those troublous days. However, he always found consolation in his favorite maxim: "Qui Deum habet pro se turbatur in nulla re." Who has God on his side is never disturbed by anything.

The Sovereign Pontiff, accompanied by several bishops, likewise paid a visit to Prémontré at this time. His Holiness did so to show

[14] Cfr. Hugo o. c., p. 316, who bases his assertion on a manuscript life of St. Norbert. Cfr. also P. Alph de Liguori, p. 292.

his appreciation of all Norbert had done in his behalf.[15] "What the Pope witnessed," the writer further continues,

> "fully confirmed all he had heard concerning the fervor of these religious, who at this period were the admiration of the whole Church. With his own eyes he saw how men of noble birth and great learning practiced joyfully the most rigorous austerities of privation and religious discipline. Five hundred religious he found living together as brethren, united by the same spirit and working for the same end. He further saw how many of them, while strictly observing the monastic exercises of the contemplative life, fulfilled at the same time the priestly functions of the active ministry. The virtuous lives of these fervent religious so edified Pope Innocent, that he again confirmed, now as Sovereign Pontiff, the Order which he had formerly confirmed as Legate to Pope Honorius. He further confirmed and approved the resolutions of the General Chapter, by which unity of discipline had been established for all Premonstratensian foundations, and by which the Abbot of Prémontré had become Abbot-General."[16]

After the Pope's departure Norbert spent a few more days in his dear solitude, and then at the special command of Innocent, hastened back to Germany that he might confer with Lothaire on the proposed expedition into Italy.

[15] Cfr. Madelaine, pp. 416-417.

[16] According to Le Paige, 419-448, both these "Bulls" are dated April 12, 1131.

CHAPTER VI
THE ITALIAN EXPEDITION

Schisma Anacleti quando Norberte! coerces,
Clara tibi comitem vallis amica dedit.
Innocui papae partes meliusne tueri
In mundo quis, quam Lilium, apisque, queat?

When Norbert was engaged in suppressing the schism of Peter di Leone, Clairvaux offered him as helper St. Bernard. Who, of all men, were more able to defend the cause of Pope Innocent than these two Saints?

HILE nearly the whole Catholic world recognized Innocent as the rightful pastor of the Church, Anacletus with all his power and the influence of his wealth, had managed to remain master in the Eternal City. Roger, Duke of Sicily, who was ambitious to wear the royal crown, and William, Count of Poitou and Duke of Aquitaine, both recognized his authority, for which they were naturally amply repaid by Anacletus. Thus the latter had even given to Roger the hand of his sister in marriage, adding by this to his domains the principality of Capua and the lordship of Naples. One of the biographers of St. Bernard observes that Anacletus had promised the pontifical sanction to his election to the kingdom of Sicily and Italy, in return for Roger's formal engagement to lend a helping hand against the pretensions of Innocent. "It is even asserted," he continues, "from some documents found in Roger's papers, that, in order to attach the kingdom of Sicily more closely to the cause of the Holy See, the schismatical pope promised him the dignity of patrician of Rome, and, perhaps, even the crown of the German Empire."[1]

But Pope Innocent, relying on the promises of King Lothaire, which were communicated to him through Norbert at the Council of Rheims, namely, that Lothaire was ready to open the campaign in Italy with all the forces of his Empire, set out for Rome in the company of St. Bernard, hoping to be able at last to put an end to the schism. In the words of one of the oldest chroniclers, this was the situation: "Anacletus occupied the seat of authority, Innocent had with him the churches; the former was master of Rome, the latter reigned over the "Catholic world."[2]

"However," says the biographer of St. Bernard,

> "the critical state of affairs in Germany was far from justifying the ostentatious promises of Lothaire. Obstacles arose on every side to his Italian campaign... The princes of the empire, whose esteem Lothaire had not been able to gain, remained shut up in their capitals, in displeasure at the decay of the German Empire and thus testifying their disapprobation of the enterprise which they considered to be ill-timed, and beyond the power of Lothaire to accomplish."[3]

Norbert, who by this time had returned to Germany, had been instructed by the Holy Father to use his influence to strengthen the King in his resolve to send an army. Moreover, it must also be observed that Lothaire's expedition into Italy had another object be sides giving assistance to the Pope. Innocent had promised to crown Lothaire Emperor as soon as Rome and the church of the Lateran would be in his possession, and "Lothaire was aware that the imperial crown alone could strengthen his tottering authority in Germany, and enhance the majesty of his throne in the eyes of the

---

[1] Cfr. "The Life and Times of St. Bernard," by Mons. L'Abbé Ratisbonne, p. 174.

[2] Hugo "Sacrae Antiq. Monum." I. Chron. fr. Balduini Ninov., p. 165.

[3] Ratisbonne, o. c., p. 189.

German princes."[4]

Thus we might say that Lothaire at last undertook the perilous expedition, by the persuasion of Norbert, and through personal ambition. His vassals having refused him their assistance, he succeeded with infinite difficulty in collecting an army of from fifteen hundred to two thousand men. On Easter Sunday of the year 1132 (April 10), he solemnly announced his determination to undertake the expedition, and confided the care of the kingdom to Henry, Duke of Bavaria. He further commanded the army to meet at Wurzburg, and when Norbert gave his consent to accompany the King into Italy, Lothaire appointed him his Chancellor, since this office was vacant on account of the death of the Archbishop of Cologne.[5]

At first the Saint had refused the honor on account of failing health. Worn out by austerities of more than seventeen years, by hard missionary labors, and not the least by the numerous hardships endured by him during his episcopate, Norbert now began to feel that his earthly career was drawing to a close. However, when both King Lothaire and Pope Innocent insisted on his coming, and convinced him that his presence was necessary for the welfare of the Church, the Saint finally yielded. It is to be noted here that the last years of Norbert's life, to his great credit, were entirely spent for the welfare of the Church in general. Might we not infer from this fact that conditions in his own diocese were such that his

[4] Ibidem, p. 190.

[5] Upon this matter, says S. J. Eales, o. c., General Preface, p. 43, there is a letter of the Emperor Lothaire in the Spicilegium, vol. VI, in which Norbert, Archbishop of Magdeburg, has the title of Chancellor. Returning to Magdeburg after his visit to France, Norbert had been present at the election of the new Archbishop of Cologne. First, Godfrey, who afterwards entered the abbey of Steinfeldt, had been elected, but was prevailed upon to make room for Bruno, whom St. Bernard in letter VIII refers to St. Norbert for advice. According to Hugo, the bishop-elect at this time was in a monastery preparing himself for his consecration and hence unable to accompany the King. Cfr. Hugo, o. c., p. 329.

presence was no longer absolutely required to insure regularity?

King Lothaire, surrounded by his Court and many Prelates of the Church, met his army at Wurzburg, and celebrated the feast of the Assumption. From here the army went to Augsburg, where they arrived on the 27th of August, 1132, and, says a contemporary author, Norbert's first visit was to the Cathedral. As was his wont, on entering, he knelt at the threshold and said: "Peace be to this house and to all who dwell therein." Scarcely had he said these words when he turned to his deacon and said: "Brother, I have prayed for peace in behalf of this place and wished for it; but I have seen that peace has not been received. Take good care of my pallium and all the things I have entrusted to you, for the inhabitants will soon be in arms, and there will be a great confusion in the city."[6]

These prophetic words of Norbert were soon fulfilled, for when, on the next morning, the citizens offered resistance to the royal troops, a sanguinary battle ensued, and but for Norbert's prompt action, even the life of their venerable Bishop Hermann would not have been spared.[7] In less than two hours the greater part of the city was reduced to ashes and the king's army dispersed in all directions; and what was far worse, when, with the greatest difficulty the army had been reassembled, many of the soldiers looked upon this catastrophe as a bad omen, and refused to continue the expedition. On this occasion especially did Norbert make use of his power of eloquence, and so effectually convinced the soldiers of the greatness of the cause for which they were going to fight and of the sure protection from above, that with renewed courage they continued their march.

During this interval, Innocent had gone to Italy in the company of St. Bernard, to await there the army of Lothaire. Their unexpected arrival, added to the news of the expedition of Lothaire,

---

[6] Acta SS. XX. Anacleta Norb. Append, fratr. Cappenb., p. 846.

[7] VandenElsen, p. 327, says that the venerable bishop had been thrown out into the street during the night, and Norbert found him and cared for him.

made a deep impression upon the Italians; and whilst the adherents of Conrad and Anacletus maintained a prudent reserve—the partisans of Innocent and Lothaire took fresh courage. St. Bernard, in obedience to the Pope's orders, went preaching peace in the principal cities of Lombardy, and was so successful that under the footsteps of St. Bernard, as the prophet expresses it, "The valleys were filled, the mountains were brought low, the ways were made plain, and the crooked ways straight."

The army meanwhile had reached Milan, where shortly before, Lothaire's great opponent and competitor, Conrad, had received the royal crown. But Conrad, who had learned that Lothaire was on his way to Italy with a numerous army, and believed the rumor, went back to Germany, says Otto of Frisingen, to hide his shame.[8]

Between Plaisance and Cremona is the plain of Roncaglia, where at last the king, anxiously awaited by Pope Innocent, arrived. Here Innocent and Lothaire, after deliberating with their trusted advisers, Norbert and Bernard, on the best means of bringing the expedition to a successful issue, decided that the Pope should go along the seacoast of Viterbo, while the troops should continue their march by a different route. The details which now follow are entirely new to history[9] and based on a biography of St. Norbert, recently published in Germany. King Lothaire made a halt along the shore of Lake Bolsena, in a place called Valentano, and Pope Innocent was resting not far from there at Viterbo. This was in March, 1133.

Anacletus, who had been struck with fear when told of Lothaire's approach, and who, besides, was at that moment in no position to defend himself, contrived to gain by cunning and delay what he was unable to obtain by force. He sent an embassy to Lothaire in order to gain time, and endeavored by promises and even by offering a sum of money, to gain him to his cause. Acting

[8] Cfr. Tenckhoff, p. 16-38; Otto, Frising. VII, 18.

[9] Madelaine, p. 430. Cr. Muhlbacher "Researches on the schism of 1130" (Innsbruck, 1877), who points out several errors in the details of the Life of Pertz. *Vita A.*

upon the advice and under the influence of Norbert, the king scarcely listened to the ambassadors, who, consequently, wholly failed in their mission. Anacletus then devised another scheme, which apparently seemed honest and just. He admitted that his own election was doubtful, but added that neither was the election of Innocent unquestionable, and that therefore a competent tribunal, where both parties could be heard, should decide the question.[10]

This appeal at once impressed the King, who did not at first stop to consider the motives of Anacletus. Fortunately, however, Norbert was still with Lothaire and prevailed on him to suspend judgment until Pope Innocent had been heard from. Without losing a moment Norbert set out at once for Viterbo to take counsel with the Holy Father and St. Bernard. The latter refers to this incident in his letter to the Bishops of Aquitaine, in the following words: "But now they demand judgement, which they ought to have waited for (expectasse) before acting. When that proposition was made to them at the proper time, they rejected it; they do this now only to appear to have right on their side, if you refuse it in your turn; and if you accept it, they hope that during the process, time may be gained by delays. . . . This is a trap. . . ." (CXXVI.)

Many of the Pope's friends and advisers opposed the scheme with all their might, but Norbert saw a great opportunity of exposing the ambition of the anti-pope by accepting the proposal. The Holy Father was of the same opinion, and thus consented to appear before the king's tribunal at the place and time appointed.[11]

That which Norbert had foreseen now soon came to pass. Anacletus had counted on a haughty refusal on the part of Innocent, and thus was embarrassed when the latter consented. He tried to

---

[10] Cfr. Madelaine, o. c., p. 431, who quotes *Vita A*, Ch. XXI.

[11] Ibidem. Cum adversus Norbertum disputaretur summum Pontificem hominis judicio subdi . . . non oportere, papa Innocentius ... se exposuit in captivitatem perpetuam detrudendum, si non loco et tempore sibi constituto . . . se presentaret. Further see "Sententia Lotharii in Anaeletum." (Pertz Legum II, p. 81.)

have recourse to his former policy of postponing things in order to gain time, and of humoring King Lothaire by vain promises. However, public opinion could no longer fail to recognize the personal ambition of Anacletus; those who had been wavering, now admiring the noble conduct of Innocent, went over to his party.[12]

King Lothaire himself, seeing clearly the drift of the intrigues of Anacletus, now lost all patience and marched his army to Rome, concentrating his men on a hill called "Mons Latronum". The Romans, in consternation, and destitute of succor, were unable to defend themselves; and in their perplexity sent an embassy of peace to Lothaire to disarm his vengeance, and to offer him admission into their city. Lothaire thus entered Rome on the 14th of April, 1133,[13] without meeting any opposition, and mustered his troops on the Aventine Hill, while the Pope took up his abode in the palace of the Lateran. As to the anti-pope, continues the biographer of St. Bernard, he did not hazard an attempt at resistance. He retired to the Castle of St. Angelo with his adherents, and remained master of that quarter of St. Peter's, which he surrounded with fortifications and barricades. Anacletus did not fail to see how great a check his cause would receive, in case Lothaire were to be crowned Emperor by Pope Innocent; for this reason he persistenly refused to vacate St. Peter's, where coronations had always taken place. He moreover again manifested a desire of entering into a negotiation with Lothaire, but the latter, in concert with the Pope, "sent to him St. Bernard and St. Norbert, the Archbishop."[14] But the two servants of God found the antipope so hardened in pride, that they soon gave up all effort at reconciliation.

Norbert, having tried in vain to make Anacletus realize the

[12] *Vita A.* Ibidem. "Inde accidit ut tergiversatio Petri Leonis circa papatum rugientis frustaretur. . . ." Cfr. Also Litterae Lotharii, l. c.

[13] This date differs from that given by Ratisbonne, who again differs from Otto of Frisingen. That their dates must be incorrect, subsequent events will prove.

[14] Cfr. Ratisbonne, o. c., p. 197.

hopelessness of his cause, and to vacate St. Peter's, now endeavored to induce Lothaire to be satisfied if his coronation took place in the Church of the Lateran instead of in St. Peter's. Although Lothaire feared that his enemies would find in this an excuse to declare his coronation of no value, yet under the circumstances he considered it best to consent, and Norbert at once informed Pope Innocent to this effect. "But to Norbert's great disappointment the Pope refused, for the condition agreed upon for the coronation was, that Anacletus should be driven from Rome, and Innocent placed on the pontifical throne."[15] However, Norbert in his capacity as Chancellor of the King, used his diplomacy, and at last succeeded in convincing the Pope of the reasonableness of the demand. Since Lothaire's present army was too small to carry out his plans, the Pope was satisfied with the king's promise to return later to Rome with a larger force. Finally, preparations were made for the solemn coronation of Lothaire, on the 4th of June, in the Church of the Lateran.

When the rumor of these coming events reached the ears of Anacletus and his adherents, they at once realized their importance and were furious with rage. Seeing that this coronation would be their ruin, they did all in their power to stir up the populace of Rome and prevent, if possible, the proceedings. The result of their agitation was that on the day of the coronation, in the midst of the solemnities, a large number of disturbers tried to invade the sacred edifice and prevent Innocent from crowning Lothaire. Not without the greatest difficulty did the soldiers of the King succeed in keeping the crowd at a distance, and prevent them from committing murder and sacrilege. However, at the altar the coronation went on undisturbed, and the Pope solemnly placed on the head of Lothaire the crown of Charlemagne. His Holiness likewise crowned the Empress Richenza. Baronius speaks of the oath which the new Emperor took before God and His Vicar, to defend the Church and

[15] VandenElsen, o. c., p. 335.

the Pope, to protect the possessions of the Holy See and to recover those that had been usurped.[16]

The author of the first manuscript life of St. Norbert, having chronicled these events, then describes an incident which was as unexpected as it was compromising, especially for our Saint. "Lothaire now being crowned Emperor, had the bad taste to ask at this particular time, that the Holy Father grant him, for the honor of the empire and the stability of the compact which he had made with him, the privilege of Investiture."[17] Strange inconsistency on the part of a monarch who but a moment before swore on the Holy Gospels to defend at all times the rights of the Pope and the Bishops! All present, and even the Pope himself, were staggered by this bold request. But before anyone present had time to raise his voice in protest to this most pretentious demand, Norbert arose, and in the presence of the Emperor, whose Chancellor he was, and of a number of German Officers, fearlessly addressed the Holy Father in these words:

> "What do you mean to do, O Father? To whom would you deliver the sheep entrusted to your care, to be torn to pieces? The Church which you have received in freedom, will you reduce her again to slavery? The Chair of St. Peter requires actions worthy of Peter. I have promised obedience indeed to Blessed Peter and You in the name of Christ; but if you accede to the demands now made upon you I declare in the presence of the whole Church that I gainsay you, and will oppose the measure you will take."[18]

The eyes of all were fixed upon Norbert, as he thus boldly spoke, and stood in their midst like a messenger from God speaking with

[16] Baronius XVIII, p. 488. Pertz "Legum," II, p. 81. There is still in the palace of the Lateran a painting on which is represented Lothaire receiving the crown from the hands of Pope Innocent.

[17] *Vita A*, Ch. XXI. This same demand had been made by Lothaire at Liège two years before, but without success.

[18] Ibidem. In medium procedens, presente imperatore cum multo milite "Quid," inquit "Pater agis?"...

authority. However, his was the last word spoken in this unfortunate affair, for the Emperor dared no longer urge his unreasonable request, nor had the Pope any desire of making so culpable , a concession. "For Lothaire," continues the same author, "feared God ... and loved Norbert as a man sent from heaven, by whose advice he had oftentimes been guided, and from whom he daily received the Word of God." Thus did God on this day protect His Church from a great calamity, through His servant Norbert, and Pope Innocent himself was the first to shower upon our Saint numerous tokens of heartfelt gratitude. There still exists a Bull of Pope Innocent, dated June 4, the very day of the coronation, addressed to Norbert, and in it we read:

> The Roman and Apostolic Church has, in consequence of unmistakable signs, favorably approved of your ardent devotion and energy in her times of trial. Since the time it pleased Divine Providence to call Us, notwithstanding Our unworthiness and insufficiency, to the administration of the Holy See, an admirable devotedness has shown forth more and more in your person; and the constancy of your faith and piety has become renowned not only among the people near you, but even among the most remote nations. For neither have infirmities nor promises nor threats prevented you from placing yourself as an unassailable wall against the tyranny of Peter Leonis, nor from working effectively in gaining over the King and other princes to the obedience of St. Peter. . . .[19]

Truly a magnificent testimony to the work done by our saintly Archbishop in the great struggle of the Papacy! And to further reward Norbert for the great services done in the interest of religion, Pope Innocent by this same document raised Norbert to the

[19] Cfr. Muhlbacher in his "Die streitige Papstwahl des Jahres 1130" (Innsbruck 1876). Also Acta SS. T. XX. Append, p. 50.

dignity of Primate of Germany.[20]

Thus was peace again restored to the Church, and the two great powers, Church and State, were once more consolidated. Innocent, for the moment at least, resided in Rome, and Lothaire had been crowned Emperor, protesting his fidelity to the cause of Innocent. The Emperor decided to leave at once the Eternal City with his troops, and recrossing the Alps he returned into Germany, in order to set before the eyes of the princes of the empire the glorious advantages he had gained. On the 8th of September he reached Wurzburg, where the Sovereigns of Germany, who were in astonishment at the almost miraculous success of his intrepid undertaking, encircled him with their homage. Fortune having favored his arms, they all magnified his valor; and his most implacable enemies dared not disturb the unanimous concert of applause. Norbert, who at this time seems to have been very delicate in health, for he had suffered much from the Italian climate, was with the Emperor on his return journey.

Among those who had come to Wurzburg to welcome the Emperor were the newly elected bishops of Augsburg and Regensburg. The latter had been consecrated without the knowledge of Lothaire, which was not in accordance with the decisions of the Concordat of Worms. Norbert, however, used his influence with the Emperor and succeeded in inducing him to confirm this election. This, no doubt, meant a great sacrifice for Lothaire, especially since the new appointment had come about through the influence of his competitor, Conrad; but Lothaire yielded for the sake of peace for the Church.[21]

In order to show how Norbert, notwithstanding his numerous

---

[20] In regard to this Primacy of Norbert see Madelaine, p. 438. He quotes Acta SS. T. XX. p. 914. Append. 46-52. "De Primatu Germaniae Magdeburgensis Ecclesiae . . . Cfr. also DuPré Ann. breves Ann. 1133 "Pater Norbertus. . . accipit laborum praemium ab Innocentio Germaniae ecclesiarum Primatiam."

[21] Cfr. VandenElsen, o. c., p. 344.

occupations of a worldly nature, remained nevertheless a man of true humility and prayer, a miraculous incident is related by the different biographers, which occurred in Rome when the army was about to undertake its return journey. One of the soldiers was possessed by the evil spirit, and before leaving Rome his companions brought him before the Holy Father, and entreated him to deliver their comrade from this woeful torment. But Pope Innocent sent the men to Norbert, whom they found in the church, humbly praying before the altar. Deeply moved at the sight of the sick man, he said to them: "Let us all with a humble and contrite heart approach the Lord, and beseech Him to be merciful to this unfortunate man." All immediately began to pray, and the Saint remained in supplication from noon until evening, and finally obtained through the prayers of all, the deliverance of the possessed soldier; "for in the evening, with a fearful noise the evil spirit left him." The man fell exhausted into the arms of his companions, but after a refreshing sleep completely recovered his former strength. The Saint then exhorted him to make his confession, and prescribed for him, both as a penance for his past sins and as an act of thanksgiving for his deliverance, to abstain for a number of days from a certain kind of food, remarking that if he dared break these rules of abstinence, he would certainly fall back into the same misfortune. The soldier returned with the army to Germany, and there, having broken the rules laid down by the Saint, became again possessed by Satan. They brought him again before Norbert, and he was for a second time released through the mercies of God and the ministry of the Saint.[22]

[22] *Vita A*, Ch. XXI.

CHAPTER VII
The Death of St. Norbert

Finis adest vitae, finis Norberte laborum,
Ad sua Te Christus regna vocat,

Thy combat o'er, thy work is done.
The arms of Mary and her Son
Are clasped around thee. ...

URING his absence Norbert had entrusted the care of his Church to the Benedictine Abbot of Bergen, who had with great prudence and wisdom continued the government of the archdiocese according to the views and principles of the Saint. The year 1133 was drawing to a close when Norbert, physically weak and exhausted, reached his episcopal city. The fatigues of the journey, the great heat of the Italian summer, added to his austere mortifications, had greatly aggravated the infirmities of the Saint, and thereafter he was continually subject to acute bodily pains. The great desire he had of being once more in the midst of his flock, seemed, however, to make him unconscious of pain. This longing was at last gratified and the people of Magdeburg greatly rejoiced to see their beloved Archbishop again. They had reason indeed to be proud of their beloved Bishop who now was proclaimed the Founder of a Religious Order, the heroic Reformer of clergy and people, the Liberator of the Church, and the Chancellor of the German Empire. He had been laden with honors by Pope Innocent and by their Emperor, and his name was celebrated throughout the Empire. Still these good people must have honored him above all as the simple and holy religious, the Saint through whose instrumentality God performed miracles. Says the early chronicler:[1]

> Hardly had the Saint arrived, when the people brought before him a man possessed by the evil spirit. In spite of repeated exorcisms by others, Satan still refused to abandon his victim. Though he boasted that he would never depart, not even at the command of the Arch- bishop, no sooner had the unfortunate man been brought before Norbert, than the devil left him. In fact, while the Saint was blessing water, before he was able to sprinkle the holy water over the unfortunate man, the evil spirit had departed. This incident naturally intensified the love and veneration of the people for their saintly Archbishop.

It is beyond doubt that for a long time Norbert had been regarded by the people as the great Thaumaturgus of his days. He had repeatedly triumphed over Satan, and, as observed, even dumb animals obeyed his voice. It now pleased God to show forth Norbert's great sanctity through his power over death. The power God had given at one time to St. Martin, and which in later days He was to give to St. Dominic, He now gave to our dear St. Norbert.

One day the people brought before him the corpses of three men, begging Norbert in the name of the destitute relatives, to bring them back to life. Having invoked the help of Almighty God, he bent over the dead bodies, and commanded in the name of God that life should return to them. His prayer was heard; the three men rose up and walked, and Norbert restored them to their relatives.[2] This fact, chronicled by many contemporary writers, was ridiculed by Abelard, as we observed above; but his ridicule only makes it the more incontestable.

By Christmas, Norbert's state of health was so much improved

---

[1] *Vita B,* Appended. Can. Capp. Ch. X.

[2] *Vita B.* Notationes Dni Hertoghe, p. 429-434. Dupré. Annal. Ord. Praem. (MS. of the Library of Laon.) Annal. breves ann. 1134—miraculis illustris triumque mortuorum suscitator magnificus. . . . Also De Waghenaere, p. 66.

that he was able to go to Cologne and confer the Pallium upon the new Archbishop. The Emperor and his Court also assisted at this solemnity, and had left for Aachen the day before Epiphany, at which time messengers came from the Countess of Holland, announcing that her son Floris had been murdered. We mention this incident here, because the murder of Floris led indirectly to the founding of the abbey of Berne,[3] the Mother-Abbey of our American foundation in Wisconsin.

Fulco of Berne, who with the Counts of Kuik had been the cause of the murder, changed his castle into a monastery by way of doing penance for the rest of his life. The monks he introduced were quite lax in the observance of their rules, and thus it happened that six months later, Fulco invited the Premonstratensians into his castle. Berne was therefore the last abbey founded by Norbert himself.

The Emperor was still at Aachen when Norbert submitted to him for approval, the Charter of the abbey of Clarholt, which abbey however, had been founded and endowed the year before by Rudolph of Stenford, and was situated in the diocese of Osnabruck. Lothaire confirmed the foundation most willingly, and the Charter was signed by the Emperor, by Cardinal Gerard and by Anselm, Bishop of Havelberg.[4]

---

[3] VandenElsen on p. 345, observes, speaking of the transfer of the abbey of Berne to the Premonstratensians, that the Prior, Frederic of Grevenrath, had accompanied the Emperor Lothaire on his Italian expedition. The monks and the founder, Fulco, had made use of his absence to lodge complaints against his ill-government. When Frederic heard of this he resigned his charge, and since Norbert was at court at the time, the monastery was offered to him and his canons. Premonstratensians of Marienweerd were at once introduced.

[4] This Charter deserves special mention since in it we read that it was delivered "by the hand of Norbert, Archbishop of Magdeburg and Archchancellor of the Empire." Lothaire confirmed the same, in 1134, "in favor of men serving the Lord according to the Rule of St. Augustine." Cfr. VandenElsen, p. 347, Madelaine, p. 441, who further quotes Hugo "Annales Ordinis Praemonstr. T. I. Clarholtum, Probat. CCCXCIV- CCCXCV.

Meanwhile, Norbert's health was gradually declining; he remained in the service of the Emperor until the beginning of the month of March, 1134, since Lothaire refused to do anything of importance without the advice of Norbert. In the beginning of Lent, however, he declined all participation in State affairs, and Lothaire was obliged to go to the Saint and find him in Magdeburg, since he was no longer able to make the journey. When, at Easter, Lothaire sent messengers to Norbert requesting him to come to Halberstadt, the Saint was on his bed of suffering, where for four months he awaited the hour of death.[5]

High fevers were undermining what little strength remained in Norbert's emaciated body; but though a burning fever robbed him of his physical strength, his mind was ever clear and alert, and from his bed of pain he ceased not to direct and look after the welfare of his diocese. Feeling his end to be near, this faithful servant of God took special pains to regulate the interests of his Master. "Still," adds the biographer, "Lent must have seemed terribly long to the Saint of such astonishing activity! His great and only consolation was the frequent reception of Holy Communion."[6]

At last Holy Week approached, bringing with it the remembrance of all the Savior had suffered. The Archbishop made a great effort to forget his own suffering; he gently dismissed all those that were around him, and, notwithstanding their loud protestations, went once more to his Cathedral, there to perform the services of Holy Thursday. He would have spent the whole night there in memory of Jesus' agony in the Garden, but his physical state rendered it impossible. Utterly exhausted, he returned to his palace. Still, supported by the energy of his strong will, the Saint rose once more from his bed of pain, on Easter Sunday, and celebrated the Holy Sacrifice, which was to be the last Mass offered by St. Norbert. Completely exhausted and suffering untold pain, the

---

[5] *Vita B*, Ch. LII. Per spatium quatuor mensium...

[6] Cfr. Acta SS. T. XX. Chron. Magdeb., p. 53.

Saint was carried to his bed, never to rise from it again.[7]

From now on his condition from day to day grew worse; still Norbert, though his head was deluged in pain, refused to spare himself, and not being able to rise, he desired his brethren to gather around him, that he might give them his last instructions. In these his last moments he urged upon them the practice of faith and patience especially, two virtues which all during his life he had most cherished. "As when striking flint with steel, you thereby obtain sparks of fire, so also, does lively faith striking a heart of stone, produce sparks of divine love. ... Do you suffer persecution? be patient. Are you better than your Master?" He then continued to comfort them and to exhort them with a smiling countenance to practice these virtues.

Blessed Hugh, the General of the Order, was sent for upon the request of the Saint. Somehow, he was prevented from making the long journey from Prémontré to Magdeburg. Madelaine observes that Blessed Hugh could not believe that the hour was so near. On the other hand, Evermode, who for a long time had been Norbert's constant companion, never left the sickroom for a moment. He had always been Norbert's most beloved disciple, and none more closely resembled the Saint in character than he did. As for the absence of Hugh, the biographer says that Norbert felt assured that the future of the Order was safe in his hands, and thus when the brethren seemed overwhelmed with grief at his departure, and asked with the disciples of St. Martin: "Why, O Father, dost thou leave us?" he spoke to them of the great virtues of his first disciple, Hugh.

The future of his diocese caused Norbert far more anxiety than the future of his Order. During eight years he had worked incessantly for reform, and undoubtedly he accomplished great things, notwithstanding the fiercest opposition. Recall but his captivity in the tower—his flight from Magdeburg—the hatred many

---

[7] Winter. "Chron. Gratiae Dei," p. 334. Excussa modicum aegritudine, Chrisma consecravit, et die sancta ... divina celebravit...

of the nobles, in the beginning especially, bore him. What was to become of his work after he was gone? Would all his labor be really in vain? The Saint, however, considered these thoughts but temptations of the evil one, and at once dismissed them from his mind as sinful, as showing a lack of confidence in Divine Providence. Still his mind was at times disturbed on this point, so it pleased God to set his mind entirely at rest.

The Emperor, as well as the Canons of the Cathedral, assured Norbert that after his death the diocese was to be confided to the care of Conrad of Querfurt, a saintly man, who had received his priestly ordination from Norbert himself. This knowledge greatly pleased the Saint. He sent for Conrad at once and, like a dying father who is about to entrust the care of his household to his eldest son, thus also did Norbert explain conditions to Conrad and give him wise counsel as to the government of the diocese. He further recommended to him in a special way a young community of Premonstratensians in the abbey "Gottesgnade," which abbey had a great future before it.

Meanwhile his illness increased, and the Saint, fully realizing his condition, asked to receive the last Sacraments, which were administered to him by Bishop Anselm, who had been constantly at the Saint's bedside. Norbert received the Body of Our Lord with extraordinary piety and fervor. With the Holy Unction it seemed as if a new effusion of the Holy Spirit had entered his soul, and, regaining for a moment his former strength, he once more addressed his disciples in a clear and distinct voice. This was on the day of Pentecost, June 3, 1134.

Still in the afternoon of the same day he began sinking so rapidly that all present could see that death, in a very short time, would rob the diocese of its Archbishop, and the brethren of a loving father. Bathed in tears, the brethren began reciting the prayers for the dying, but his hour was not yet come. The Saint lingered till Wednesday, when finally, in the full possession of his senses, he gave his last blessing to the Archdiocese and his Order, and then invoking the Holy Names of Jesus, Mary, Joseph, Norbert peacefully expired, casting a last glance of angelic sweetness towards heaven. "Subvenite, Sancti Dei; occurrite Angeli Domini..." thus the brethren prayed, while the Saints were conducting his soul to the heavenly Jerusalem.[8]

> Then the fulness of fruition
> Came at last. The combat oer,
> Norbert gazes on the vision
> Changeless on the golden shore.

The Saint died on the sixth day of June, 1134, in the fifth year of the Pontificate of Innocent II—the ninth year of the reign of Lothaire. The Saint had lived 54 years, nineteen of which had been devoted to a strict life of penitence, eighteen in the apostolic ministry. He had been Archbishop during seven years, ten months and twenty days.

The brethren stood weeping around the corpse, while the sad news spread through the city of Magdeburg. Though the tidings were not unexpected, still the people were all profoundly touched, and hastened in great numbers to the episcopal palace. "Alas!" exclaims a Saxon historian of the time,

> "the universal law of death has taken him away from our midst ... him the great Archbishop, the eminent preacher, the man great in words and in works, the founder of numerous monasteries, the great apostle and propagator of our holy religion, the fearless defender of the Catholic Pope, Innocent, the irreconcilable adversary of the schismatic, Peter Leonis! He has been taken away from his Order, his Diocese, the Empire, the Church!"[9]

---

[8] Acta SS. T. XX. l. c. "In confessione nominis Christi." *Vita B*, Ch. LII. "Cum omni integritate sensus sui, astantibus benedictione data..." Cfr. also Pertz Script. XII, p. 451.

[9] Cfr. Pertz Script. XII. Sigeb. Contin. Praem., p. 451. VandenElsen, p. 355; Madelaine, p. 450.

Since the Saint before dying had confided the care of his body to his beloved disciple, Evermode, the latter began at once to make preparations for a proper burial. However, a serious dispute soon arose as to where the sacred remains were to be interred. First, there were the Canons of the Cathedral, who demanded that the body of their Archbishop should be buried in the Cathedral. On the other hand, the Premonstratensians of St. Mary's quite naturally insisted that the body of their holy Founder should find a last resting place in their church. For a while it seemed impossible to come to any agreement.

For six days the remains of our dear Saint were daily carried from one church to another, where amidst a great concourse of people Masses were daily celebrated, and the solemnities of the "Absolution" repeated. To the people this very procession meant rather the veneration of the relics of a Saint than a funeral procession, especially after they noticed that, notwithstanding the excessive heat, the corpse did not show the least sign of corruption. On the contrary,

Aemula dum sacro certant de pignore Templa,
Coelesti semper Corpus odore fragrat.

Meanwhile, the Canons of the Cathedral and of St. Mary's had agreed on having their difficulty solved by the Emperor Lothaire. Each sent deputies to Merzburg, in Swabia, where at that time the Emperor was holding his court. Evermode was one of the deputies of St. Mary's, and he pleaded with such energy in favor of the Premonstratensians, that Lothaire decided in favor of St. Mary's.

According to the Chronicles of Magdeburg the solemn obsequies took place on Monday, the 11th of June. Several of the most prominent men of the Empire, who at the time were assisting at the Diet of Merzburg, came to assist at the Saint's burial. Among these were the Duke Henry of Bavaria, the Margraves Conrad of Misnie, Henry of Glogau, Albrecht of Nord Marche, and the Landgrave

Louis of Thuringen.[10] Several German writers are of the opinion that the Emperor himself came from Merzburg to assist at the solemnity. There were also present Cardinal Gerard, the Archbishop of Mainz, and the Bishops of Halberstadt, Hildesheim, Naumburg, Merzburg and Meissen. An immense multitude from the surrounding country had come to Magdeburg to tender a last tribute of respect to their beloved Archbishop. The three suffragan Bishops, Godebald, Ludolph and Anselm, performed the solemn rites, "and," adds the biographer,[11] "the abundant tears of all present spoke louder than the most eloquent funeral sermon."

The corpse was buried in the nave of the Church of St. Mary, before the altar of the Holy Cross. The Saint's body was vested in full archiepiscopal ornature, namely, in Cope, Pallium and Stole, Mitre, Ring and Crozier. A few years later the Canons decided to transfer the body to the sanctuary, and place it before the High Altar. To their unspeakable joy, they found then that the body had still preserved its freshness of color, and it seemed to them as if the Saint were but sleeping. A sweet-smelling odor was exhaled from the body, which, in the words of Bl. Hugh, manifested the glory of this temple of the Holy Ghost in heaven. The brethren now placed a marble slab on the grave of their beloved Father. The following words were engraved on it in letters of gold:

> HERE, UNDER THIS MARBLE, RESTS NORBERT, BY THE GRACE OF GOD ARCHBISHOP OF THE CHURCH OF MAGDEBURG, FOUNDER OF THE ORDER OF PRÉMONTRÉ, AND RESTORER OF THIS MONASTERY. HE DIED IN THE YEAR OF OUR LORD, 1134, ON THE SIXTH DAY OF JUNE.[12]

"Mirabilis Deus in Sanctis Suis." As God had singularly blessed

---

[10] Winter. The Premonstratensians of the 12th century. Ch. III.

[11] Chron. Magdeb. Tenckhoff, p. 42.

[12] Le Paige Biblioth. Ord. Praem., p. 401; also Annales breves, p. 7.

the birth and the life of our Saint, so He also made the death of His faithful servant glorious in the sight of men. Immediately after his death the Saint, clad in white and holding an olive branch in his hand, appeared to one of the religious who at that moment happened to be on one of the granges of the abbey of Prémontré. The brother asked with timidity: "Father, whence have you come and whither are you going?" To this the Saint replied that he came from heaven and that he was going to transplant the green olive branch, the symbol of peace and victory, in the house of his poverty. By this name the Saint always had loved to call his dear abbey of Prémontré. When afterwards it was found that this apparition had taken place, not only on the day, but at the very hour that the Saint had died in Magdeburg, great importance was attached to it.[13]

Some days later another religious, this time one of the priests, also had a vision, and at once recognized his saintly father. Little by little he saw Norbert's figure change into a lily of remarkable whiteness, which was then carried to heaven by angels.

Lilia Candorem, fructum dant pacis Olivae,
Has Norbertus ovans, Angelus illa tulit.

This religious spoke at once of this vision to the prior of the monastery, and was told to mark down the exact day and hour. Afterwards these were found to correspond exactly with the day and hour on which the burial had taken place.[14]

The consolation of a similar vision was also granted to Bl. Hugh. He saw his beloved Father seated in a palace of exquisite beauty and splendor. Prostrate before him, Hugh asked the Saint regarding the future happiness of his own soul. Norbert then raised him from the ground and, embracing him most tenderly, said: "My son, you ask me something difficult to explain; but as God opens the door to

---

[13] *Vita B*, Ch. LIV.

[14] Ibidem.

those that knock, come and sit at my side." Then when both were seated the Saint continued: "I am in peace and in repose. Take courtage and work with confidence in the service of God. You also will one day enter into the joy of the Lord." He then disappeared, leaving his disciple enraptured and consoled.

Let all who believe in miracles and visions believe these with that same simplicity of faith with which they were first written down. For, having related the above, Bl. Hugh adds: "After this none of the faithful will doubt the beatitude of the man who lived as we have related, and who, after his death, by the Providence of God, gave such unmistakable signs of his happiness. You all may believe what I have written, for I take God to witness that I am speaking the truth." Bl. Hugh further appeals to his own experience and the veracity of eye and ear witnesses, so that little room can be left to doubt the sanctity and beatitude of Norbert.

From the very time of Norbert's burial his holiness was proclaimed by the "Vox populi." When shortly after the new Archbishop, Conrad of Querfurt, drew up, in accordance with his promise to Norbert, the Charter for the foundation of the abbey "Gottesgnade," he spoke of Norbert as "Blessed," and with the consent of numerous Bishops, Norbert, from that time on, received in particular churches the "cultus" of a Saint. Moreover it pleased the Almighty to manifest the glory of His servant by making his tomb glorious. Many miracles were wrought over the Saint's tomb through his intercession, and Norbert's name was invoked throughout Saxony. The brethren of St. Mary's kept a book in which were recorded the numerous miracles, and they also wrote the Saint's biography within six years after his death. Alas! these writings are lost to us. The fire, which according to the Saxon Chronicler, destroyed the Provostry of St. Mary, consumed also this register, and most of the personal writings of the Saint. From what people remembered and a few scattered documents, a new register was made, to be used later at the time of Norbert's canonization.

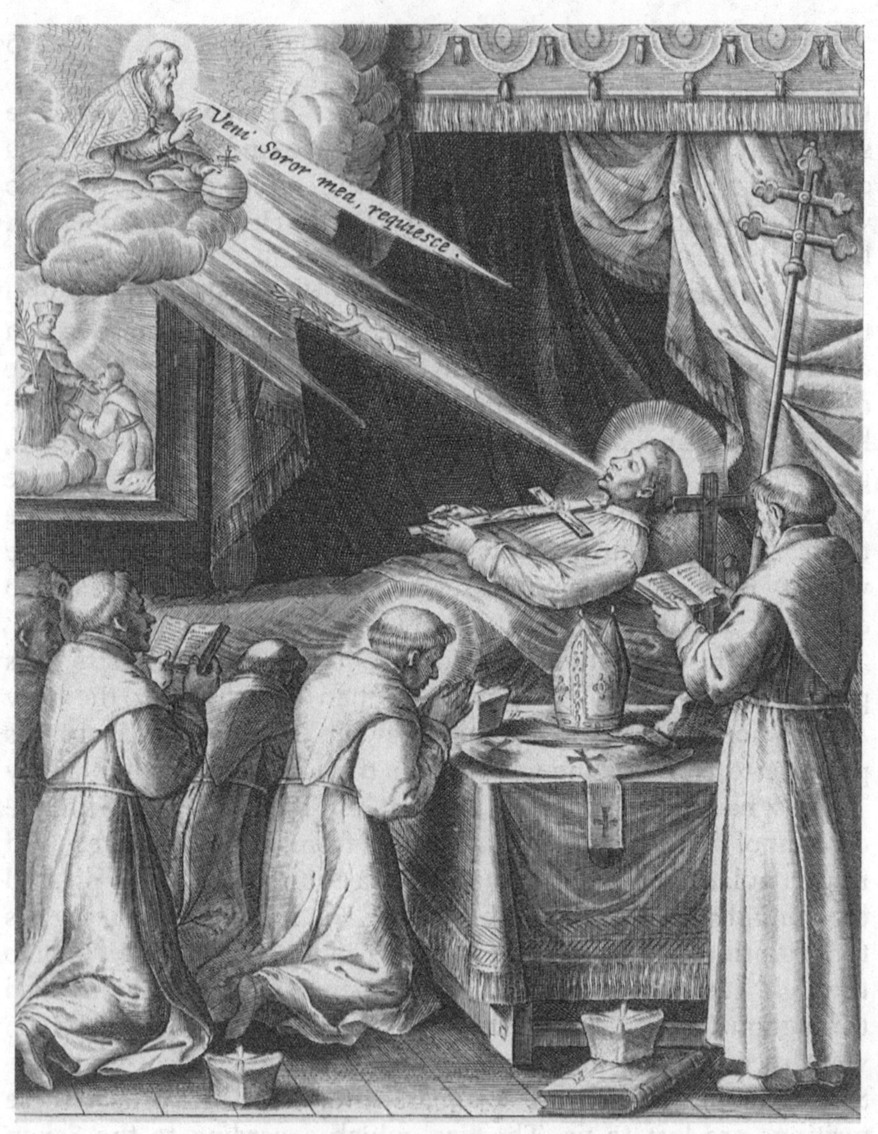

THE DEATH OF ST. NORBERT

❧✿❧

CHAPTER VIII
TRANSLATION OF RELICS

Divorum cineres dum Islebica turba profanat,
Tu procul antiqua de Statione fugis,
Inter Virgineos recipit Te Praga Penates:
Lilia Stare loco num meliore queant?

When in later years the relics of St. Norbert were exposed to profanation in Magdeburg, they were translated with great solemnity to the abbey of Strahov, near Prague.

HE great diversity of events related in this history of St. Norbert, have manifested the beautiful and sterling qualities and strong virtues of our dear Saint. He comes down to us in history as Norbert the Great, and Norbert the Saint, and a short retrospect of his life will show how well merited are the titles.

We remember the young man surpassing his fellow students at the University of Cologne. His inborn eloquence, his wide knowledge of literature—sacred and profane—his noble birth and genteel appearance, and above all his quick and penetrating intellect had made him at the age of twenty, a veritable leader among men. At the court of the Archbishop of Cologne, as well as at the court of the Emperor, Norbert was the favorite of all and was everywhere applauded. Of a firm will and an impetuous nature, he gave himself over to the world with an ardor and zeal worthy of greater objects.

By a miracle God changed the worldly young man into a second Paul, and with his characteristic ardor and impetuosity he entered into God's service. He bade farewell to the world and its allurements, and retired to a monastery to learn heavenly wisdom from the image of Christ Crucified, and the illustrious and saintly abbot Conon. He was ordained "Priest of the Most High" and at once strove to do all in his power to make others share in his newly found happiness. Neither ridicule, nor sarcasm, nor abuse could withhold him from pointing out to others the very mistakes he himself had once made. He became the great "Reformer." His life of penitence subdued the striking appearance of the brilliant courtier, and he went forth preaching penance by word and example. Led by Divine Providence, he left his native land and, in a deserted and marshy valley, found the realization of his life's ideals. Many devoted men gathered around him, and Norbert, like a grain of wheat apparently dry and dead, soon, under the influence of Divine light and love, sent forth shoots of inexhaustible fecundity. A new Order was founded, an Order of priests, practicing at the same time monastic exercises and priestly functions. Foundations were made in France, Belgium and Germany, and a new era of true religious fervor had been inaugurated.

He was led by Divine Providence to the archbishopric of Magdeburg, and again went heart and soul into the work before him. No opposition, be it calumny or even bodily injury, could make him lose sight, for a single moment, of the ideal he had placed before himself, the work of "Reform." His wonderful conversion, his continual preaching, and the fecundity of the Order founded by him, made him great in the eyes of King and Pope. He was the able guide of Lothaire in his struggle against the Hohenstaufen, and in the schism of Anacletus he directed political life in Germany with such success that Germany actually became the champion of Pope Innocent. It is written of him:

> Norbert is in every respect a reflection of his time and a worthy representative of the first half of the twelfth century. The religious enthusiasm and the maturity of diplomatic sense which distinguish the German princes of this period, the high culture in which the clergy of this time could glory, all this appeared in its true sphere

under the activity of Norbert: More than any of his contemporaries he had in view as cleric, depth of religious sentiment; as prince of the Church, purity of life and of morals; as prince of the Empire, a clear view of his duties towards Church and State. Hence it was through the energetic and powerful part he took in the leading questions of his day that he created a situation which gave him a wide-spread influence over his own age and over all succeeding ages.[1]

His power as an orator has been highly extolled by numerous contemporaries. If, in the words of St. Augustine, "Real eloquence has two sources, namely, love for man and love for truth," it is almost impossible to calculate how great was the influence of Norbert over his age, through his powerful eloquence.

Norbert was also an author. Though constantly occupied in preaching, founding monasteries, and later in the administration of his vast diocese, historians are unanimous in ascribing to Norbert several works. Thus, in his "Catalogue of Witnesses to the Truth," Mr. William Eisengreim ascribes the following works to Norbert:

1. The three books of Visions. Although a Lutheran author, Samuel Halter, speaks of them disdainfully as the product of a fanatical imagination, we can only express our deep regret that the books are lost to us, for the marvelous revelations with which heaven favored the Saint during the years following his conversion, were given in these books.
2. The sermons delivered on his missions and in the monastery to his disciples were also recorded by Norbert. The titles of some have come down to us. "On the Death of a Saint"—"The Shortness of Life"—"The Sweetness of the Yoke of Christ"—"The Reestablishment of Regular Discipline." At present we have nothing but part of his discourse to the brethren at Prémontré, previously mentioned. This ascetic discourse has, during the last century, been deemed worthy of a place in the Library of the

[1] Rosenmund. "The most ancient biographies." Sect. IV. "The Norbert of History," pp. 122-123.

Fathers.

3. An Office of the Most Pure Conception of the Blessed Virgin Mary. The antiphon composed by Norbert, "Ave, Virgo, quae, Spiritu Sancto praeservante, de tanto primi parentis peccato triumphasti innoxia," has been inserted in the new Office of the Immaculate Conception.

4. A treatise on the nullity of the election to the Papacy of Peter di Leone.

5. A book on the "Priesthood."

Father LePaige, who enumerates these different works, further adds a list of Homilies on the Sacred Scriptures from the the hand of Norbert, and assures us that the manuscripts were kept, as late as the year 1633, in the celebrated monastery of Cappenberg.[2] It seems inexplicable how these works, still existing in the seventeenth century, are all lost to us today. But the severe trials of the abbeys during the period that followed the Protestant Reformation, of which we shall speak later, and also the great fire at Magdeburg in 1631,[3] may, in some measure account for their loss. Yet, as Madelaine observes, it is quite possible that Norbert's manuscripts do exist today, in some forgotten corner of a library.

It is evident to any student of the history of St. Norbert that "authorship" was by no means his main object in life. Norbert was a man of action, and we have found his life full of high activity, which, however, did not interfere with his sanctity. If he was considered great in the eyes of the world, it was not that he sought it. Since the day of his conversion his one aim was to live the life of Jesus Christ. Most unjustly, therefore, has Norbert been referred to as the Luther of the twelfth century.[4]

---

[2] Cfr. Madelalne, p. 458—Le Paige Biblioth. Ord. Praem., p. 304—also Lienhart "Spiritus literarius Norbertinus," pp. 6-8.

[3] Cfr. Cath. Enc., Vol. IX, p. 525.

[4] See Madelaine, p. 471.

True, the sudden death of a friend was to Luther what a storm was to Norbert. Both realized the vanity of earthly things and withdrew from the world. However, instead of founding a religious Order, Luther condemned them all; instead of working for the restoration of Christ's kingdom in the hearts of men, Luther did all in his power to destroy God's kingdom. Norbert was instrumental in restoring a Pope to the throne of St. Peter, Luther was the sworn enemy of the papacy. Norbert, following the example of Saul of Tarsus, had from the day of his conversion placed himself under the guidance of a saintly abbot, and true humility and mistrust of himself had been the foundation, the beginning of his subsequent virtuous life. Luther, on the other hand, was guided by pride and self-love, and thus threw not only himself into the abyss but millions of others.

The poles are not farther apart than are the character, life-work and aims of Norbert and Luther. The virtue which especially characterized Norbert, was his deep faith. As we read in the MS. Life by Bl. Hugh: "Bernard of Clairvaux was known especially for his charity; Milo for his humility, but Norbert for his faith." Seeing God in that clear light of faith, he must needs love Him with his whole heart, and seek to make Him loved by others. Thus we see in Norbert a ceaseless burning thirst for the salvation of souls, and it is difficult for the historian to keep pace with the wonderful development of the Saint's great faith. It is written of him:

> The period of his conversion at first indicates only an illustrious penitent; soon the penitent is eclipsed by the apostle. For a moment we lose sight of the apostle and consider the founder of a new religious Order. The Founder himself seems to disappear when the Archbishop commands our attention. How can one follow him at the court of kings, whose oracle he is; among heretics to whom he is a powerful opponent, or in the midst of ravages produced by a schism whose executioner he is?[5]

[5] Cfr. Migne "Orateurs sacrés" T. LIII., col. 344.

Recall but to mind Norbert's lively faith in the Holy Eucharist. This great mystery has been called the "dogma generating true and solid piety." Daily did Norbert offer up the Holy Sacrifice, and on many occasions, several times in one day. God permitted His greatest miracles through the Saint when he was celebrating the Great Sacrifice, and in Antwerp we found Norbert to be its great advocate and apostle. It was while celebrating Mass that Norbert especially reconciled enemies, drove out evil spirits, and even restored sight to the blind.

Of his austerities, mortifications and self-denial, enough has been said to convince the most skeptical mind of Norbert's holy life. His devotion to the Blessed Virgin was so great that he devoted all new foundations to her honor, and dedicated them to her name. In recognition of his filial piety the Queen of Heaven showed Norbert the habit of his Order and always protected him and his Order in a most special manner. Norbert, from the very day of his death, was proclaimed by the "Vox populi" a true Saint; and the bishop who succeeded him in Magdeburg spoke of him as "Blessed." It may perhaps seem strange to us, therefore, that Norbert's solemn canonization did not take place till the year 1582.

Various biographers give different reasons to account for this delay. It is very probable that Norbert's canonization was asked for as early as 1163, when the cause of St. Bernard was first introduced at the Council of Tours.[6] At that time the Pope rejected all applicactions for the simple reason, as he explains in a Brief of Jan. 18, 1174, that there were entirely too many; and not to give offense, His Holiness postponed them all. During the reign of Pope Innocent III, Norbert's cause was once more introduced by the Saxons, who laid before the Holy Father the scattered documents regarding Norbert s miracles. "Jealousy on the part of the abbey of Prémontré," continues the same historian,

> prevented Norbert's canonization at this time, because the

[6] Thus VandenElsen, o.c., p. 375.

> Abbot-General, Gervase by name, refused to use his influence with the Pope as long as the sacred remains were kept in Magdeburg. Naturally Prémontré, the cradle of the Order of Norbert, thought it had the first right to preserve the body of the Saint. We might feel inclined to overlook this petty jealousy on the part of the abbey of Prémontré, did it not lead to a long postponement of Norbert's canonization. Several other abbeys took the stand of the Abbot-General, and for years after, as often as the canonization was asked for, the cause was always introduced as a petition of a single abbey, and not of the whole Order."

The Provostry of Magdeburg became soon after the Saint's death one of the most celebrated houses of the Order, and the mother-house of ten abbeys. It had even certain rights over the bishopric of Brandenburg, Havelberg and Ratzeburg, the bishops of which dioceses were elected by the Norbertine canons attached to these cathedral churches. Adding to this ascendency the fact that St. Mary's was the actual guardian of the tomb of the Saint, it is not difficult to find the cause of the petty jealousy between the two leading abbeys.

However, in the fifteenth century, a time of general relaxation in monastic discipline, the Fathers of Saxony unfortunately lost more and more the spirit of Norbert, and in several monasteries they began to be replaced by other religious. When, in the year 1541, the General Chapter introduced the cause of Norbert's canonization, Magdeburg had entirely lost its former glory. Like the whole Catholic Church in fact, the Premonstratensian Order at this time was passing through a severe crisis, and once more did lack of unity among the different houses prevent the canonization. Only, when in 1573 the Order had once more its Abbot-General, and unity and discipline had been re-established, Norbert's cause was at last introduced successfully, and was Norbert solemnly canonized by Pope Gregory XIII, on the 28th of July, 1582.

"We have heard from trustworthy witnesses," thus says the

Holy Father in the Bull of Canonization,

> and especially from Cardinal Philippe Buoncompagni, our Great-Penitentiary, and John, Abbot of the monastery of Prémontré, in the diocese of Laon, that Blessed Norbert, Archbishop of Magdeburg and a man of eminent sanctity, founded, more than four hundred years ago, the Premonstratensian Order. We therefore consider it Our duty to have him honored and venerated on earth as he is venerated and honored in heaven, since his life, so pleasing to God, has been glorified by so many miracles. In consequence we authorize the Abbot John and all the Superiors of the Order to show themselves forever grateful sons and devoted to their Father, and to celebrate the feast of St. Norbert, Confessor and Pontiff, on the sixth day of June, the day on which he emigrated to heaven, solemnly as a feast Double with an Octave, and then make the common suffrage according to the monastic rite of the Order; and further to inscribe Norbert's name, which is found already in several martyrologies consecrated to the use of the Catholic Church, to inscribe, I say, in the Calendar of said Order, under the rite of Double with an Octave . . .
>
> Given at Rome the year of the Incarnation, 1582, the fifth of the Kalends of August.[7]

Rightly do the Bollandists observe that in this document Pope Gregory speaks of Norbert as it were of a Saint who had been canonized long before.[8] Further, Pope Gregory also granted a plenary indulgence to all Premonstratensians on that day. Pope Urban VIII finally made the feast of St. Norbert a general feast to be observed by all the churches and all religious Orders.

The act of Pope Gregory was the occasion for a general outburst of devotion for our dear but forgotten Saint. His name was once more on the lips of all, and his powerful intercession was invoked by the Church Universal for guidance in the lamentable days of Luther's revolution. Alas! the heresy of Luther, himself a Saxon by

---

[7] Miraeus Chron. Ord. Praem., p. 232, App. No. XV.

[8] Acta SS. T. XX.

birth, had made sad ravages in Saxony especially, and in 1540 had expelled the sons of Norbert from St. Marys Chapter. As a consequence the body of the Saint had come into the hands of Lutherans, who persistently refused to part with it. In the year 1596 the different abbots met to find means of removing Norbert's tomb from Magdeburg, for they greatly lamented the fact that the relics of their Holy Founder had fallen into the hands of these sacrilegious reformers, to whom nothing was sacred. The religious of Steinfeld had failed in their efforts to secure it, and thus John Lohelius, Abbot of Strahov and later Archbishop of Prague, John de Pruetis, Abbot-General of Prémontré, and Denis Feyten, Abbot of St. Michael's at Antwerp—three influential men—united their efforts and went to the German Emperor. The latter consented to send a man of influence to Magdeburg to urge their request, but under pretext that the body would be used as an object of idolatry, the Lutherans persisted in their refusal. Moreover, the Catholics themselves of Magdeburg, who looked upon Norbert as their special Protector in those evil days, were loath to part with the remains.[9]

Thirty years more passed during which numerous efforts were made, but always in vain. Meanwhile John Lohelius had died, and Gaspar von Questenburg had succeeded him in the abbatial dignity. He went to the Emperor, Ferdinand II, in the year 1625, and obtained a letter from him in which His Majesty urged his civil and military officials in the district of Magdeburg to support the request made by the abbot of Strahov. The abbot went to Magdeburg in person and saw the tomb of his spiritual Father; but, influenced by the Lutheran Provost of St. Mary's, the officials still refused to let him have the body. Abbot Gaspar returned to Prague, sick at heart, and in utter despair of ever being able to obtain the sacred relics of Norbert. Repeatedly did he return to Magdeburg and use his eloquence as well as the influence of powerful friends, but without success. At one time he even went with forty armed men to take the

[9] Cfr. VandenElsen, p. 383—Madelaine 492—Le Paige Biblioth. Ord. Praem., p. 408—and Pére Alphonse de Liguori "Vie de Saint Norbert," p. 314.

relics by force, but still in vain. Only after the people of Magdeburg had suffered defeat upon defeat in battle, and had begun to fear provoking the anger of the Emperor, did they consent.

It was on December 3, of the year 1626, that the Abbot of Strahov once more entered Magdeburg, in company of the Provost of Doxan, and was allowed to proceed to an official inspection of the tomb of St. Norbert in the presence of the Lutheran Provost and canons of St. Mary's, the civil and military authorities, and numerous lay and clerical witnesses. He made the verification and found the body of the Saint intact, robed in the sacred vestments in which Norbert had been buried nearly 500 years before.[10]

On the following day Abbot Gaspar and the Provost left Magdeburg under good escort, carrying their precious treasure to the convent of Norbertine Nuns at Doxan, where the relics of the Saint were first deposited. The good Sisters received them with indescribable joy, on the 16th of December, 1626. On the same day a message was sent to Prague, where the people at once began to make preparations for a solemn reception. The relics had been deposited only temporarily at Doxan, six miles from Prague. In Prague there was a universal rejoicing when the good people heard of the great treasure they were about to possess. On the 30th day of April the civil and ecclesiastical authorities solemnly proclaimed Norbert as their chosen Protector and as the Patron Saint of the kingdom of Bohemia. Great festivities were arranged for the Solemn Translation of Norbert's Body, which finally took place on the 2nd day of May, 1627.

Meanwhile the Abbot of Strahov had invited the abbots of Bohemia, Poland, Germany, France, Holland and Belgium to come

[10] The various circumstances related here are taken from a process-verbal made up on this occasion by a Lutheran notary of the senate of Magdeburg. Cfr. Madelaine, p. 494. VandenElsen, on p. 387, relates the same facts, and has taken them from VanderSterre, who received them from the mouth of some of the canons of the abbey of Steinfeldt, who had been present on this occasion. Further confer also Le Paige, loc. cit.

to Prague to take part in the triumph of their Holy Father, and thus was the Solemn Translation carried out in the presence of an immense crowd of people with the greatest magnificence. The Sacred Remains were carried in triumph through the city on the shoulders of eight abbots vested in pontifical attire, and were followed by a countless multitude carrying banners and singing hymns in honor of St. Norbert. Silver coins made in remembrance of this occasion, were distributed among the people, and the festivities lasted for a whole week.[11] During the Octave, sermons, in which Norbert's glory was proclaimed, were preached in every church of Prague, and on the last day the procession was repeated with the same solemnity.

God deigned to work a great many miracles through the intercession of St. Norbert during the solemn celebrations. A record of these is still preserved in the office of the Chancellor of the Diocese, among which is related, as the greatest and the most remarkable of all, the abjuration of not less than 600 Protestants, who, during this Octave, were reconciled to the Church.[12]

Part of the relics of St. Norbert were transferred to Antwerp, in Belgium, where, upon their arrival, the festivities were no less glorious, and it is a most remarkable fact that in these two countries, Bohemia and Belgium, where the Saint's relics have been kept and venerated, the Order has ever since flourished. The Premonstratensians in Germany and in France, who had withstood the Protestant Reformation, came to dishonor in the days of the Revolution, while the abbeys of Belgium and Bohemia were never in a more flourishing condition than in those very days of rebellion; and what is more, they have continued their glorious record until our times.

The canons of Strahov are still the custodians of the relics of St.

[11] Cfr. VandenElsen, p. 390.

[12] Cfr. Madelaine, p. 495.

Norbert, and whenever the feast of the Solemn Translation is being commemorated, thousands of people sing before the shrine:

> This Saint is a vessel of election filled with the Holy Ghost. This is Norbert, the great friend of God. He is the valiant champion who fought with the serpent of old. An angel of peace, a herald of penance, he is powerful in words and deeds by miracles and prophecies. We, his children, approach Him, our Father; we, his clients, approach Him, our Patron. O, let us pray to Him and say: O, Saint of God! O, Friend of the Spouse! Father and Guardian, Thou the glory of our holy mountain, pray to the Lord for us. Hear us, O hear us, St. Norbert! Make those whom thou hast deemed worthy to guard the treasure of thy sacred body, ever feel the benefit of thy powerful intercession. Amen.

These great celebrations naturally gave a new impetus to the cultus of St. Norbert, and thus it is that since this memorable event especially, historians in their annals, poets in their verses, and artists on their canvas, began anew to proclaim the greatness of our dear Saint. His statue soon decorated the portico of the Vatican, and was placed also within the walls of St. Peter's. It is seen in the left transept between the statues of St. Juliana Falconieri and St. Peter Nolascus, with this inscription:

S. NORBERTO
PATRI SUO INSTITUTORI
POSTEA ARCHIEP. MAGDEBURG.
CANONICI PRAEMONSTRA. EREXERUNT
ANNO MDCCLXVII

Different paintings from the hand of the great Rubens himself, representing the Saint, were at one time found in the Abbey of St. Michael, in Antwerp. One of these, representing St. Norbert, St. Clare and St. Thomas of Aquin, in adoration before the Blessed Sacrament, decorates even to this day the entrance of the museum

Kensington in London. But it is especially in the city of Antwerp that one finds numerous representations of St. Norbert, because since his victory over Tanchelm he has been rightly considered the apostle of that city.

In closing the "Life" of the glorious patriarch, we know of no more fitting tribute we can give to his greatness than a sketch of the history of his Order, which is about to celebrate its eighth centenary, and this will form the second volume.

www.ingramcontent.com/pod-product-compliance
Lightning Source LLC
Chambersburg PA
CBHW011128070526
44583CB00023B/2954
9781953746559